Study on
China's Belt & Road Investment and
Financing Cooperation
in Australia

中国在澳大利亚
"一带一路"投融资合作研究

（中英文双语版）

孟 刚◎著

人民出版社

序

林毅夫

　　中国自改革开放以来，取得了人类经济史上不曾有过的奇迹。习近平主席倡议的"一带一路"建设是我国对外开放的一个新举措，不仅能够帮助中国创造一个有利的外部环境，以实现中华民族的伟大复兴，同时能够帮助其他发展中国家实现他们国家现代化的梦想，也有利于发达国家和全球经济的复苏和大发展。

　　我国现在是一个中等偏上收入的国家，中华民族的伟大复兴要求我国跨过中等收入变成一个高收入国家。从过去30多年改革开放经验来讲，应该更充分利用国内和国际两个市场以及国内和国际两种资源。并且我国现在是世界第一大贸易国，同时按照市场汇率计算，是世界第二大经济体，按照购买力平价计算，则已经是世界第一大经济体。在国际上，我国应该承担相应的责任，也应该有相应的影响力和发言权。

　　"一带一路"是应上述要求而提出，经由多国参与的高层次全球协同发展的倡议。政策沟通、设施联通、贸易畅通、货币流通、民心相通，建立所有参与国家的利益共同体、责任共同体、命运共同体。这个愿景的落实非常需要倾听海外一线的声音，需要在境外工作的各界人士的具体推动。

　　孟刚博士是北大毕业生，在国家开发银行海外一线工作，致力于"一带一路"建设的实践，做出了很多成绩。《中国在澳大利亚"一带一路"

1

投融资合作研究》这本著作为"一带一路"建设融入了海外一线金融实务专家的智慧和经验。希望孟刚博士能够再接再厉，兼顾理论和实践，在"一带一路"建设这个广阔的大舞台上，展现精彩人生，做出更多贡献！

林毅夫

全国政协常委

中华全国工商业联合会副主席

北京大学国家发展研究院名誉院长、教授

世界银行原首席经济学家兼高级副行长

2017 年 3 月

中国国家发展和改革委员会西部开发司巡视员

欧晓理：

澳大利亚是"一带一路"建设的重要合作国家，和中国建立了全面战略伙伴关系，经济高度互补，合作发展空间较大。孟刚博士的著作《中国在澳大利亚"一带一路"投融资合作研究》，有高度，接地气，是在推动中澳经贸合作实践基础上的理论研究成果，更是来自"一带一路"建设最前沿的金融实务专家的真知灼见，对推动中澳企业合作以及"一带一路"建设具有参考借鉴意义。鉴此，我郑重推荐此书。

中国社会科学院—上海市人民政府上海研究院常务副院长

中国社会科学院研究生院教授，博士生导师

上海大学副校长

文学国：

孟刚博士致力于研究"一带一路"和国际产能合作，针对中澳经贸合作的热点领域展开了系统的高水平研究，取得了丰硕的成果。他长期负责国家开发银行在澳大利亚和南太地区的"一带一路"投融资合作，实务经验丰富，理论水平扎实，在该领域发表了许多研究成果。《中国在澳大利亚"一带一路"投融资合作研究》这本著作填补了该领域的空白，具有非常重要的理论和现实意义。我对本书的顺利出版表示祝贺并郑重推荐！

中共中央党校国际战略研究院教授

"'一带一路'百人论坛"发起人

赵　磊：

　　当前，在稳步推进"一带一路"建设进程中，需要在四个方面寻求突破：服务于丝路建设的现代思路需要进一步明晰，尤其应拓展国际化视野、提升品牌意识；需要着力打造具有强大软实力的世界一流企业；急需培养真正专业的丝路专家与智库；需要确定并实施支撑"一带一路"的标志性项目。孟刚博士的著作《中国在澳大利亚"一带一路"投融资合作研究》，就是一种专家和智库成果的体现，是在融资支持"一带一路"标志性项目过程中的智慧结晶和理论升华，对推动中资企业在中澳经贸合作中打造世界一流企业具有指导性意义。我郑重推荐本书！

中国建设银行悉尼分行总经理

金扬统：

　　国家开发银行是支持中资企业在澳大利亚"走出去"和参与"一带一路"建设的主力银行。中国建设银行和国家开发银行在澳大利亚有很好的合作关系，我和孟刚博士不仅是工作上的合作伙伴，更是相知相交的好朋友。孟刚博士的著作凝聚了他在澳大利亚开展开发性金融业务的多年心血，立意高，落脚实，前瞻性强，既是银行同业了解中澳两国政府合作热点的理论佳作，也是中资企业在澳大利亚开展投融资合作必不可少的经典读物。郑重推荐！

中国五矿 MMG 公司执行董事兼执行总经理

徐基清：

国家开发银行对中国五矿在澳大利亚的投资并购和 MMG 公司的后续投资及日常运营给予了大力支持。孟刚博士作为国家开发银行澳大利亚工作组负责人，潜心研究中澳两国政府合作热点和市场化合作领域，积极推进"一带一路"建设，为在澳中资企业提供了大量非常有价值的高端智库型信息和建议。孟刚博士经常和中资企业驻澳大利亚负责人在一起深入探讨各行业前沿和热点问题。因此，本书中各个领域的研究既有战略高度又具行业专业性，对中资企业的可持续发展，提供了很强的理论指导性和实际操作性。好书！值得推荐！好书！值得收藏！

兖州煤业澳大利亚公司副董事长和执行委员会主席

张宝才：

在孟刚博士的大力推动下，国家开发银行和兖州煤业澳大利亚公司签署了《"一带一路"建设专项财务顾问协议》。这是中国的银行支持中资企业在澳大利亚开展"一带一路"建设的第一个专项财务顾问合作成果，具有非常重要的标志性意义。本书是孟刚博士基于丰富金融实务经验而撰写的理论著作。全力推荐！

3

丰盛控股集团澳大利亚公司总经理

余翼：

　　为推动中澳两国领导人倡议的"一带一路"建设对接澳大利亚"北部大开发"战略，孟刚博士领导的国家开发银行澳大利亚工作组充分发挥融智融资优势，和澳大利亚联邦、昆士兰州以及维多利亚州等各级政府开展了密切合作，为中资企业在澳大利亚开展经贸合作产业园区建设给予了有力支持！极力推荐该著作！

中节能风力发电股份有限公司总会计师

罗锦辉：

　　在孟刚博士团队的专业优势支撑下，国家开发银行作为主牵头行，和澳大利亚国民银行、西太银行以及中国工商银行和中国建设银行，一起成功支持了中节能和金风科技在澳大利亚非常有影响力的白石风电项目。该项目最终获得上海市银行同业公会2016年度最佳项目奖及牵头银行奖。本书是理论和实践合一的著作。强烈推荐！

浙江交工集团股份有限公司海外分公司总经理

宋智鹏：

　　"一带一路"建设已经从顶层设计阶段进入到了全面务实推进阶段。孟刚博士的著作不仅是中澳"一带一路"合作的最前沿理论研究，还为中资企业在澳大利亚及大洋洲地区开拓国际工程承包业务提供了方向性指导。强烈推荐！

目　录

CONTENTS

前　言

"一带一路"建设要与其他国家战略对接

    2013 年 9 月,习近平主席在哈萨克斯坦纳扎尔巴耶夫大学发表演讲,回顾了古丝绸之路的重要贡献,进而提出在当代建设"丝绸之路经济带"的倡议。习近平说:为了使我们欧亚各国经济联系更加紧密、相互合作更加深入、发展空间更加广阔,我们可以用创新的合作模式,共同建设"丝绸之路经济带"。同年 10 月,习近平在印尼国会发表演讲时表示:东南亚地区自古以来就是"海上丝绸之路"的重要枢纽,中国愿同东盟国家加强海上合作,使用好中国政府设立的中国—东盟海上合作基金,发展好海洋合作伙伴关系,共同建设"21 世纪海上丝绸之路"。作为中国外交的新提法,"丝绸之路经济带"和"21 世纪海上丝绸之路"共同构成了"一带一路"重大倡议。

    "一带一路"建设提出后,在党中央的重大会议、国家重要政策文件和领导人外事活动中多次提及。2013 年 11 月,党的十八届三中全会通过的《中共中央关于全面深化改革若干重大问题的决定》明确指出:"加快同周边国家和区域基础设施互联互通建设,推进丝绸之路经济带、海上丝绸之路建设,形成全方位开放新格局。"在"博鳌亚洲论坛"2015 年年会上，习近平主席呼吁各国积极参与"一带一路"建设。随后，中国政府发布《推动共建丝绸之路经济带和 21 世纪海上丝绸之路的愿景与行动》，明确了"一带一路"的共建原则、框架思路、合作重点、合作机制等。

2016 年 3 月，中国"十三五"规划纲要正式发布，其中有一章专门围绕"推进'一带一路'建设"。这意味着在未来 5 年，"一带一路"将是我国经济社会发展的重要抓手和战略任务。中国秉持共商、共建、共享原则，推动"一带一路"沿线国家发展战略对接，已同 20 多国签署"一带一路"合作协议，初步形成覆盖亚、非、拉、欧四大洲的国际产能合作布局，带动了中国与世界各国共同发展，开创了南北和南南合作新模式。在全球经济低迷不振形势下，"一带一路"为欧亚大陆乃至世界经济发展带来了新希望，开辟了新前景，注入了新动力。

2014 年 7 月，习近平主席在澳大利亚堪培拉演讲，正式提出"一带一路"对接澳大利亚"北部大开发"的倡议，中澳建立全面战略伙伴关系。2016 年 4 月，习近平主席和李克强总理在北京分别和澳大利亚特恩布尔总理宣布"一带一路"和澳大利亚"北部大开发"对接，中澳创新驱动战略对接。

国家开发银行是服务"一带一路"建设的主力银行。自"一带一路"倡议提出以来，国家开发银行积极配合"一带一路"建设，主动作为，以配合高访和规划先行为切入点，为沿线国家经济社会发展提供融智融资支持。国家开发银行以基础设施互联互通和国际产能合作为重点，紧密围绕基础设施互联互通、能源资源合作、装备制造出口等，在油气、核电、高铁、装备、港口、园区等重点领域，支持中资企业和优势产能"走出去"，为重大项目建设提供资金支持，为促进多双边政府间合作机制建设奠定坚实的政治互信基础。

本书作者作为国家开发银行澳大利亚工作组负责人，在澳大利亚具体负责落实中澳政府和企业间"一带一路"投融资合作。本书是作者在澳大利亚开拓开发性金融业务的理论思考成果。本书的撰写得到了中澳政府有关部门、企业高管和各界朋友的大力支持和帮助。本书在分析中资企业在澳大利亚投资历史和现状的基础上，研究内容基本涵盖了中澳"一带一路"投融资合作的热点领域，具体包括：(1) 21 世纪海上丝绸之路在南太平洋地区（以下简称南太地区）四国投融资合作研究；(2) 新形势下中国在澳大利亚加强国际产能合作研究；(3)"一带一路"和澳大利亚"北部大开发"的对接路径和融资合作研究；(4) 中方对接澳大利亚创新驱动战略的路径和融资合作研究；(5) 中资企业在澳大利亚建设经贸合作区的投融资合作研究；(6) 中资企业在澳大利亚基础设施领域的投资合作研究；(7) 推动中资企业在澳大利亚能矿领域的投资合作研究。

澳大利亚是中国全球直接投资的第二大目的地国，发挥着连接亚太地区和欧美发达国家的桥梁作用。本书以中澳"一带一路"投融资合作为研究框架，从以经济外交应对全球经济秩序重构、共同迎接新一轮全球科技创新革命、巩固能源资源领域传统合作保障中国经济安全、拓宽中资企业"走出去"的合作空间等方面阐述了新形势下中国在澳大利亚加强投融资合作的战略意义，分析了中国在澳大利亚"一带一路"和国际产能合作的主要领域，就从政府层面构筑支持体系，以及从企业层面探索投融资合作模式提出了中肯务实的思路建议，对中资企业在澳大利亚以及其他国家投融资实践具有理论指导意义。

"一带一路"顺大势应民心。中澳两国共同推进"一带一路"建设需要总结研究实实在在的合作成果，需要让人才和思想在"一带一路"上流动起来，需要充分发挥教育在"一带一路"中的基础性、先导性、引领性作用，为"一带一路"建设的可持续发展提供优质服务、智力支撑和人才保障。据澳大利亚联邦政府公布的数据显示，仅 2016 年当年，就已有 5 万多名中国留学生来澳大利亚学习，同比增长 23%，中国留学生在澳大利亚教育出口业发展中占据重要地位，且大多学习专业为商业、金融、工商管理、法律等内容。因此，本书非常适合中国学者、留学生作为专业读物，了解中澳"一带一路"投融资合作的热点领域和发展方向，传播"一带一路"文化，加强"一带一路"软实力建设，引导和带动更多的优秀国际人才积极投身"一带一路"建设的理论和实践！

21 世纪海上丝绸之路南线四国投融资合作研究 *

一、澳新巴斐：开发性金融在南太地区的重点合作国家

21 世纪海上丝绸之路南线建设是"一带一路"建设的重要组成部分。2014 年 11 月，习近平主席在访问澳大利亚、新西兰和斐济期间，明确提出南太地区是中方提出的 21 世纪海上丝绸之路的自然延伸，热诚欢迎相关国家共同参与海上丝绸之路建设，推动经贸合作取得更大发展。在双边关系方面，中国与澳大利亚、新西兰已从战略伙伴关系提升为全面战略伙伴关系，与巴布亚新几内亚（以下简称巴新）和斐济等南太地区建交岛国的双边关系提升为战略伙伴关系。

目前，南太地区除澳新外共计有 14 个独立国家[①]，从地理上属于大洋

---

* 本文部分公开发表于《开发性金融研究》2016 年第 1 期。

① 按照独立的先后顺序分别是：1. 澳大利亚（1901）；2. 新西兰（1907）；3. 萨摩亚（1962）；4. 瑙鲁（1968）；5. 汤加（1970）；6. 斐济（1970）；7. 巴布亚新几内亚（1975）；8. 所罗门群岛（1978）；9. 图瓦卢（1978）；10. 基里巴斯（1979）；11. 马绍尔群岛（1979）；12. 瓦努阿图（1980）；13. 帕劳（1994）；14. 密克罗尼西亚（1986）；15. 库克群岛（1989）；16. 纽埃（2006）。其中，10 个国家和中国已建交，它们是澳大利亚、新西兰、斐济、巴布亚新几内亚、密克罗尼西亚、萨摩亚、瓦努阿图、汤加、库克群岛、纽埃。

洲，是区域组织太平洋岛国论坛的正式成员。由于这些国家主要分布在太平洋赤道以南，因此，国际社会一般称其为南太岛国。2015 年，整个南太地区（含澳大利亚、新西兰、巴新）、斐济和其他所有岛国、地区）人口总计为 3935.9 万人，陆地面积总计为 895 万平方公里，海洋面积总计为 4662 万平方公里。在南太地区，澳大利亚和新西兰是发达国家，经济发展遥遥领先于其他国家，巴新和斐济是经济实力较强的发展中国家。根据 IMF 的数据，2014 年澳新巴斐四国的 GDP 总量是 16584 亿美元，在南太地区占比 99.99% 以上。南太地区其他国家经济总量较小，主要依靠政府间发展援助开展国际合作，如最小国家瑙鲁，陆地面积仅 21 平方公里，人口约 1.08 万，2014 年 GDP 0.48 亿美元。

表 1　南太地区部分国家 2014 年 GDP 全球排名

单位：百万美元

国家	澳大利亚	新西兰	巴布亚新几内亚	斐济	瓦努阿图	密克罗尼西亚联邦	帕劳	基里巴斯
GDP	1444189	198118	16060	4212	812	315	269	181
排名	12	53	114	154	177	183	184	186

资料来源：IMF。

"一带一路"建设是党中央、国务院的重大战略决策。落实该战略的重要支撑是资金融通，特别是要加大开发性金融对重大项目的支持力度。目前，中国主导的致力于服务"一带一路"建设的开发性金融机构主要有亚洲基础设施投资银行、丝路基金和国家开发银行(以下简称国开行) 等。截至 2015 年 9 月末，国开行资产总额超过 11 万亿人民币，外汇业务余额超过 3200 亿美元，其中为"一带一路"沿线国家提供融资项目超过 400 个，贷款余额 1073 亿美元，在支持"五通"方面取得了良好成效。澳新巴斐四国在南太地区政治上有影响力，同时也是经济发展的主力军，基础设施建设需求强劲，能矿资源丰富，和中国经济契合度高，合作基础扎实，合作意愿强烈，是开发性金融机构参与南太地区融资合作的重点国家。

二、四国经济的优劣势分析

（一）澳大利亚

1. 优势

在政治环境方面，澳大利亚实行英联邦制，划分为六州两领地，政治制度稳定，政权更迭合法有序，投资环境良好，并将与美国、日本、中国、印尼的关系作为澳最重要的四大双边关系。在经济基础方面，澳大利亚经济高度发达，产业结构合理，是南半球经济最发达的国家和全球第 12 大经济体，人均 GDP 约 6.8 万美元，服务业、制造业、采矿业和农业是四大主导产业。在自然资源方面，澳大利亚矿产和农业资源丰富，铁矿石、煤、黄金、锂、锰矿石等产量居世界前列，多种矿产出口量全球第一；农业高度现代化、机械化，是全球第四大农产品出口国。在对华关系方面，2015 年澳正式加入亚投行，签署双边自贸协定，就"21 世纪海上丝绸之路"和"北部大开发"共建战略达成共识。

2. 劣势

一方面，"中国威胁论"在一定程度上影响着两国关系。一是少数政客崇尚"中国威胁论"，无根据地指责中国岛礁建设，对南海等问题指手画脚，不利于中澳双边经贸关系的深化。二是政界少数反对派人士认为将关键资产出售给中国国企将引发民众的抵制情绪。如，禁止中国投资者购买大片土地，对北领地将达尔文港出租给中方表示不满等。另一方面，大宗商品价格暴跌，政府面临一定的货币贬值和财政赤字问题。铁矿石、煤炭等主力大宗商品价格下跌趋势明显，其中铁矿石从 2011 年每吨 190 美元高位一路暴跌至 2015 年 12 月每吨 40 美元左右。大宗商品价格下跌刺激澳元持续贬值，汇价均值降至 0.71 美元，创六年新低。同时，大宗商品价格大幅下跌对政府税收造成影响，2014—2015 年预计财政赤字为 411 亿澳元。截至 2015 年第一季度末，澳大利亚净外债已攀升至 9550 亿美元，约占 GDP 的 60%。

（二）新西兰

1. 优势

在政治环境方面，新西兰政治稳定，投资环境良好，实行英联邦制，划分为 11 个大区，5 个单一辖区，政治制度稳定，政权更迭合法有序，并将亚太地区作为对外关系的优先领域。在经济基础方面，新西兰是贸易立国的"小型开放经济体"，经济增长以出口为核心，农产品是最大的出口商品。在对华关系方面，两国政治上互信，在重要多边机制及重大国际和地区问题上保持良好沟通协调，《中华人民共和国政府和新西兰共和国政府自由贸易协定》是中国与其他国家达成的第一个全面自贸协定，新西兰是第一个加入亚投行谈判的发达国家。

2. 劣势

一方面，地震、干旱等自然灾害影响经济发展。新西兰是地震频发国家，2009 年、2010 年南岛发生两次强震，当地第二大城市克赖斯特彻奇市地区经济损失惨重。此外，2012 年至今，北岛地区多次遭遇大旱，对新西兰畜牧业等支柱产业发展造成一定影响。另一方面，新西兰将建设出口市场列为首要目标，经济结构相对单一，易受到国际市场的需求和价格冲击。近年来，新西兰国内经济有衰退迹象，税收减少，支出上升，政府财力有所减弱。

（三）巴布亚新几内亚

1. 优势

在政治环境方面，巴新实行英联邦君主立宪制，划分为 21 个省和首都行政区，2012 年以来大力推行政府改革，争取党派合作，政治环境相对稳定。在经济基础方面，2002 年 8 月以来，巴新政府大力推动"以出口带动经济复苏"，加大勘探和开发矿产资源，放缓私有化改革，经济持续快速增长，最近五年的 GDP 增速保持在 5%—15%，农业、工业和服务业各占比三分之一左右。巴新立法规定外债不得超过 GDP 的 35%，有效控制了财政风险。在自然资源方面，巴新能源矿石（以下简称能矿）等自然资源丰富，是世界第十大铜生产国和第十一大黄金生产国。此外，巴新的淡水、热带雨林和海产资源也比较丰富。

2. 劣势

主要包括：(1) 社会治安问题突出。大城市抢劫、谋杀、械斗等刑事案件数量呈逐年上升趋势，部分高地地区部落冲突加剧，安保花费在投资成本中占比较大。(2) 基础设施滞后。主要交通方式为空运和水运(货物)，没有铁路运输，没有连接全国的公路网，码头容量不足，农村地区通信不发达，供电能力较低，无国家电网系统，全国只有约 15% 的人口能用到电，电力缺口较大。（3）人口素质不高。本国青年计算能力偏低，识字率低于 70%，多数学龄儿童无法上学，师资不足，教学质量差，劳动力供给不能满足经济增长和可持续的社会发展需要。(4) 土地产权管理不规范。巴新实行土地私有化，97% 的土地被各个部落占有，没有明确的土地登记制度，土地界限不清晰，一旦开发，许多土地主会主张收益权利，合作机制存在很大不确定性，土地资源难以发挥优势，甚至成为制约经济发展的瓶颈。

（四）斐济

1. 优势

在政治环境方面，斐济政治相对稳定，1970 年独立后成为英联邦成员，1987 年政变后改称共和国，并脱离英联邦，是太平洋岛国中外交较为活跃的国家。2010 年以来斐提出"向北看"战略，积极发展同亚洲各国以及非洲和美洲国家的关系。在经济基础方面，斐济是太平洋岛国中经济相对发达的国家，经济一直处于良性发展中，2010 年以来实现了连续五年稳健增长，建筑、制造、批发零售、金融、保险、农业、通信、运输仓储等行业发展势头良好。斐济海岛众多，旅游资源丰富，政府高度重视旅游产业，建立了一套较为完整的旅游发展和管理体系。

2. 劣势

一方面，由于全球金融危机、国际市场价格下跌和国内产业结构调整等原因，斐济以制糖业、旅游业和服装加工业为主的三大传统支柱产业受到一定程度的冲击，产业结构有待进一步优化。另一方面，土地产权问题对基础设施建设等形成瓶颈制约。斐济全国土地只有 10% 是可以自由买卖、移转的私人土地（Freehold Land），土著拥有全国 88.37% 的土地，任何外人的租赁及使用，除先需与各部落达成协议外，还受到斐济原住民土地基金会（NTLB）监督。斐济的土地产权问题很大程度上限制了能源电力、道路港口等基础设施建设。

表2 2004年、2009年和2014年四国的宏观经济数据

年份	国家	GDP（亿美元）	经济增长率（%）	人口（万人）	人均GDP（美元）
2004 年	澳大利亚	6130	4.2	2013	30452
	新西兰	1040	3.8	409	25428
	巴新	39	2.7	595	655
	斐济	27	5.3	82	3293
2009 年	澳大利亚	9000	1.5	2169	41494
	新西兰	1200	−0.47	430	27907
	巴新	81	5.5	670	1209
	斐济	28	−1.3	85	3294
2014 年	澳大利亚	14444	2.5	2349	61728
	新西兰	1981	3.3	451	43925
	巴新	161	5.4	748	2139
	斐济	42	3.8	89	4494

资料来源：IMF。

三、四国投融资合作的重点领域

（一）能矿资源领域

1. 现状

自 1997 年我国实施充分利用"两种资源、两个市场"的"走出去"战略以来，我国能矿资源类境外投资逐步进入了一个高峰时期。但是，自 2012 年起，由于大宗商品价格的暴跌，我国能矿资源类境外投资又呈现了断崖式下跌态势。在南太地区，中资企业在澳大利亚的能矿资源类投资最多，比较有影响力的有中信泰富、鞍钢等的铁矿石项目，兖州煤业等的煤矿项目等。此外，中冶在巴新的镍矿项目和中石化参与的美孚 LNG 项目也得到了广泛关注。中资企业在南太地区的能矿资源领域"走出去"主要集中于 2007—2008 年左右，正是市场泡沫高企时期，成功案例不多，教训和代价不少。

2. 机遇

由于市场的无法预测性，国际巨头也犯了同样的错误，矿业能源危机下大量国际能矿公司出现巨额亏损。例如，某国际矿业巨头 2011 年用 40 亿美元买下了一个矿床，三年后卖出仅 5000 万美元。目前，全球能矿市场极其低迷，相当部分的能矿资源价值趋于理性甚至被严重低估。这为中资企业以"一带一路"战略为契机，参与全球能矿市场的合作与竞争，提供了难得机遇。中国是全球第二大经济体，是全球最大的能矿资源需求市场。长远看，中资企业更大程度上参与全球能矿领域的竞争是大势所趋，南太地区更是中资企业打造具有重要国际影响力的能矿跨国集团的必争之地。

3. 风险

澳新等发达国家的能矿资源领域风险更多是市场风险和企业运营风险，导致影响投资回报率。巴斐等发展中国家，政治风险和政策法律风险则更为突出。政治风险是与东道国主权有关的不确定因素，如政局不稳、政权更迭、武装冲突、社会不稳定、政策不稳定等情况。

(二) 基础设施领域

1. 现状

中资企业积极参与澳新巴斐等国的基础设施建设，业务大体上可以分为国际工程承包和海外投资两大类。经过近十年的发展，业务范围已经从房建、路桥等劳动密集型领域逐渐扩展到冶金、电力等资金技术密集型领域，业务模式从劳务分包、结构分包等简单承包逐渐发展成行业主流的施工总承包，业务规模从初期承接几十万美元的小型施工项目到现在承接几十亿以上的大型、特大型综合项目。

2. 机遇

澳大利亚的基础设施较为完善，但是许多基础设施已经接近使用年限，港口、道路、机械、电力等新合作机会也不断涌现，据测算建设资金缺口在 7700 亿澳元以上。新西兰经济体量较小，基础设施需求规模不大，但受地震灾害的影响，基督城等地区的基础设施重建缺口也达到 50 亿美元以上。巴新和斐济是快速增长的发展中经济体，电力港口道路等基础设施需求强劲，中资企业的低成本优势非常明显，虽然单一项目规模有限，但数量越来越多。

3. 风险

在澳新等发达国家，中资企业由于缺少发达国家的项目建设和运营经验，很难独立中标并参与基础设施项目，进入的门槛较高，且本国施工人员签证较难获得，环境保护和原住民土地权益保护问题突出，劳工成本较高，商业和文化差异较大。在巴斐等发展中国家，需要充分考虑政治风险、开发风险（如投标程序、腐败、保密规定、恶性竞争等）、建设期施工风险（如环境保护、获取全流程的批准文件等）、施工完成后的项目运营风险（如和当地社区的关系、本地员工的职业健康安全等）以及商业风险等。

（三）农业领域

1. 现状

历史案例分析显示，投资四国农业领域需要面对政府的审查和媒体民众的舆论压力，且大多数投资标的为中小型家族企业，规模化经营能力有限，可供投资者参考的财务等信息相对缺乏。在澳新巴斐四国农业领域，中资企业的总投资相对较小，适合介入的农业项目主要为农地、林地、渔业和大中型农企的并购或绿地投资。以农业领域投资最多的澳大利亚为例，外国公司在澳拥有近 11.3% 的土地，而中国公司可能仅拥有不到 1% 的澳洲土地，以 2006 年以来高于 500 万澳元的投资统计，中资进入澳农业领域已完成的交易仅有 10 余项，总投资 10 亿多澳元。

2. 机遇

从规模角度分析，相比能矿资源领域的投资，中国在澳新巴斐农业领域的投资仍处于起步阶段，尚不是这四国农业领域的重大投资来源国，但中国又是农产品消费大国。因此，在四国的农业领域，蕴藏着较大的国际合作空间。

3. 风险

农业的前期成本投入较大，需要熟悉当地市场，处理好和当地社区特别是原住民的关系，充分了解和中国不尽相同的气候条件等自然因素，大量投入水利等基础设施建设，等等。因此，四国的农业合作是否成功较大程度上取决于中资企业的前期调研是否扎实、介入后的管理经营是否到位、市场开拓是否顺畅等诸多因素。

（四）装备制造等领域

1. 现状

随着"一带一路"战略的实施，我国国际产能和装备制造合作面临难得的发展机遇。在南太地区，合作的重点国是与我国装备和产能契合度高、合作愿望强烈、合作条件和基础较好的巴新、斐济等发展中国家，澳大利亚和新西兰等发达国家也是积极开拓的市场。

2. 机遇

就澳新巴斐四国而言，深化能矿资源、基础设施、农业等领域的合作无疑将带动国际产能和装备制造合作，达到以点带面的效果。可以此为基础，进一步推动双方在钢铁、有色、建材、铁路、电力、化工、轻纺、汽车、通信、工程机械、航空航天、船舶和海洋工程等重点行业的全面合作。

3. 风险

南太地区诸国传统上是欧美等发达国家的重点合作区域，在装备制造等方面欧美跨国集团具有先发优势。四国特别是澳新对装备制造的产品标准、质量等有较高的要求，客户忠诚度较高，很难改变消费习惯，之前失败案例较多。因此，中资企业在四国装备制造领域的介入，需要做好全方位的细致准备，充分发挥自身的比较优势。

四、开发性金融参与南太地区投融资合作的思路和建议

（一）对接规划，加强重大项目储备

在澳新巴斐四国，融资合作的重要抓手是规划先行。开发性金融机构和四国开展规划合作，应当紧密围绕"一带一路"建设的整体战略布局，并和四国自身的重大经济发展规划紧密结合，如澳大利亚的"北部大开发"战略和巴新的"基础设施建设"规划，在推动整体规划合作的同时，围绕重点领域，发挥所在国知名咨询公司、律师事务所、高校科研机构等社会力量的本土化优势，深入开展专项规划，包括基础设施、能源资源、经贸合作、产业投资、金融合作、人文交流、生态环保和海上合作等，实现点面结合的规划合作战略布局。在做好整体规划的基础上，着重加强重点领域重大项目的谋划和融资方案的策划，以基础设施、能矿资源、农业、装备制造和国际产能合作等为重点，加强重大项目储备。

（二）以澳大利亚为平台，发挥综合经营优势辐射南太各国

澳大利亚在南太地区的经济总量绝对领先，分别是排名第二的新西兰和排名第三的巴新的 8 倍和 90 倍左右。澳大利亚的资本市场高度发达，金融业占全国经济总量的比重最大，约占 GDP 的 8.4%，拥有亚太地区第二大股票市场，澳元在全球的交易量位居第五。澳大利亚始终作为最重要的外部因素，影响南太地区诸岛国[①]，和南太地区诸岛国保持紧密的经贸合作，并有直接到达大多数岛国的便捷交通渠道。因此，开发性金融机构在澳大利亚设立经营性分支机构，可以起到辐射南太地区诸岛国的作用，并将双边与多边合作相结合，将投贷等金融产品相结合，加大金融产品和模式创新力度，探索投融资合作新模式，全面开展项目融资、贸易融资、国际结算、财务顾问、离岸资产证券化、银团贷款等综合金融业务，为南太地区的中资企业提供全方位的一站式服务。

（三）结合四国政府热点，积极参与重大基础设施项目建设

在能矿等大宗商品价格暴跌背景下，四国均将加大基础设施建设作为新的经济增长点，如澳大利亚的"北部大开发"、新西兰的基督城震后重建、巴新和斐济的电力交通等领域。以澳大利亚的"北部大开发"为例，联邦政府设立了总额 50 亿澳元的北部地区基础设施贷款计划，以优惠利率贷款吸引全球投资者加入该区域的港口、公路、管线、电力、水利等基础设施建设，并将直接投资约 10 亿澳元先期进行重点基础设施改造。建议开发性金融机构结合四国政府热点，引导中资企业探索"EPC+F"（工

[①] 2007 年后，澳大利亚加大了对南太地区诸岛国的援助力度，投入大量资金实施"南太伙伴计划"。2006—2013 年，澳大利亚在太平洋地区的双边援助是中国的 6 倍。澳大利亚援助额是 68 亿美元，中国是 10.6 亿美元。

程总承包加融资)、PPP（公私合营）、BOT（建设—经营—移交）、PFI（私营主动融资）等多种合作模式，积极参与重大基础设施建设，进一步推动国际产能合作和重大装备制造业"走出去"。

（四）设立大宗商品平稳基金，股权布局四国重点能矿企业

从短中期趋势分析看，能矿资源等大宗商品价格还有一定的下行空间。国际大宗商品价格的进一步急剧下跌将给澳大利亚和巴新等资源型出口国带来更多问题，包括引发急剧的货币贬值、外汇短缺、通货膨胀或者削弱主权偿还外债能力等。但从另一个角度分析，这也是开发性金融逆周期介入，支持中资企业投资境外能矿资源领域的一个战略机遇。建议开发性金融机构可探索设立能矿等大宗商品平稳基金，在适当时机对澳大利亚和巴新等大宗商品出口国施以援手，支持中资企业在互利共赢前提下，以股权投资优先的模式开展商业合作，短期帮助缓解大宗商品价格下跌对出口国经济的崩盘式冲击，长期增强中资企业在国际大宗商品定价方面的话语权甚至主导权。

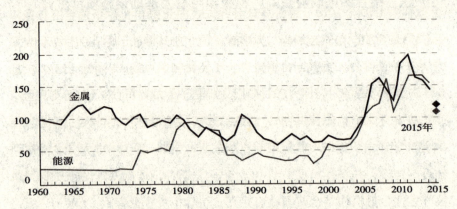

图 1　国际金属及能源类大宗商品价格走势（1960—2015 年）

注：某类商品的实际价格指数是该类商品全球美元价格的贸易加权平均值，按发达国家制造业价格指数平减，并将 2005 年的数值设定为 100。

资料来源：IMF 初级商品价格体系；美国能源信息署；世界银行全球经济检测数据库。

（五）加强和四国的银行同业合作，共同支持重大项目

澳大利亚的金融监管法律严格。澳新银行、国民银行、西太银行、联邦银行等澳大利亚四大商业银行，在新西兰、巴新、斐济等主要南太地区岛国都设立了分支机构，深耕多年，实力较强，是南太地区金融市场的主力银行。建议开发性金融机构加强与多边金融机构、中资银行、澳大利亚四大主力商业银行以及巴新的南太银行等本地银行的合作，以银团贷款、直接授信和转贷等方式共同支持南太地区的重大项目开发建设，在产品开发、风险控制、信息技术、经营管理等方面，全面提升在南太地区的综合经营能力和影响力。

（六）为具有开发性的商业项目设计更市场化的金融品种

境外具有开发性的商业项目竞争激烈，主要体现为：一是很多赴境外投资的中资企业自有资金充足，融资需求综合化，更看重银行财务顾问等中间业务的服务能力；二是海外同业特别是外资银行的融资成本较低，融资决策较快，审批流程较高效，贷款币种较丰富，能够满足客户"子弹式"还款（贷款到期一次性还本）等不同金融产品的需要。因此，建议开发性金融机构为境外具有开发性的商业项目创新设计出不同的金融产品，对项目的风险偏好、风险容忍度、信用结构、贷款定价、贷款品种、审批流程等做出不同的标准和要求，满足开发性金融机构在境外以市场化的方式支持具有开发性的商业项目，实现"一带一路"建设整体战略布局的需要。

参考文献:

胡怀邦:《以开发性金融服务"一带一路"战略》,《中国银行业》2015 年第 12 期。

"Oceania 2015", Population Pyramids of the World from 1950 to 2100, http://populationpyramid.net/oceania/2015/.

Rom Crocombe, *The South Pacific*, IPS Publications, University of South Pacific, 2008.

喻常森:《21 世纪海上丝绸之路南线建设:中国与大洋洲关系》,《大洋洲发展报告 (2014—2015)》,社会科学文献出版社 2015 年版。

陈景河:《经济新常态下中国矿业的现状与未来》,第十七届中国国际矿业大会,2015 年 10 月。

李铮:《国际工程承包与海外投资业务融资》,中国人民大学出版社 2014 年版。

花旗集团:《澳大利亚基础设施大循环》,2008 年 6 月 20 日。

澳大利亚工程师论坛:《2010 年澳大利亚基础设施报告》,2010 年。

Philippa Brant, Lowy Institute for International Policy, http://www.lowyinstitute.org/chinese-aid-map/.

中国在澳大利亚的国际产能合作研究 *

国际产能合作是通过国际贸易和投资等方式，将产能在不同国家或地区间转移，从而实现在全球范围内配置和组合生产要素。19 世纪末的德国、20 世纪 50 年代的美国以及 90 年代的日本都曾通过对外投资和贸易在全球范围内转移产能、化解国内产能过剩、助推国内产业结构升级、改善贸易条件并向他国输出本国技术和产业标准，进而控制整个产业链。2015 年 5 月，中国正式发布《关于推进国际产能和装备制造合作的指导意见》，强调抓住全球基础设施建设和产业升级的历史机遇，将钢铁、有色、建材、铁路、电力、化工、轻纺、汽车、通信、工程机械、航空航天、船舶和海洋工程等十二大产业作为国际产能合作的重点，分类实施，有序推进，打造中资企业在境外投资的升级版。

一、中资企业在澳大利亚的投资历史和现状分析

澳大利亚国土辽阔，自然资源丰富，较早步入发达国家行列，2015 年 GDP 约为 1.598 万亿美元，人均 GDP 约为 6.658 万美元，是全球第 12

---

* 本文部分公开发表于《开发性金融研究》2016 年第 3 期。

大经济体，政治和法律环境稳定，市场机制规范，产业结构合理，可投资领域较多，投资回报较为稳定，具有国际领先的技术和管理经验，是连接亚太地区和欧美发达国家的桥梁。2005—2015年，澳大利亚成为中国全球直接投资的第二大目的地国。2013—2015年，中国成为澳大利亚第一大海外直接投资来源国。中资企业在澳大利亚的境外投资有着多年的探索历程和投资领域的逐渐变化过程。

（一）1980—2005年：起步阶段

中资企业在澳大利亚开展了少量投资活动。这个阶段，中国在澳大利亚的投资合作尚不成规模，典型案例有中信集团投资波特兰铝厂，中钢集团投资力拓治那铁矿，中远集团成立中澳合资企业——五星航运代理有限公司，中国中纺投资棉花行业，中国银行恢复在澳营业等。

（二）2006—2012年：能矿资源领域

中资企业开始大规模投资澳大利亚。这个阶段，中国的投资合作项目集中在能矿领域，累计投资总额的73%于矿业，18%于天然气行业，主要集中在西澳大利亚州和昆士兰州，包括中海油的250亿澳元LNG项目，中信泰富的99亿美元铁矿石项目，兖州煤业的60亿美元煤矿项目，中国五矿的20亿美元MMG收购项目等。由于投资行业多为能矿领域，较多的案例为大规模投资。中资企业在澳大利亚的直接投资由2007年的15.4亿美元猛增到2008年的162亿美元。2012年中资企业在澳大利亚的投资是101亿美元，超过半数的投资项目高于2亿美元。

（三）2013 年至今：多元化趋势

中资企业在澳大利亚的投资开始呈现多元化趋势。这个阶段，除能矿领域外，中资企业在澳大利亚投资项目还包括基础设施、农业、制造业、高端食品、休闲、零售业、物流业等，典型案例有中交建 11.5 亿澳元收购约翰荷兰建筑公司，中国招商局 8.75 亿澳元获得纽卡所港口的 99 年租赁权，山东岚桥集团 5.06 亿澳元获得达尔文港 99 年租赁使用权，国家电网收购当地电网公司的股权，上海中福集团收购北领地的农地，新希望投资奶牛场和乳品加工厂，绿地等多个知名房企投资商业地产，万达院线收购澳洲影院，联想控股投资海鲜产业，阿里巴巴布局电商平台等。

（四）现状分析

2006—2012 年，中国总投资额的 2/3 是在西澳大利亚州和昆士兰州的能矿资源领域。2013 年，中资企业在澳大利亚的直接投资是 91.9 亿美元；从投资总额占比分析，输电 40%，矿业 24%，天然气 21%，房地产 14%，农业 1%。2014 年，中资企业在澳大利亚的直接投资是 83.5 亿美元；其中，民营企业在澳大利亚的投资首次在交易数量（占比 85%）和投资总量（占比 66%）上都超过国有企业；从投资总额占比分析，房地产 46%，基础设施 21%，休闲和零售 12%，矿业 11%，石油和天然气 7%，制造 2%，农业 1%；新南威尔士州成为中国直接投资的首选目的地，占投资总额的 72%。2015 年，中资企业在澳大利亚的直接投资是 111 亿美元；从投资总额占比分析，房地产 45%，新能源 20%，健康医疗 17%，矿业 9%，石油和天然气 3%，基础设施 3%，农业 3%；农业项目有 12 个，总投资达 3.75 亿美元；民营企业交易数量占比 78%；新南威尔士州吸引中国直接投资保持第一，占投资总额的 49.3%，维多利亚州排第二，占比 34%。

二、新形势下中国在澳大利亚加强国际产能合作的意义

（一）以经济外交应对全球经济秩序重构

金融危机发生后，美国推出了以高标准和排他性为特征的新一轮全球经贸规则，如跨太平洋伙伴关系协定（TPP）、跨大西洋贸易与投资伙伴协议（TTIP）。这些协定具有很强的排他性，会严重影响中国以及新兴市场和发展中国家。面对这种情况，在对 TPP 持开放态度的同时，中国提出了"一带一路"倡议，强调用投资输出和资本输出而不是商品输出构建连接亚太经济圈和欧洲经济圈的发展平台。澳大利亚是亚太地区政治上和经济上都具有很强影响力的发达国家，积极响应"一带一路"建设，是亚洲基础设施投资银行的创始成员国，2015 年 6 月和中国正式签署了《中华人民共和国政府和澳大利亚政府自由贸易协定》（以下简称《中澳自贸协定》），是中国主动适应经济全球化新形势的重要合作国。在澳大利亚深化国际产能合作，对中国以经济外交应对全球经济秩序重构具有重要战略意义。

（二）共同迎接新一轮全球科技创新革命

2015 年 6 月，中国公布《关于大力推进大众创业万众创新若干政策措施的意见》，强调创新是引领发展的第一动力，必须摆在国家发展全局的核心位置，深入实施创新驱动发展战略。2015 年 12 月，澳大利亚公布《全国创新和科学工作日程》，全面推进创新驱动战略。从历史上的几次全球化科技革命看，科技创新始终是提高社会生产力和综合国力的重要战略支撑。在世界新科技革命中抢得先机的国家，必将成为世界经济的领头羊。澳大利亚是资源、能源、农产品、健康产品等的输出大国，中国是消

费大国和制造业大国。中澳两国在科技创新领域的合作，具有极强的互补性，是两国共同迎接新一轮全球科技创新革命的必由之路。

（三）巩固能源资源领域传统合作保障中国经济安全

澳大利亚矿产和农业资源丰富，铁矿石、煤炭、黄金、铀、锌铅、铝土、锰、石油、天然气、页岩气等产量居世界前列，农业高度现代化、机械化，是全球第四大农产品出口国。澳大利亚已探明的铁矿石资源约有160亿吨，勘探开发较为成熟，是力拓、必和必拓、FMG 等世界前几大矿商以及中资企业铁矿石投资的重点国家。澳大利亚是世界最大的煤炭出口国，黑煤地质储量约575亿吨（工业经济储量397亿吨），居世界第六，褐煤地质储量约418亿吨（工业经济储量为376亿吨），占全球褐煤储量的20%，居世界第二。加强和澳大利亚的国际产能合作，对保障中国经济发展所需要的能源资源的安全性具有重要的战略意义。

（四）拓宽中资企业"走出去"的合作空间

过去，中资企业"走出去"主要是贸易，也就是产品输出，通过贸易将中国制造的产品向外输出。在经济全球化的新形势下，中国推进国际产能和装备制造合作，核心就是要把中资企业的产品贸易和产品输出升级到产业输出和能力输出，从出口中低端产品到出口高端制造业产品，实现贸易驱动到投资驱动和金融驱动的新型对外经济合作模式。中资企业在澳大利亚开展多元化投资，是机遇也是挑战，如果投资成功，不仅可以将国内优势产业转移到澳大利亚，取得稳定的投资收益，更可以获得国际先进的技术及管理经验，为成长成为具有全球影响力的跨国公司打下扎实的基础。

三、中国在澳大利亚国际产能合作的理论基础

在总结大量实践案例的基础上,各国专家学者深入研究,形成了国际产能转移的诸多理论,对中国在澳大利亚更好地开展国际产能合作具有非常有益的启示。

(一) 产品生命周期理论

产品生命周期理论是解释制成品贸易和企业对外直接投资战略选择的著名理论。该理论没有从产品自然属性逐渐消失的角度考虑问题,而是从产品创新、产品成长和成熟、产品标准化等三个阶段来分析企业所做出的对外直接投资决策。产品创新阶段,市场需求主要在国内,创新国主要通过出口而不是直接投资来满足其他国家需求。产品成长和成熟阶段,创新国的市场竞争日益激烈,逐渐出现跨国生产以规避进口国关税等贸易壁垒,成本要素成为市场竞争的主要手段,开始向市场结构相似、消费者偏好相似、相对成本较低的其他国家进行直接投资。产品标准化阶段,竞争更加激烈,企业开始在世界范围内寻找生产成本最低的生产地区,此时自然资源丰富和具有低成本优势的国家成为企业对外投资的最佳选择。

(二) 投资要素诱发组合理论

投资要素诱发组合理论 (Theory of Investment-Induced Factors Portfolio) 产生于 20 世纪 80 年代后期。该理论认为,任何形式的国际直接投资都是在直接诱发要素和间接诱发要素的组合作用下发生的。直接诱发要素是指各类生产要素,包括自然资源、劳动力、资本、生产技术、知

识信息以及管理技能等，诱发了投资国对外直接投资。间接诱发要素是指直接诱发要素以外的其他要素，一是投资国的诱发因素，如国家鼓励企业对外投资、与东道国签署合作协议等；二是东道国的诱发因素，如优越的投资环境、优惠的吸引外资政策、健全的法律法规等；三是全球性的诱发因素，如经济全球化、科技创新等。

（三）国家比较优势理论

国家比较优势理论是国际直接投资理论的最新研究成果，对企业如何形成并保持可持续的竞争优势进行了分析。该理论将国家经济发展划分为生产要素驱动阶段、投资驱动阶段、技术创新驱动阶段和财富驱动阶段，并将影响一国国际竞争力的主要因素细分为四点：一是自然资源、资本资源、知识资源、人力资源、基础设施等；二是较易产生规模经济、较高需求层次和具有超前性的国内需求；三是得到上游原材料供应和下游销售渠道支持的产业因素；四是支持企业创建、战略规划、组织和管理的条件。该理论认为国内的激烈竞争会导致对外直接投资的发生，为了确保对外直接投资成功，企业必须获得充分的竞争优势。

（四）跨国公司全球战略理论

跨国公司全球战略理论是指跨国公司在经济全球化的时代背景下，充分结合和利用投资国与东道国的比较优势，合理配置生产和营销资源，谋求最大利益。该理论指出跨国公司全球化战略的目标不能限于东道国，而应追求全球范围内的利润最大化，强调全球性、整体性和协同性，通过合理配置、协调和管理各国各项资源，实现采购、生产、营销、研发和财务等环节的一体化，真正实现专业化生产，增强企业的国际竞争力和风险防范能力。

23

四、中国在澳大利亚国际产能合作的主要领域

(一) 能矿资源领域

自 1997 年我国实施充分利用"两种资源、两个市场"的"走出去"战略以来，能矿资源类境外投资逐步进入了一个高峰时期。但是，自 2012 年起，由于大宗商品价格的暴跌，我国能矿资源类境外投资又呈现了断崖式下跌态势。中资企业在澳大利亚的能矿资源类投资正是市场泡沫高企时期，成功案例不多，教训和代价不少。目前，全球能矿市场有触底反弹趋势，相当部分的能矿资源价值趋于理性甚至被严重低估。这为中资企业以"一带一路"战略为契机，参与全球能矿市场的合作与竞争，提供了难得机遇。中国是全球第二大经济体，是全球最大的能矿资源需求市场。长远看，中资企业更大程度上参与全球能矿领域的竞争是大势所趋，澳大利亚是中资企业打造具有重要国际影响力的能矿跨国集团的重要战略性合作国家。

(二) 基础设施领域

澳大利亚政府于 2016 年 2 月正式宣布《澳大利亚基础设施规划》（*Australian Infrastructure Plan*）。此纲领性文件针对未来 15 年内澳大利亚基础设施领域面临的需求与挑战，重点提出了 93 项优先建设项目列表（Infrastructure Priority List），并对各级政府发展基础设施提出 78 项建议，内容涵盖改扩建悉尼、墨尔本等首府城市轨道交通，霍巴特等老城区翻新改造，大力发展收费公路，扩建大型机场枢纽，改革电力、供水、宽带等领域融资和运营方式。澳大利亚的基础设施较为完善，但是许多基础设施

已经接近使用年限，港口、道路、机械、电力等新合作机会也不断涌现，据测算建设资金缺口估计在 7700 亿澳元以上。中资企业由于缺少发达国家的项目建设和运营经验，很难独立中标并参与澳大利亚的基础设施项目，进入的门槛较高，且本国施工人员签证较难获得，环境保护和原住民土地权益保护问题突出，劳工成本较高，商业和文化差异较大。

(三) 农业领域

从规模角度分析，相比能矿资源领域的投资，中国在澳大利亚农业领域的投资仍处于起步阶段，尚不是农业领域的重大投资来源国，但中国又是农产品消费大国。因此，在澳大利亚的农业领域，蕴藏着较大的国际产能合作空间。农业的前期成本投入较大，需要熟悉当地市场，处理好和当地社区特别是原住民的关系，充分了解和中国不尽相同的气候条件等自然因素，大量投入水利等基础设施的建设。在澳大利亚的农业合作是否成功还取决于中资企业的前期调研是否扎实、介入后的管理经营是否到位、市场开拓是否顺畅等诸多因素。适于中资企业在澳大利亚的农业投资项目主要是畜牧养殖类农场、乳业等畜产品加工、渔业捕捞和贸易、粮食作物种植加工和贸易、水果种植加工和贸易、园艺以及林业等。

(四) 装备制造领域

澳大利亚和我国的经济契合度高、合作愿望强烈、合作条件和基础较好，随着"一带一路"战略的实施，应当是中资企业积极开拓装备制造业合作的发达国家市场，并可以辐射到周边国家。深化能矿资源、基础设施、农业等领域的合作无疑将带动装备制造合作，达到以点带面的效果。中资企业可以此为基础，进一步推动双方在钢铁、有色、建材、铁路、电力、化工、轻纺、汽车、通信、工程机械、航空航天、船舶和海洋工程等重点行业的全面合作。传统上，欧美等发达国家在装备制造方面和澳大利亚合作较为广泛，具有先发优势。澳大利亚对装备制造的产品标准、质量等有较高的要求。澳大利亚企业的客户忠诚度较高，很难改变消费习惯。因此，中资企业介入澳大利亚装备制造领域前，需要做好全方位的细致准备，能够充分发挥出自身的比较优势。

五、从政府层面构筑中国在澳大利亚国际产能合作的支持体系

（一）以两国政府战略对接为契机

2014年11月，中国与澳大利亚从战略伙伴关系提升为全面战略伙伴关系。2015年8月，中澳第二轮战略经济对话在堪培拉举行，双方达成共识，要通过两国发展战略的对接进一步提升合作的领域和层次。2016年2月，中澳两国外长级会谈进一步明确了两国战略全面对接的具体内容。2016年4月，习近平主席、李克强总理和来访的澳大利亚总理正式宣布了中方"一带一路"倡议同澳方"北部大开发"、中国创新驱动发展战略同澳方"国家创新与科学议程"的对接。2016年4月19日，澳大利亚维多利亚州丹尼尔·安德鲁州长宣布本州的《中国战略》计划，一是要加强与中国中央政府及各友好省政府的往来，明确工作开展方向及目标，同时为更广泛的中澳合作奠定基础；二是推动维多利亚州成为全澳对亚洲有深入了解、具备亚洲能力的卓越中心；三是通过文化交流合作，建立联系，并为人文交往搭建新的平台；四是为政府大型基础设施项目等吸引投资，为维多利亚州经济的持续增长提供支持；五是为成功的中澳商业交往提供支持；六是根据维多利亚州的竞争优势以及中国特定的市场机会，有

针对性地开展贸易活动。中澳两国政府的全方位战略对接，为中资企业在澳大利亚开展国际产能合作提供了前所未有的机遇。

（二）以两国自由贸易协定为保障

2015 年 6 月，中澳两国政府签署了《中澳自贸协定》。一是在货物领域，双方各有占出口贸易额 85.4% 的产品将在协定生效时立即零关税。过渡期后，澳大利亚最终实现零关税的税目占比和贸易额占比会达到 100%，中国实现零关税的税目占比和贸易额占比会分别达到 96.8% 和 97%，都远超过一般自贸协定中 90% 的降税水平。二是在服务领域，澳方承诺协定生效后对中方以负面清单方式开放服务部门，是世界上首个对中国以负面清单方式就服务贸易承诺的国家。中方会以正面清单方式向澳方开放服务部门。此外，澳方还对中方在假日工作机制等方面作出专门安排。三是在投资领域，双方自协定生效后相互给予最惠国待遇，澳方同时降低中国企业赴澳投资审查门槛，并给予便利化安排。四是协定还在"21世纪经贸议题"的电子商务、政府采购、知识产权、竞争等十几个领域作了双方交流合作的推进规定。

（三）以两国产业支持政策为指引

国际产能合作是两国政府合作推动的发展模式，不能完全依靠市场，一定程度上需要政府有意识引导。中澳两国政府要通过产业支持政策的指引发挥引导与推动作用，搭好国际产能合作信息平台，为项目对接牵线搭桥，解决市场调节难以解决的信息不对称、贸易成本较大、投资风险较高等问题。中澳两国政府应当建立国际产能合作的产业支持政策指引平台，形成政策指引信息网络体系，了解企业对国际产能合作的供求状况，不定期地发布产业合作项目的供求信息和调查分析报告。我国驻外使领馆、驻外新闻机构、商会协会、金融机构等，应当与澳大利亚有关政府部门积极开展沟通和协调，尽早获得澳大利亚政府的产业支持政策以及重大项目开发信息，协助中资企业积极跟进项目并建立对接与合作关系。

六、从企业层面探索中国在澳大利亚国际产能合作的基本路径

（一）中资企业是中国在澳大利亚国际产能合作的主体

国务院发布的《关于推进国际产能和装备制造合作的指导意见》提出了"企业主导、政府推动，突出重点、有序推进，注重实效、互利共赢，积极稳妥、防控风险"的基本原则。企业作为最具活力的经济体，应当在中澳国际产能合作方面发挥最重要的作用。只有以企业为主体，才能坚持市场导向，反映市场需求。企业主体地位能否确立，主导作用能否发挥，很大程度上决定了中澳两国的国际产能合作的成败。中资企业可以通过在澳大利亚开展国际产能合作获得设计、研发、营销、服务、再创新能力等高端生产要素，逐步提高在全球价值链、产业链、物流链和创新链的地位。

中资企业可以从不同角度形成自己的战略目标，例如：结合澳大利亚基础设施的市场需求，推动钢铁、有色、建材行业等优势产能的国际合作；结合澳大利亚可能推进的"高铁"建设，加快拓展轨道交通装备的国际市场；开发和实施澳大利亚的境外电力项目；继续推动能矿等重点领域的境外投资；提高农业行业的国际合作水平；提高信息通信行业的国际竞争力；推动工程机械等制造企业在澳大利亚布局，完善全球业务网络；推动航空航天装备对澳大利亚的输出；开拓澳大利亚的船舶和海洋工程装备

高端市场。中资企业在澳大利亚开展国际产能合作更要尊重市场规律，要通过在澳大利亚的境外并购加快企业走向国际市场。中澳政府也应该给予必要的政策引导和支持，应当以企业为主体统筹规划，为两国企业的国际产能合作搭建平台，推动和支持两国企业的重大经贸合作项目。

（二）以规划先行作为在澳大利亚开展国际产能合作的先导

规划先行是中资企业在澳大利亚开展国际产能合作的重要抓手，可以从银政企三个方面共同推动。中资企业在澳大利亚开展国际产能的规划合作，应当紧密围绕"一带一路"建设的整体战略布局，充分对接澳大利亚自身的重大经济发展战略。在推动整体规划合作的同时，中资企业要围绕重点领域，发挥知名咨询公司、律师事务所、高校科研机构等社会力量的本土化优势，深入开展专项规划，以基础设施、能矿资源、农业、装备制造等为重点，加强国际产能合作的重大项目储备。

以澳大利亚"北部大开发"为例。澳大利亚政府设立了总额 50 亿澳元的北部地区基础设施专项贷款，以优惠利率贷款吸引全球投资者加入该区域港口、公路、管线、电力、水利等基础设施建设；此外，澳大利亚北部地区能矿资源极其丰富，主要有铁矿石、煤炭、黄金、铀、锌铅、铝土、锰、石油、天然气、页岩气等，北领地正在运营的有八大矿山，2014—2015 年矿业产值超过 32 亿澳元，LNG 的年产能为 1200 万吨，2014 年石油勘探投资达 5.5 亿澳元，页岩气资源潜力超过 200 万亿立方英尺，有 17 个成熟项目正在寻找投资机会；澳大利亚高度重视和中国在农业方面的合作，在 2015 年 12 月正式实施的《中澳自贸协定》中，农业领域合作涉及最多最全面，西澳大利亚州、昆士兰州和北领地政府每年都会组织中澳两国企业家参加以农业合作为重要内容的论坛和座谈会，宣介和对接合作项目，畜牧业、种植业、渔业、林业等适于中资企业投资开发。

(三) 共建国际产能合作产业园区服务产业集群需要

新形势下，共建产业园区是中澳国际产能合作的重要方式。新建的产业园区作为世界新技术革命和知识经济时代的产物，应当以科技创新型为主，能够高效率地实现国际产能合作的"产学研"三位一体发展目标，极大地推动产业转型升级。中澳两国共建产业园区，要协调好两国政府之间以及政府和市场及企业之间的关系，发挥好研究性大学在技术创新中的作用，构建完善的支持创新体系，创造有利于企业国际产能合作的文化氛围。在产业园区内，中资企业不仅可以共享配套基础设施和各类标准化服务，还能因配套企业和合作企业的地理位置邻近而降低物流等交易成本，更能发挥集体效益，享受两国政府的优惠政策支持和便利制度安排。成功的产业园区可以促进两国形成国际产能合作的新产业合作链条和产业合作集群，助力两国企业繁衍、发展和壮大，成为企业间互动和创新合作的发动机。

中澳两国共建国际产能合作产业园区，要特别注意文化差异、法律制度体系差异、区域内的合作模式差异、资本投入的差异。一是国际产能合作产业园区内的企业边界不能过于清晰，否则不利于企业间沟通合作，不利于产业集群的未来深化发展。二是国际产能合作的中澳企业合作力量不能过于分散，要提高生产资源的孵化效率，将高科技和创新作为中澳企业国际产能合作的主要动力，否则会形成劳动密集型和低增加值的低端产业特征。三是应当整合金融资源，为中澳企业国际产能合作提供成熟的金融产品，更好地推动国际产能合作产业园区的可持续发展。

(四) 搭建金融平台支持中澳国际产能合作项目

澳大利亚资本市场高度发达，金融业占全国经济总量的比重最大，是

GDP 的 8.4%，拥有亚太地区第二大股票市场，澳元在全球的交易量位居第五。应当在澳大利亚打造支持中澳国际产能合作的金融合作平台，发挥好中国的开发性金融、政策性金融、商业性金融等各种金融形态的优势和作用，加强同澳大利亚的澳新银行、国民银行、西太银行、联邦银行等本地银行、产业投资基金、保险公司、风险资本等金融机构的合作，畅通投融资合作渠道，在产品开发、风险控制、信息技术、经营管理等方面，全面提升自身的综合经营能力和影响力，全面开展项目融资、贸易融资、国际结算、财务顾问、离岸资产证券化、银团贷款等综合金融业务，为中资企业提供全方位的一站式服务，共同支持中澳国际产能合作重大项目的开发建设。

特别要指出的是，与商业性金融不同，开发性金融不以利润最大化为目标，可以在早期率先进入中澳国际产能合作的利润相对较低的领域，是中国在澳大利亚国际产能合作的先行者和开拓者。在中澳国际产能合作的起步阶段，大项目的投资回报期较长、利润率较低、资金缺口较大，商业性金融很难参与其中。因此，开发性金融可以自身的经验、影响力和资本投入，为其他金融形式的进入提供前期的支持与保障，优化中澳国际产能合作的金融支持生态环境。

参考文献：

胡怀邦：《以开发性金融服务"一带一路"战略》，《中国银行业》2015 年第 12 期。
张燕生：《"一带一路"的战略背景与实践机遇》，《清华金融评论》2015 年第 9 期。
白春礼：《以"四个全面"统领"创新驱动发展"》，《人民日报》2015 年 3 月 19 日。
孟刚：《21 世纪海上丝绸之路南线四国融资合作研究》，《开发性金融研究》2016 年第 1 期。

Department of the Prime Minister and Cabinet, *Our North, Our Future: White Paper on Developing Northern Australia*, Australia, 2015.

National Innovation and Science Agenda, Australia commonwealth government.

Department of the Prime Minister and Cabinet, *Green Paper on Developing Northern Australia*, Australia, 2014.

Australian Bureau of Statistics, Australia.

孟刚:《中澳创新驱动战略的对接路径和融资合作研究》,《全球化》2016 年第 6 期。

夏先良:《构筑"一带一路"国际产能合作体制机制与政策体系》,《国际贸易》2015 年第 11 期。

澳大利亚中国总商会:《中资企业在澳大利亚》,中国人民大学出版社 2015 年版。

严俊:《国际产能合作:全球经济治理的义利观典范》,《国家治理》2015 年第 42 期。

高薇:《国际直接投资理论的演变及其对中国的启示》,吉林大学博士学位论文,2011 年。

孟刚:《澳大利亚"北部大开发"为开发性金融带来战略新机遇》,《中国银行业》2016 年第 4 期。

蒋群英:《中国企业对外直接投资现状与对策研究》,复旦大学博士学位论文,2003 年第 4 期。

林莎:《中国企业绿地投资与跨国并购的差异——来自 223 家国内企业的经验分析》,《管理评论》2014 年第 9 期。

卓丽洪:《"一带一路"战略下中外产能合作新格局研究》,《东岳论丛》2015 年第 10 期。

武文卿:《中国制造追梦 2025 投资助推国际产能合作》,《中国招标》2015 年第 27 期。

李锦:《中央企业参与"一带一路"应把握七要点》,《中国远洋航务》2015 年第 8 期。

"一带一路"对接澳大利亚"北部大开发"投融资合作研究 *

一、两大战略对接是南太平洋地区的重要经济合作

　　21世纪海上丝绸之路是"一带一路"建设的重要组成，主要有两条线路，一是从中国沿海港口过南海到印度洋，延伸至欧洲，二是从中国沿海港口过南海到南太平洋。2014年11月，国家主席习近平在澳大利亚联邦议会发表《携手追寻中澳发展梦想，并肩实现地区繁荣稳定》的重要演讲，指出南太平洋地区是古代海上丝绸之路的自然延伸，对澳大利亚参与"21世纪海上丝绸之路"建设持开放态度，表示中方将支持澳大利亚实施"北部大开发"计划，双方要巩固能源资源等传统强项合作，加快培育基础设施建设、农业等新的合作增长点，实现两国经贸关系多元化。这为"一带一路"建设和澳大利亚"北部大开发"计划两大战略的对接指明了方向。

　　澳大利亚在南太平洋地区政治上有影响力，同时也是经济发展的主力军，和中国经济契合度高，合作基础扎实，合作意愿强烈。中国与澳大利

---

* 本文部分公开发表于《全球化》2016年第11期。

33

亚的双边关系已经从战略伙伴关系提升为全面战略伙伴关系。2014年6月，澳大利亚联邦政府对外发布绿皮书，宣布了"北部大开发"计划。2015年6月，澳大利亚联邦政府正式公布了《我们的北部，我们的未来——发展澳大利亚北部构想》白皮书，全面系统地阐述了"北部大开发"计划，提出了未来20年澳大利亚北部地区发展的愿景和蓝图。澳大利亚"北部大开发"的区域包括西澳大利亚州和昆士兰州的南回归线以北的北部地区以及北领地全境，面积为300万平方公里左右，约占澳大利亚总面积的40%，人口120万左右，约占澳大利亚人口总数的5%。根据2012—2013年的统计，55%的澳大利亚出口是从北部地区通过港口海路运输出境。澳大利亚北部地区能矿资源丰富，农业潜力巨大，基础设施建设需求强劲，离中国等亚洲国家地理位置最近，特别是达尔文港等几个主要港口是海上丝绸之路进入南太平洋地区的门户。

2015年8月，中澳第二轮战略经济对话在堪培拉举行，双方达成共识，中国的"一带一路"倡议和国际产能合作与澳大利亚的"北部大开发"倡议和国际基础设施发展计划有许多共同点，要通过两国发展战略的对接进一步提升合作的领域和层次。2016年2月，中澳两国外长共见记者时表示，促进两国发展战略对接，重点推动中方"一带一路"倡议与澳方"北部大开发"计划对接。2016年4月，习近平主席在北京会见澳大利亚总理特恩布尔，再次重申，希望双方做好中方"一带一路"倡议同澳方"北部大开发"计划、中国创新驱动发展战略同澳方"国家创新与科学议程"的对接，实施好《中澳自贸协定》，探讨开展更多务实合作项目。可以预见，中国政府倡导的"一带一路"战略和澳大利亚政府自身的重点发展规划对接的最佳会合点将会是在澳大利亚北部地区，"一带一路"建设对接澳大利亚"北部大开发"计划无疑将成为南太平洋地区的重要标志性合作内容之一。

二、"一带一路"和"北部大开发"对接的重点建设领域

"一带一路"建设的实施将促进沿线国家和地区经贸合作自由化、便利化和一体化，带动沿线基础设施建设和产业发展，在全球化范围内促进经济要素有序自由流动、资源高效配置和市场深度融合，实现互利共赢的战略目标。搞好"一带一路"建设，参与国际产业链的分工合作，可以增强中资企业在能源资源、基础设施、农业等领域的国际产能和装备制造合作能力，对中国经济结构转型升级具有巨大推动作用。"21世纪海上丝绸之路"优先推进基础设施互联互通、产业金融合作和机制平台建设，以政策沟通、设施联通、贸易畅通、资金融通、民心相通为主要内容，加强沿线国家区域经贸合作。澳大利亚联邦政府将农业食品、能源矿产、旅游度假、海外教育、医疗养老等作为将来支撑北部发展的五大支柱产业，并强调加大投入基础设施建设是落实"北部大开发"计划的前提和重中之重。在"一带一路"建设对接澳大利亚"北部大开发"计划方面，可以重点关注以下几个合作领域。

(一) 基础设施

基础设施互联互通是"一带一路"建设的优先领域。"一带一路"战略倡导国家间加强基础设施建设规划合作，抓住交通基础设施的关键通道、关键节点和重点工程，共同推进港口等国际骨干通道建设，实现国际运输便利化。澳大利亚北部地区由于人口分布较少，基础设施发展相对薄弱。澳大利亚政府在公路、铁路、港口、机场、管线等基础设施领域主要发挥制订规划、落实政策、推介投资等宏观管理职能，不直接参与基础设施项目的投资和建设。为了推动落实"北部大开发"计划，2014年，澳

大利亚政府打破惯例，专门设立了总额 50 亿澳元的北部地区基础设施专项贷款，以优惠利率贷款吸引全球投资者加入该区域港口、公路、管线、电力、水利等基础设施建设，并将直接投资约 10 亿澳元先期进行重点基础设施改造，其中包括 2 亿澳元的水资源开发工程、1 亿澳元的活牛运送通道建设以及 6 亿澳元的包括大北高速在内的公路改造项目，2015 年，白皮书又提出了金额达 12 亿澳元的投资计划，作为对之前 50 亿澳元基础设施投资的补充。

（二）能矿资源

"一带一路"建设倡导国家间加大煤炭、油气、金属矿产等传统能源资源勘探开发合作，加强能源资源深加工技术、装备与工程服务合作，积极推动水电、太阳能等清洁和可再生能源合作，形成能源资源合作上下游一体化的国际合作产业链。澳大利亚北部地区能矿资源极其丰富，主要有铁矿石、煤炭、黄金、铀、锌铅、铝土、锰、石油、天然气、页岩气等。澳大利亚已探明的铁矿石资源 90% 都集中在西澳大利亚州，勘探开发已经较为成熟，占据了全球铁矿石贸易的半壁江山，是力拓、必和必拓、FMG 等世界前几大矿商以及中资等各国企业铁矿石投资的重点地区。昆士兰州的黑煤资源丰富，且以露天矿藏为主，已探明工业经济储量占全澳的 62%，煤质较好，发热量高，硫、氮含量和灰分较低。焦炭、动力煤等黑煤的出口约占澳大利亚矿产和能源出口的四分之一[①]。北领地的能矿资源主要为黄金、铀、锌铅、铝土、锰、石油、天然气、页岩气等，目前正在运营的有八大矿山，2014—2015 年矿业产值超过 32 亿澳元，LNG

---

① 澳大利亚是世界最大的煤炭出口国，黑煤地质储量约 575 亿吨（工业经济储量 397 亿吨），居世界第六，褐煤地质储量约 418 亿吨（工业经济储量为 376 亿吨），占全球褐煤储量的 20%，居世界第二。

的年产能为 1200 万吨，2014 年石油勘探投资达 5.5 亿澳元，页岩气资源潜力超过 200 万亿立方英尺，有 17 个成熟项目正在寻找投资机会。

（三）农业

"一带一路"建设倡导国家间开展农林牧渔业、农机及农产品生产加工等领域深度合作，积极推进海水养殖、远洋渔业、水产品加工等领域合作。沿线国家深化农业领域合作，可以以彼此的对外依存度较高的农产品为重点，提高重要农产品安全保障能力，帮助促进合作国的农业出口。澳大利亚北部地区的土壤和气候适于多种农业生产，农业发展主要依靠畜牧业、种植业、渔业、林业等，农产品主要用于出口，最大的出口市场是东北亚、东盟、中东地区，农产品以产值为序依次为：小麦，油菜，大麦，羊毛，肉牛，蔬菜，绵羊和羔羊，水果和坚果，干草，牛奶，燕麦，园艺花卉及幼苗，蛋，鳄梨等。昆士兰州总面积 173 万平方公里，农业用地面积约为 147 万平方公里，占全州面积的 85%，68% 的面积用于天然林草场的放牧。西澳大利亚州总面积 252 万平方公里，农业用地面积 109 万平方公里，占全州面积的 43%，由于存在大面积的沙漠，全州的 37% 为极少使用土地。北领地总面积 135 万平方公里，农业用地面积 67 万平方公里，占 50%，最主要的土地利用类型为天然放牧，占 50%。澳大利亚高度重视和中国在农业方面的合作，在 2015 年 12 月正式实施的《中澳自贸协定》中，农业领域合作涉及最多最全面。西澳大利亚州、昆士兰州和北领地政府每年都会组织中澳两国企业家参加以农业合作为重要内容的论坛和座谈会，宣介和对接合作项目。目前，适于中资企业在澳大利亚北部地区投资的农业项目主要集中在畜牧养殖类农场、乳业等畜产品加工、渔业捕捞和贸易、粮食作物种植加工和贸易、水果种植加工和贸易、园艺以及林业等领域。

（四）产业园区

"一带一路"建设倡导国家间发挥比较优势，探索投资合作新模式，合作建设境外经贸合作区、跨境经济合作区等各类产业园区，促进产业集群发展。通过共建海外产业集聚区，推动当地产业体系建设，在教育、科技、文化、旅游、卫生、环保等领域共同拓展合作空间。澳大利亚北部地区有各类产业园区，虽然与中国模式不尽相同，但同样具有产业集聚区的功能，并以推动教育、科技、医疗、农业、旅游等当地产业体系建设为目标。中资企业可以发挥建设产业园区的比较优势，与西澳大利亚州、昆士兰州和北领地探索投资合作新模式，与澳大利亚本土企业以及其他跨国企业合作建设经贸、经济、高科技合作区等各类产业园区，促进澳大利亚北部地区的产业集群发展，在教育、科技、文化、旅游、卫生、环保等领域共同拓展合作空间，深化中澳两国的国际产能和装备制造业的产业体系合作。

三、澳大利亚"北部大开发"的主要内容

澳大利亚设立了由联邦政府的总理和副总理，西澳大利亚州、昆士兰州和北领地的州长共同组成的"北澳战略合作伙伴论坛"（The Northern Australia Strategic Partnership Forum），力图发挥各级政府的合力，共同负责领导、协调和执行"北部大开发"计划。2015 年，澳大利亚联邦政府公布了《"北部大开发"未来 20 年的发展规划（2015—2035 年）》，成立了由产业、创新和科技部部长担任负责人的"北部大开发"办公室，将从以下 6 个方面推动落实"北部大开发"计划。

（一）为支持投资制订更简便的土地政策

澳大利亚政府将在 2—5 年内梳理畜牧业改革的原则，对土著居民土地权管理提供更多支持，由澳大利亚政府会议（COAG）就土著居民土地管理和使用情况提交报告，就开发土著居民土地的新模式开展公众咨询，在澳大利亚北部建立适合商业使用的土地所有权信息数据，在土著居民土地管理方面引入新的基于成果的拨款模式，由澳大利亚政府会议开展土地调查取得进展，研究土著居民土地用于商业用途的排他性使用模式并取得进展。在此基础上，澳大利亚政府将就北部试点地区的土地所有权管理总结经验教训，在北领地就村镇土地长期租赁进行协商，在牧场租赁管理中减少规定要求，在北部对于个人拥有土著居民土地采用更简便的管理方式。在 10—20 年内，澳大利亚政府将解除所有的牧场租赁规定要求，争取实现排他性土著居民土地权租赁，土著居民土地和牧场土地的农业潜能信息容易获取，以吸引投资者，争取完成现有的土著居民土地认定工作，确保有更多确定权属的土地可用于投资和开发，在土地方面为澳大利亚土著居民带来更多机会。

（二）开发北部地区水资源

澳大利亚政府将在 2—5 年内建立总金额 2 亿澳元的水资源基础设施开发基金，在昆士兰州（以下简称昆州）Mitchell 水库、西澳州 Fitzroy 水库和北领地达尔文地区进行水资源评估并完成相关评估，完成昆州 Nullinga Dam 项目和西澳州奥得河三期项目可行性研究（视调研结果考虑推动这两个项目），启动大自流盆地可持续性计划第四期，以控制该地区空洞形成，确定水资源基础设施开发基金将支持的北部地区重点项目，决定重点水库的用水总量上限，修复大自流盆地空洞取得显著进展，在重点水库推广用水许可拍卖等方式的水资源交易市场，考虑对更多有产业利用潜力的水库进行水资源评估。在 10—20 年内，澳大利亚政府将完成对北领地、昆州和西澳州法定水资源计划的复评，按需建设更多的水资源基础设施，帮助投资者了解水资源位置信息，在北部实现清晰、受法律认可的水权体系，在北部地区利用水资源更为方便，在水库和地下含水层建立有效的水资源交易体系。

（三）发挥北大门作用，促进和亚太各国的经贸投资合作

澳大利亚政府将在 2—5 年内发布北部地区成熟招商项目的价值评估信息，开展调研，确定渔业和水产业的简化管理制度，推动北部科研机构和当地合作伙伴就热带地区健康问题开展合作，开展新的热带研究和商业化运用项目，帮助咨询顾问业进入北部地区的商业运营，对低风险渔业的环境许可有效期延长至 10 年，与土著居民及商业企业协商历史遗产保护管理体系，建立新的北部地区开发合作研究中心并投入运营，在达尔文开放新的边境口岸，在中国和印度开放旅游签证电子递交，试点快速通道服务，强化北部地区的生物安全管理，由澳大利亚北部保险专门团队提供推荐方案，更多土著居民担任生物安全巡查员，发布渔业和水产业评估报告，引进 10 年多次往返签证并试点简体中文的签证申请流程，将水产养殖管理权限由联邦下放到各州及领地，投入运行新的北部地区渔业联合管理窗口，涉及鳄鱼制品贸易、使用受保护动物的土著艺术品、袋鼠及澳洲鸵鸟出口管理简化措施到位，在进行咨询后，考虑修订联邦土著遗产立法，减少重复内容，增加相应保护，对于管理情况良好的渔业公司延长出口许可有效期至 10 年，评估北领地的出入境口岸并考虑在昆州和西澳州增设口岸。在 10—20 年内，澳大利亚政府将促进科研机构与外国合作伙伴通过强有力的合作获取以产业为导向的成果，将热带健康问题研究成果

转化为商业机会，促使澳大利亚北部成为全球领先的热带健康研究中心，促进澳大利亚北部与 APEC 及东盟国家建立更紧密的联系，通过世界级的研发建立一个规模庞大、不断成长、具有可盈利性的农业产业，建立清晰、低成本的监管体系，以支持有弹性的商业发展，在更为广阔的产业中有更多投资项目。

(四) 有序加快推进北部地区基础设施项目

澳大利亚政府将在 2—5 年内发布北部地区基础设施审计报告，建立总金额 50 亿澳元的北部地区基础设施专项贷款，建立一个商业小组为改善北部地区航空运输现状做准备，启动为期四年的地区航空运输及偏远地区机场升级计划，提高北部地区养牛产业供应链的生产力，为应对汤斯维尔机场新增的国际旅客，增加边检和生物安全相关设施投入，宣布总金额 6 亿澳元的道路相关一揽子计划，发布并不断更新北部基础设施建设计划，宣布牛肉运输道路拨款项目，开始 Mount Isa 至 Tennant Creek 铁路预调研，考虑降低检查和治疗壁虱的成本，宣布道路相关一揽子计划项目的开工时间，完成编制改善北部地区航空运输的计划，解除目前的沿岸航运管理框架，促进沿岸航运高效发展，力争北部地区基础设施专项贷款支持的项目取得显著进展，促使道路一揽子计划对于重点发展的道路产生预期的改善，在牛肉运输道路拨款项目内改善关键道路，建立更短和更直接的运输线路。在 10—20 年内，澳大利亚政府将改善偏远地区机场，有更高质量的信息可以支持北部地区基础设施的强劲发展，修建更多牛肉重型车辆运输可使用的道路，牛肉产业的生产力更强和稳健，更好地利用北部地区基础设施，由政府和商业界共同投资支持更多现代的、高效的基础设施。

（五）提高北部地区的劳动力数量和质量

澳大利亚政府将在 2—5 年内启动新的全国促进就业服务，在包括北领地在内的北部地区推行定点移民协议取得进展，扩大并简化季节性劳工项目以包括更多的农业和住宿相关产业，允许打工度假签证持有人在有需求的地区工作更长时间，启动面向太平洋岛国居民的低技能劳工试点计划，加大对北部地区商业界在产业技能拨款方面的支持，支持北领地简化工作技能执照相关流程，为公路建设项目准备的土著雇佣政策到位，旅游业提交季节性劳工试点方案，发布入境澳大利亚劳工情况报告，发布劳工关系框架报告，扩大简化北领地职业技能执照自动认定的适用范围，评估打工假期签证对国内劳动力市场的影响，在与昆州政府、商业界和社区讨论后，在昆州北部实行定点移民协议，评估面向太平洋岛国居民的低技能劳工试点计划实施情况。在 10—20 年内，澳大利亚政府将实现更多澳大利亚人在北部工作，土著居民社区有更多就业机会，北部商业界有更多打工度假劳动力，北部的劳动力需求基本得以满足，有技能的国内劳动力能得到低成本、高效的外国劳动力项目的补充。

（六）加强政府和非政府机构等的共同治理结构建设

澳大利亚总理将和昆州、西澳州、北领地行政首长保持战略合作关系，寻求澳大利亚国会的支持，将议会北部联合委员会设为常设委员会，继续开展"全国地图开放数据行动"在北部的工作，启动政府借调项目，首次开展由副总理向议会就北部开发进行报告的工作，并在今后每年度进行，在国防年度白皮书中增加北部地区内容的比重，将澳大利亚北部办公室搬迁至北部地区，强化北部生物安全管理，配置更多的一线执法人员，减少北部相关议题的过多公文，发布联邦改革白皮书，建立一个新的合作研究中心用于研究北部澳大利亚开发，在达尔文建立一个出入境口岸，议会北部联合委员会向议会提交年度报告，通过战略合作延续领导力，基于国防年度白皮书确定国防投资重点项目，通过人员借调改善政府机构工作能力，各层级的政府间建立更优化的联席会议和更强有力的合作，共同建设澳大利亚北部地区。

四、开发性金融支持两大战略对接的思路建议

落实"一带一路"建设的重要支撑是资金融通，特别是要加大开发性金融对重大项目的支持力度。开发性金融是以实现长期经济增长以及政府意图为目标，由一个或多个国家建立具有国家信用的金融机构，为特定需求者提供中长期信用，建设市场和制度，以大额中长期投融资为载体，引导社会资金投入具体项目，最终实现国家战略。中国主导地致力于服务"一带一路"建设的开发性金融机构主要有亚洲基础设施投资银行、丝路基金和国家开发银行等。国家开发银行目前是世界上最大的开发性金融机构和对外投融资银行。党的十八届三中全会，中共中央文件首次提出"开发性金融机构"。2015年3月，国务院正式批复将国家开发银行的定位明确为开发性金融机构。近年来，国家开发银行积极发挥金融引擎和先导作用，以市场化方式大力开拓国际合作业务，全力服务"一带一路"建设的实施，与沿线国家和地区建立了良好的合作基础。在"一带一路"建设对接澳大利亚"北部大开发"方面，开发性金融机构可以从多个方面发挥支持作用。

（一）配合双边政府，通过规划合作开展项目对接

开发性金融机构可以紧密围绕"一带一路"建设的整体战略布局，通

过规划合作和澳大利亚"北部大开发"计划充分对接。在推动整体规划合作的同时，围绕重点领域，发挥所在国知名咨询公司、律师事务所、高校科研机构等社会力量的本土化优势，深入开展专项规划，包括基础设施、能源资源、农业、经贸合作、产业投资、金融合作、人文交流、生态环保和海上合作等，实现点面结合的规划合作战略布局。在做好整体规划的基础上，以基础设施、能矿资源、农业、装备制造和国际产能合作等为重点，着重加强重点领域重大项目的谋划和融资方案的策划。

（二）以较成熟地区为重点，发挥示范作用和虹吸效应

"一带一路"和澳大利亚"北部大开发"的对接，可以较为成熟的地区为重点，培育和支持重大项目合作。2016 年 6 月，中国驻布里斯班总领事馆在澳大利亚布里斯班举办了"一带一路"对接"北昆大开发"论坛，昆州政府部门和企业及中国在澳企业、银行，国内江苏、山东、陕西等省企业代表共 200 多人参加了论坛。在昆士兰州副州长杰琪·特拉德和中国驻布里斯班赵永琛总领事的见证下，昆士兰州贸易投资局局长、中国驻布里斯班总领事馆商务领事以及国家开发银行共同签署了《"一带一路"对接"北昆大开发"投资机会合作会议纪要》，明确三方共同支持两国战略对接，在基础设施、能源资源、农业、产业园区等领域加强规划合作。昆士兰州贸易投资局、中国驻布里斯班总领事馆将在其政府能力范围内，对中国投资者提供最大限度的便利，国家开发银行将在符合内部授信审批管理制度的前提下支持中国企业投资，为其提供融资支持，以共同促进投资、实现互利共赢。三方将根据工作需要，不定期交换意见、沟通商业计划，并适时开展特色领域的规划合作，支持昆士兰州政府重点推动的中国丰盛集团在北昆的农业产业示范园区、码头和机场改扩建、健康医疗产业园区等综合产业园区的项目开发，发挥重大项目的示范作用和虹吸效应。

（三）打造银行同业合作平台，提升综合服务能力

开发性金融机构应当发挥好政策性金融、商业性金融等各种金融形态的优势和作用，加强同国际金融机构、澳大利亚的澳新银行、国民银行、西太银行、联邦银行等本地银行、产业投资基金、保险公司、风险资本等金融机构的合作，提高综合金融服务能力，全面开展项目融资、贸易融资、国际结算、财务顾问、离岸资产证券化、银团贷款等综合金融业务，打造金融合作平台，畅通投融资合作渠道，在产品开发、风险控制、信息技术、经营管理等方面，全面提升自身的综合经营能力和影响力。开发性金融机构可以在澳大利亚设立经营性分支机构，以银团贷款、直接授信和转贷等方式联合本地金融机构共同支持澳大利亚北部地区的重大项目开发建设，为参与澳大利亚"北部大开发"计划的中资企业提供全方位一站式服务，引导中资企业探索"EPC+F"（工程总承包加融资）、PPP（公私合营）、BOT（建设—经营—移交）、PFI（私营主动融资）等多种合作模式，积极参与重大基础设施建设，进一步推动国际产能合作和重大装备制造业"走出去"。

（四）创新金融产品，建立长效合作机制

澳大利亚是成熟的发达市场经济体，"北部大开发"计划中的很多开发性项目也多以市场化、商业化模式运作，融资领域竞争激烈。主要体现为：一是澳大利亚投融资法律体系错综复杂，涉及劳工保护、环境保护、原住民保护、土地水源等各个方面，中资企业融资需求更综合化，非常看重银行提供的财务顾问等中间业务的服务能力；二是海外同业特别是外资银行的融资成本较低，融资决策较快，审批流程较高效，贷款币种较丰富，能够满足客户"子弹式"还款（贷款到期一次性还本）等不同金融产

品的需要。开发性金融机构应当将投贷等金融产品相结合，加大金融产品创新力度，探索投融资合作新模式，为具有开发性的商业项目创新设计出不同的金融产品，对项目的风险偏好、风险容忍度、信用结构、贷款定价、贷款品种、审批流程等做出不同的标准和要求，建立长效合作机制，满足开发性金融机构以市场化、商业化的方式支持各类开发性项目，更好地可持续服务"一带一路"建设和澳大利亚"北部大开发"计划对接的战略需要。

参考文献：

胡怀邦：《以开发性金融服务"一带一路"战略》，《中国银行业》2015 年第 12 期。

Department of the Prime Minister and Cabinet, *Our North, Our Future: White Paper on Developing Northern Australia*, Australia, 2015.

孟刚：《21 世纪海上丝绸之路南线四国融资合作研究》，《开发性金融研究》2016 年第 1 期。

Department of the Prime Minister and Cabinet, *Green Paper on Developing Northern Australia*, Australia, 2014.

Australian Bureau of Statistics, Australia.

孟刚：《澳大利亚"北部大开发"为开发性金融带来战略新机遇》，《中国银行业》2016 年第 4 期。

孟刚：《中国在澳大利亚的国际产能合作研究》，《开发性金融研究》2016 年第 3 期。

孟刚：《中方对接澳大利亚科技创新战略的路径和融资合作研究》，《全球化》2016 年第 7 期。

中方对接澳大利亚创新战略的
路径和融资合作研究 *

一、创新驱动战略合作是中澳两国合作重点

2014 年 11 月，习近平主席在澳大利亚首都堪培拉发表重要演讲，将中国与澳大利亚从战略伙伴关系提升为全面战略伙伴关系，强调中澳双方要巩固能源资源等传统强项合作，加快培育新的合作增长点。2015 年 6 月，中国国务院印发《关于大力推进大众创业万众创新若干政策措施的意见》，这是推动大众创业、万众创新的系统性、普惠性政策文件，更是加快实施创新驱动发展战略的纲领性文件。2016 年 3 月，李克强总理在《政府工作报告》中强调，创新是引领发展的第一动力，必须摆在国家发展全局的核心位置，深入实施创新驱动发展战略。2015 年 8 月，中澳第二轮战略经济对话在堪培拉举行，双方达成共识，要通过两国发展战略的对接进一步提升合作的领域和层次。2016 年 2 月，中澳两国外长进一步明确了两国创新驱动等发展战略全面对接的合作目标。

面向未来，世界主要国家为了迎接新科技革命带来的挑战，纷纷把科

＊ 本文部分公开发表于《全球化》2016 年第 7 期。

技创新作为国家发展战略的核心，陆续出台创新战略和行动计划。中国科学院白春礼院长认为，世界科技革命有两种驱动：一种是社会需求驱动，一种是知识与技术体系内在的驱动。迄今为止，全球发生了五次科技革命（两次科学革命，三次技术革命）。一是16世纪和17世纪，以伽利略、哥白尼、牛顿等为代表的科学家，在天文学、物理学等领域带来了第一次科技革命。这场前后经历144年的科技革命是近代科学诞生的标志。二是18世纪中后期，蒸汽机、纺织机的发明及机器作业代替手工劳动带动了第二次科技革命，这也是世界上第一次产业革命，蒸汽机的广泛使用推动了英国的工业革命与现代化。三是19世纪中后期，以电力技术和内燃机的发明为主要标志的第三次科技革命，带动了钢铁、石化、汽车、飞机等行业的快速发展。四是19世纪中后期至20世纪中叶，以进化论、相对论、量子论等为代表的科学突破引发了第四次科技革命，也促进了自然科学理论的根本变革。五是20世纪中后叶，以电子计算、信息网络的出现为标志带来了第五次科技革命。

科技革命现在还在持续地发展。澳大利亚的科技决策管理体制是联邦政府起主导作用的多元分散体制。联邦政府制定国家科技政策和重大科技发展计划，资助科研机构、大学、合作研究中心和重大工业科技计划。州政府管理和资助本州的农业、卫生、环境和能源领域的科技工作。澳大利亚本届联邦政府高度重视创新驱动，将创新和科学作为政府的核心战略。2015年12月，澳大利亚联邦政府对外公布《全国创新和科学工作日程》，从文化和资本、广泛合作、人才和技能、政府示范作用等几个方面，全面推进创新驱动战略。

二、澳大利亚创新驱动战略实施计划

2013 年至今，澳大利亚政府已经落实了十大关键性创新举措[①]：一是在具有比较优势的先进制造业，食品与农业，医疗技术与药品，采矿设备、技术和服务业，石油、天然气和能源资源等关键领域建立了产业增长中心；二是出台了企业家计划，帮助创业者初始创业成功；三是改革了员工持股制度，以便创业公司能够吸引世界各地的优秀员工；四是通过 50 亿澳元的小型企业和就业计划实施了减税政策；五是为学校各年级的计算机编码教学提供支持；六是改革澳大利亚课程，让教师有更多课堂时间教授科学、数学和英语；七是要求新的小学教师必须在精通一项专业后才能执业，优先是科学、科技、工程和数学（STEM）；八是就众筹股权融资建立监管体系；九是与中国、日本和韩国签署了三个具有历史意义的自由贸易协定，缔约了《泛太平洋伙伴关系协定》；十是在创新创业领域尽可能地采用国际标准改进监管制度。2015—2019 年，在历史成功实践基础上，澳大利亚政府将推动从文化与资本、广泛合作、人才与技能、政府示范作用等四个方面全面落实创新与科学驱动战略。

（一）文化与资本

澳大利亚政府希望引导创业文化观念的改变，强调创新是强势创业文

[①] 澳大利亚的科学技术在国际上享有盛名，农业、生物技术、地学、天文学、医学等领域的科技处于世界领先水平。基础研究与应用基础研究具有很高的水平，拥有较强的研究队伍和世界一流水平的大学和国家科研机构，曾经产生了 7 位科学和医学诺贝尔奖获得者。但是，澳大利亚科技与经济脱节的问题长期存在，企业研究开发力量相对较弱，科研成果商业化的能力也不强。

化的产物，弘扬对创业失败和勇于尝试的宽容文化，为初创企业提供更多资金来源，加大支持研究力量，为创新型企业提供全方位支持。澳大利亚政府认为，从启动资金投入到开始产生收入，这个时期是创新创业的"死亡之谷"，在这个阶段，企业极易陷入现金流无法周转的困境。因此，要立足于创业与创新文化，对税收制度和公司法律进行调整。

在税收方面：一是为创新型创业公司的早期投资者提供新的减税计划。根据投资金额，投资者将收到 20% 的非退税性税务抵免，而且免征投资者的资本利得税。此外，对新设的早期风险投资有限合伙企业（ESVCLP），按投入资本的 10% 提供非退税性税务抵免，并将新 ESVCLP 的承诺资本上限从 1 亿提高到 2 亿元。二是引入一种更加灵活的"主要类似业务测试"以放宽"相同业务测试"的要求。根据"相同业务测试"，公司在经营活动发生改变后的经营收益不可抵补之前的税收损失。按照新的要求，创业公司可引进权益合伙人，确保新的商业机会，而不用担心税务"处罚"。三是移除对某些无形资产（如专利权）按法定寿命计提折旧的限制，所取代的是允许按其经济寿命计提折旧。

在法律制度方面：一是对破产法进行改革。现有的破产法过于关注惩罚失败的企业或使其背上失败的信誉风险。因此，修改后的破产法将违约破产清算期从三年减少为一年；将为董事设置避免因破产导致个人责任的"安全港"，条件是董事指派了专业重组顾问为一家资金困难的公司制定振兴计划；将禁止"事实本身"性质的合同条款，即如果公司正在进行重组，将不允许协议仅由于破产事件就被终止。二是调整现行的员工持股制度（ESS）为更加便利，以便有前景的公司招揽、保留优秀员工。新的制度将允许公司可以不必向竞争对手透露商业敏感信息便将股份出售给员工。这些变动是基于近期对 ESS 作出的改革之上，包括推迟员工的起税日期，并为在创业公司的员工引入额外的税收优惠。

在资本投入方面：一是设立一个新的 2 亿澳元 CSIRO 创新基金，共同投资新衍生公司和现有创业公司，这些公司将开发来自 CSIRO 和其他由公共资金资助的机构及大学的技术。二是设立一个新的生物医学孵化基金，与民营领域共同投资 2.5 亿澳元，用于医学研究的商业化。三是为小型企业和创业公司提供支持，帮助它们顺利组建并发展。四是支持"孵化器"，孵化器在创新生态系统中作用至关重要，会保证创业公司能够获得所需的资源、信息和网络，以便将其想法变成全球化规模化的新产业。

（二）广泛合作

一是建设世界级国家研究基础设施。为科技前沿的国家研究基础设施提供稳定的长期融资，以保证研究项目和工作不会流出澳大利亚且始终处于全球创新最前沿水平。未来十年，澳大利亚政府将为同步加速器提供 5.2 亿元资金，为平方千米阵提供 2.94 亿元，为国家合作研究基础设施战略（NCRIS）提供 15 亿元。2016 年，澳大利亚的首席科学家将启动一套程序，辨别国家研究基础设施各类需求，以便知晓资金的未来需求领域。

二是加强大学与企业间的更大规模合作。澳大利亚政府将通过改革，安排更大比例的科研经费资助，鼓励研究者与产业之间的合作，在预算外提供 1.27 亿元的科研经费资助。在评估大学研究工作时，将采取明确且透明的措施，首次引入非学术性影响以及行业参与。该措施将于 2017 年在澳大利亚研究委员会进行试点，2018 年全面实行，将通过把更多的中小型企业与研究者连接起来，扩大并启动创新连接计划等，打开澳大利亚研究委员会项目连续申请快速通道，并于 2016 年 2 月启动新一轮合作研究中心项目申请。

三是与世界相连。加强与全球重要经济体的连接，确保澳大利亚在研究、商业化和企业效益方面取得进步，并充分进入国际供应链和全球市场。这包括为澳大利亚创业者设立在硅谷、特拉维夫、上海等 5 个地方的科创中心,并充分利用澳大利亚不同移民社群在重要市场国家的专业能力,同时为澳大利亚与国际产业研究集群的合作提供资金。

四是投资信息科技的未来。设立一个新的网络安全发展中心,为澳大利亚企业在这些关键领域创造发展机会,投资 2600 万元建立硅量子电路,推动澳大利亚的量子计算能力达到世界顶级水平,并创造就业机会和创新商业模式。

(三)人才与技能

一是培养年青一代,使其具备创新能力并使用数字技术。为帮助年轻人为未来的工作岗位做好准备,澳大利亚政府将投入 5100 万元用于:通过在线学习活动和专家指导,提升教师开设数字课程的技能,引入科学家和信息通信技术(以下简称 ICT)专业人士参与的科学、科技、工程、数学(以下简称 STEM)合作伙伴计划。

二是增加女性在 STEM 的机会。澳大利亚政府将投入 1300 多万元支持更多的女生和女性参与到研究领域、STEM 产业、新创建公司和创业型企业,树立 STEM 领域女性榜样,建立一套有助于实现职场性别平等的计划和网络,例如澳大利亚科学领域性别平等(SAGE)试点计划。

三是改进签证安排。提供一种新的创业者签证,利用现有的政府海外网络积极寻求并鼓励有才之士来到澳大利亚,优化高素质 STEM 和 ICT 研究生获得永久居留权的途径。

四是鼓励掌握 STEM 读写技能。为了鼓励新一代年轻人掌握 STEM 技能,将在整个学校教育中投入 4800 万元:鼓励在校学生参与并取得科学和数学上的成就,支持学生参加国际竞赛,并在享有声望的总理科学奖中设立青年奖项;为学龄前儿童设计以 STEM 概念为核心的趣味实验和以游戏为主的应用软件;支持社区的科学活动,比如全国科学周,激发年轻人对 STEM 知识的学习兴趣。

（四）政府示范作用

一是设立一个新的独立的法定委员会——澳大利亚创新与科学委员会。该委员会由总理主持，作为全国科学、研究和创新政策与经济的战略协调者。委员会将对制订影响创新政策进行协调，以便澳大利亚能够构建一个更强大、更具创业精神的经济体。该委员会的一项职责是梳理现有的研发税收鼓励政策，改善其有效性和完整性，包括加强对额外研发费用的鼓励和审查。

二是通过政府采购鼓励创新。澳大利亚政府将设立数字科技市场，将实现 ICT 产品与服务的标准化，打破技术采购的障碍，让创业公司和中小型创业型企业更易与政府接近，将通过企业研究与创新举措对政府采购试行一种新的方法，要求中小型企业拿出创新型方案，而不是直接对现有产品投标。企业将发现，通过新数字科技市场，竞争政府每年在 ICT 花费的 50 亿元更为简单。

三是政府加入数据革命。为了推动创新并充分利用大量的公共数据，澳大利亚政府将消除各政府部门拥有的许多不同数据之间的共享障碍。非敏感数据将默认为在 gov.au 网站上公开可用，以便私营部门可以使用并再次利用这些数据来创造新的创新型产品、流程、服务和商业模式。

表 1　澳大利亚创新和科学驱动计划一览和政府资金投入计划

单位：百万澳元（1 澳元兑换 0.75 美元）（* 表示无法量化）

分类		2015—2016	2016—2017	2017—2018	2018—2019	小计	总计
文化与资本	天使投资人税收鼓励	0	3	51	51	106	
	风险投资新计划	0	0	*	*	*	
	查看公司损失	0	*	*	*	*	
	无形资产折旧	0	0	20	60	80	
	CSIRO 创新基金 *	0	5	5	5	15	
	生物医学翻译基金 *	2	6	1	1	10	
	孵化器支持计划	0	3	3	3	8	
	修改破产法	0	0	0	0	0	
	员工持股制度	0	0	0	0	0	
合作	重要的研究设施	0	15	198	245	459	
	鼓励参与	0	25	51	52	127	
	全球创新战略	0	7	9	10	26	
	网络安全发展中心	0	4	7	11	22	
	创新连接计划	0	3	7	8	18	
	量子计算	0	5	5	5	15	
	影响衡量与参与大学研究						
	ARC 连接项目计划	0	0	0	0	0	
人才与技能	鼓励所有澳大利亚人掌握数字能力和 STEM	0	26	25	33	84	
	通过签证支持创新	1	1	0	0	1	
政府范例	数据	0	25	25	25	75	
	企业研究与创新主动性	0	4	10	5	19	
	数字市场	3	5	4	4	15	
	澳大利亚创新与科学	1	2	3	2	8	
	公共数据战略	0	0	0	0	0	
创新与科学驱动计划中澳大利亚政府总计投入资金							1097

资料来源：澳大利亚联邦政府。

三、对接澳大利亚创新驱动战略的路径分析

（一）主动适应两国新科技革命合作的需要

从历史上的几次全球化科技革命看，科技创新始终是提高社会生产力和综合国力的重要战略支撑。科技革命源于社会需求的驱动，又将极大促进社会经济的大发展。在世界新科技革命中抢得先机的国家，必将成为世界经济的领头羊。中澳两国科学家预测了新一轮科技革命可能发生的领域：一是宇宙演化、物质结构、意识本质等一些基本科学问题，如量子世界和思维机器人等新突破；二是后化石能源和可循环资源；三是网络信息；四是先进材料和制造业；五是农业；六是人口健康。以上六大领域的任何一个突破性重大原始创新，都会为引发新的科技革命打开空间。澳大利亚是资源、能源、农产品、健康产品等输出大国，中国是最大的消费市场和制造业大国。应该说，两国在科技创新领域的合作，具有极强的互补性和实用性。中澳两国的强强合作，是全球化背景下共同领潮世界新科技革命的必由之路。

（二）在“一带一路”建设中搭乘两国自由贸易协定合作的便车

“一带一路”建设不是一个国家的独角戏，而是多国的共同合作，共同参与。因此，“一带一路”建设为中国的对外经贸合作开创了和其他国家经济建设深度融合的机会。自 1972 年澳大利亚和中国建交以来，两国经济始终高度互补。澳大利亚能矿资源丰富，农产品在自己的国内市场供远大于求，是全球经济总量排名第 12 的主要发达经济体国家。最为关键的是，澳大利亚市场经济体制成熟，没有受到 2008 年全球经济危机的影

响,法律制度健全,政府治理模式稳定,社会治安良好。随着"一带一路"建设的深化,中国和澳大利亚必然将日益增强互利合作的全面战略合作关系,行业发展逐步形成全面对接的全新局面。更为重要的是,澳大利亚在南太平洋地区历史上至今都很有影响力,是我国在大洋洲地区的重要合作大国。中澳两国深化创新驱动战略对接合作,将极大地促进中国和南太地区诸国的政策沟通、设施联通、贸易畅通、资金融通和民心相通,对"一带一路"建设在南太地区取得成功将起到关键性作用。中澳两国政府签署的《自由贸易协定》涵盖范围较广,涉及货物、服务、投资、电子商务、政府采购、知识产权、竞争等十几个领域。中澳两国在协定生效时就会有占出口贸易额85%以上的产品实现零关税。在短短几年过渡期后中国和澳大利亚最终实现零关税的税目占比和贸易额占比都将接近或达到100%。这个比例是全球其他国家之间普通自由贸易协定的降税水平无法比拟的。澳方在服务贸易方面对中国承诺幅度较大,只要没有在负面清单中明确的服务部门都将对中国开放。这一点,对中国的对外贸易合作是个突破,将为其他国家以负面清单方式就服务贸易向中国承诺打开先河。作为平等回应,中国将向澳大利亚列明可以开发的服务部门的正面清单。澳大利亚由于缺乏必要的劳动力资源,还将对中国的大学生等高素质群体实施假日工作签证。目前在投资领域,中澳两国合作良好,但是也出现了澳大利亚以国防和安全为理由,禁止中资企业赴澳投资的案例。随着中澳双方自由贸易协定的逐步实施,两国将相互给予对方最惠国待遇,澳大利亚也承诺为中资企业提供便利化安排,去除不必要的投资审查门槛。

(三) 以企业为主体推动中澳两国创新驱动战略对接

按照联合国教科文组织的定义,国际科技合作是指两个或者两个以上国家的机构、企业或个人达成合作协议后,进行知识交换。科技知识的共享往往是深化经济合作和贸易的桥梁，但是只有以企业为主体，才能坚持市场导向，反映市场需求。企业作为最具活力的经济体，在促进科技、创新和经济紧密结合[①]以及国际合作方面具有主体地位。在各个科技创新领域，企业在国际合作方面可以采取多种形式，如加强互联网、数据库、云端等新基础设施建设合作，在海外设立研发机构，建立企业间技术创新联盟，并购研发公司，集聚国际优秀人才等。经济全球化拓宽了以企业为主体的科学技术创新和国际合作的广度和深度。企业创新主体地位能否确立，主导作用能否发挥，很大程度上决定了中澳两国创新驱动战略合作的成败。因此，中澳两国应当以企业为主体统筹规划，为企业搭建科技创新合作和产学转化的平台，推动和支持企业在科技创新领域的重大经贸合作。

（四）共同打造在全球具有影响力的科技创新中心

中国将北京和上海等确定为全国科技创新中心，紧紧围绕国家创新驱动发展战略，以全球视野谋划，在更高起点上推进自主创新，积极布局国家科技重大专项和重大科技基础设施建设，着力扩大科技开放合作、增强自主创新能力，提高原始创新、集成创新和引进消化吸收再创新能力，部署一批前沿性、探索性技术研发，产生一批标志性技术甚至颠覆性技术，由"跟跑者"向"并行者"和"领跑者"转变，打造全球最具活力的科技创新中心，力争率先成为全球化科技创新革命的引领者。澳大利亚计划在美国旧金山、以色列特拉维夫、中国上海等海外地区设立 5 个创新中心（Landing Pad），以帮助澳大利亚初创企业在国际市场立足，并发展成为

[①] 西方发达国家的 500 家最大的跨国公司集中控制着本国 90% 以上的生产技术和 95% 的技术贸易。

高增长、高回报企业。这五个地区将是全球创新企业的聚集地,设立创新中心将为澳大利亚科技企业提供联合办公空间以及更多市场机遇,有利于澳大利亚企业融入国际商业圈,接触到更多创业型人才和投资人。

(五) 以产业园区为平台服务创新驱动的产业集群需要

不同于将成熟的城市定位为"科技创新中心",产业园区可以定义为"一大片土地细分后进行开发,供一些企业同时使用,以利于企业的地理邻近和共享基础设施。[1]"高科技型的产业园区作为世界新技术革命和知识经济时代的产物[2],能够高效率地实现"产学研"的三位一体发展目标,极大地推动全球科技创新和产业转型升级。中澳两国共建产业园区,要协调好两国政府之间以及政府和市场及企业之间的关系,发挥好研究性大学在技术创新中的作用,构建完善的支持创新体系,创造有利于企业创新创业的文化氛围。企业不仅可以共享配套基础设施和各类标准化服务,还能因配套企业和合作企业的地理位置邻近而降低物流等交易成本,更能发挥集体效益,享受两国政府的创新创业制度安排。成功的产业园区可以促进两国形成新的产业合作链条和产业合作集群,助力两国企业繁衍、发展和壮大,成为企业间互动和创新创业的发动机。

---

① Peddle MT. , "Planned Industrial and Commercial Developments in the United States: A Review of the History, Literature and Empirical Evidence Regarding Industrial Parks", *Economic Development Quarterly*, 1993, No.1, pp.107-124.

② 世界上最早的高科技产业园区可以追溯到 20 世纪 40 年代的英国和美国,英国开始在特大城市周围建设和培育生活和工作平衡的独立卫星城,成为产城融合发展的雏形,美国则于 1951 年建立了世界上第一个高科技园区——斯坦福科学工业园,即著名的"硅谷"。20 世纪 70 年代开始,全球产业园区得到大发展,很多国家涌现了各种名目繁多的"园"和"区"(Industrial Parks, Business Parks, Office Parks, Science and Research Parks, Bio-technology Parks, Eco-industrial Parks, Creative Parks; Export Processing Zones, Free-trade Zones, Enterprise Zones)。

　　澳大利亚对产业园区的理解和中国不尽相同，特别是由于澳大利亚具有"小政府大社会"的特点，因此在产业园区建设方面政府不会出面协调沟通，这为习惯于借助政府力量统筹安排的中资企业增加了难度。在澳大利亚建设产业园区，还存在本地居民的认同感、商业文化的凝聚力、技术市场的市场化程度、创新资本的介入模式等不同的情况，中资企业应该提前做好市场调研，防止在深度介入后，由于观念和文化等方面的理解差异，给自己造成被动局面。中资企业要和澳大利亚本地企业充分沟通，着眼于未来在产业园区内产业集群的深化发展，形成区域优势和规模优势，吸引国际领先的研究力量的入驻或参与，吸引全球的风险投资资本予以关注和支持，提高智力资源和生产资源的孵化效率，对关键性技术和核心技术给予有效的市场转化空间和畅通的成果转化渠道，要形成产业联动优势，以优厚条件鼓励科技专家和技术专家在产业园区就职，为园区内的人才市场有效流通提供便利，避免发展成为劳动密集型和低增加值的低端产业集群区。

四、融资支持中资企业对接澳大利亚创新驱动战略的建议

（一）以规划先行为先导对接中澳创新驱动战略合作

　　高科技和创新产业是资本密集型发展模式，既需要财政投入，又需要政策性金融支持，更需要大量高效运作的市场资金，只有这样才能将高科技转换为最终的产品或将创新创业转化为成熟的商业模式。世界各国支持创新驱动战略均将财政融资、信贷融资和证券融资等几种融资方式紧密结合。因此，中澳两国政府要加强顶层设计，规划先行，处理好政府和市场之间的关系，出台包括融资在内的创新驱动战略合作的整体方案，给市场

以相对稳定的政策预期。在融资方案规划先行方面：一是要结合两国创新驱动合作的重点领域，谋划产融结合的整体合作布局。二是要满足为企业搭建合作平台的需要，几种融资模式相结合，支持科技创新中心、产业园区等合作基地以及互联网、数据库、云端等基础设施建设。三是要根据两国产业合作的特点，引导资金重点支持重大合作项目，力争标志性突破，实现以点带面的作用。四是要在稳定的财政投入增长机制的基础上，建立多元化和多层次的市场融资渠道，引导和激励各方面资金支持中资企业参与两国战略对接。

（二）以开发性金融为主力军支持中资企业参与重大项目

开发性金融是以实现长期经济增长以及政府意图为目标，由一个或多个国家建立具有国家信用的金融机构①，为特定需求者提供中长期信用，建设市场和制度，以大额中长期投融资为载体，引导社会资金投入具体项目，最终实现国家战略。与商业性金融不同，开发性金融不以利润最大化为目标，可以在早期率先进入"一带一路"和"科技创新"等利润相对较低的领域，是产融结合的先行者和开拓者。中澳两国的科技创新合作需要基础设施特别是科技创新中心、产业园区等合作基地以及互联网、数据库、云端等重大基础设施项目的先行建设。这些项目投资回报期较长、利润率较低、资金缺口较大，商业性金融在早期阶段很难参与其中。因此，开发性金融是支持中澳创新驱动战略合作的主力军，可以自身的经验、影响力和资本投入，为其他金融形式进入提供前期的支持与保障。开发性金融机构可以结合中澳两国政府创新驱动战略合作热点，引导中资企业积极

---

① 中国的国家开发银行目前是世界上最大的开发性金融机构和对外投融资银行。党的十八届三中全会，中共中央文件首次提出"开发性金融机构"。2015 年 3 月，国务院正式批复将国家开发银行的定位明确为开发性金融机构。

参与相关的重大基础设施建设，为商业性金融逐步进入创造良好的市场环境和市场规则，优化中澳创新驱动战略合作的金融生态环境。

（三）以银行同业合作为平台提供综合金融服务

中澳银行同业深化合作将为两国创新驱动战略对接提供长久持续的保障。截至 2016 年 1 月，澳大利亚金融市场总资产规模约为 6.37 万亿澳元，其中国民银行、联邦银行、澳新银行、西太银行等四大商业银行占比80% 左右。这四大商业银行在产品开发、风险控制、信息技术、经营管理等方面优势突出，实力较强，是澳大利亚金融市场的主力银行。中资银行应当加强与澳大利亚四大主力商业银行以及多边金融机构的合作，全面提升在澳大利亚的综合经营能力和影响力，以银团贷款、直接授信和转贷等方式共同支持中澳创新驱动战略合作的重大项目开发建设。目前，很多赴境外投资的中资企业自有资金充足，融资需求综合化，更看重银行财务顾问等中间业务的服务能力。中澳两国银行同业的合作，可以实现优势互补，为中资企业量身设计出不同的金融产品，对项目的风险偏好、风险容忍度、信用结构、贷款定价、贷款品种、审批流程等制订出符合监管规定的标准和要求，为中澳创新驱动战略合作提供更为便捷的综合金融服务。

（四）以风险管控为核心完善融资支持的长效机制

科技创新中心、产业园区等合作基地以及互联网、数据库、云端等重大基础设施项目的风险管控是两国合作取得成功的关键，也是完善融资支持长效机制的根本保障。此外，从全球而言，科技型中小企业是科技创新的主要载体，必将成为中澳创新驱动战略合作的重要力量。总体而言，科技型企业具有轻资产、高风险、高成长、信息不对称等特点。金融机构在筛选企业客户时，关注的还款来源一般有四种：一是现金流，二是抵质押，三是保证人，四是再筹资能力。因此，科技型企业经常面临着严重的融资约束。在融资支持中资科技企业参与中澳战略对接时，完善的风险管理模式是开展风险贷款和股权业务必须配备的。金融机构和企业都应当完善内部风控机制，建立预警体系，整合识别、监督和控制融资风险的流程和模式。科技企业更要提高科技成果转化率，保持良好的信用贷款记录，从而获得融资长期支持的良好信用记录。

中资企业在澳大利亚建设经贸
合作区研究 *

一、中资企业在境外建设经贸合作区的基本情况

（一）中资企业建设境外经贸合作区的基本内涵

境外经贸合作区是在国家统筹指导下，中资企业作为建区企业，多家入区企业参与，按照商业化运作模式，在境外建设的基础设施较为完善，产业链较为完整，辐射和带动能力较强的各类经济贸易合作区，名称可以为农业园区、加工制造园区、科技产业园区、综合产业园区等。

1.从所在国家角度分析。中资企业发起的境外经贸合作区多在巴基斯坦、柬埔寨、泰国等发展中国家，随着我国综合产业能力的增强，近年来在发达国家建设的境外经贸合作区开始逐步出现。

2.从行业角度分析。中资企业发起的境外经贸合作区大多数集中在矿产资源、轻纺、家电、机械、电子、汽车配件等我国产能优势较为突出的制造行业，高科技境外经贸合作区数量较少，随着中国综合国力的增强和

---

* 本文部分公开发表于《北京金融评论》2016 年第 3 期。

人均收入的大幅提高，生物科技、教育旅游、健康医疗等境外园区开始涌现。

3. 从功能角度分析。中资企业发起的境外经贸合作区又可以进一步细分为市场开拓型、出口导向型、资源开发型、技术研发型、综合产业型。在中国政府大力实施"走出去"战略的背景下，境外经贸合作区在投资和运营模式上不断创新，中国产业集群式"走出去"取得了长足发展。

（二）中资企业建设境外经贸合作区的历史溯源

1978 年改革开放之初，我国主要以引进外资为主。20 世纪 90 年代，中资企业开始探索海外投资道路。2000 年，中国政府正式提出"走出去"国家战略，并在党的十六大报告中明确，把"引进来"和"走出去"相结合，不断提高我国对外开放水平。2005 年底，经国务院批准，商务部正式启动了境外经贸合作区建设机制，由中国政府主导和支持中资企业集群式"走出去"。境外经贸合作区运行较为成熟并符合一定条件后，中国商务部将予以确认，给予更大程度上的政策支持。2006 年 6 月和 2007 年 7 月，商务部分两批在 15 个国家确定了 19 个境外经贸合作区。经过近十年的积累和发展，中国的境外经贸合作区建设机制取得了丰硕成果。

根据商务部的统计，截至 2015 年 9 月，中资企业正在建设的具有境外经贸合作区性质的项目共有 69 个，分布在 33 个国家。69 个合作区建区企业累计完成投资 67.6 亿美元，其中基础设施投资 34.2 亿美元，实际平整土地 376.6 平方公里；入区企业 1088 家，其中中资控股企业 688 家，累计实际投资 99.2 亿美元；合作区累计总产值 402.1 亿美元，缴纳东道国税费 12.9 亿美元；解决当地就业 14.9 万人。其中，在"一带一路"沿线国家建设的境外经贸合作区有 48 个，分布在 18 个国家。

（三）中资企业建设境外经贸合作区的政策支持

我国正式启动境外经贸合作区建设后，国务院、商务部和财政部等有关部委及国家开发银行、中国出口信用保险公司等相继出台了《境外中国经济贸易合作区的基本要求和申办程序》《境外经济贸易合作区确认考核和年度考核管理办法》《关于推进境外经济贸易合作区建设的意见》《关于加强境外经济贸易合作区风险防范工作有关问题的通知》等多项配套政策措施，从发展资金、授信、税收、审批、通关、安全、保险、培训等方面对境外经贸合作区的建设给予政策支持。

2013年，商务部和国家开发银行联合下发了《关于支持境外经济贸易合作区建设发展有关问题的通知》，为符合条件的合作区实施企业、入区企业提供投融资等方面的政策支持，具体措施包括：一是商务部对企业投资建设的合作区进行宏观指导，在国别和产业指引、资本投资便利化、境外投资保障等方面提供支持。二是国家开发银行根据国家对外发展战略的需要，支持国内企业集群"走出去"，为合作区建设提供投融资等服务。三是商务部和国家开发银行将支持或共同开展合作区布局和发展规划等研究工作。四是商务部与国家开发银行将建立有关合作区信息共享机制，加强信息交流，相互通报关于合作区确认考核、年度考核及投融资进展情况，引导企业有序赴合作区投资经营。五是根据合作区推动工作的需要，商务部、国家开发银行将不定期对合作区项目融资中存在的重要问题进行协调。

（四）中资企业建设境外经贸合作区的发展前景

新形势下，境外经贸合作区被赋予了新的使命。2015年3月，国家发改委、外交部和商务部联合发布的《推动共建丝绸之路经济带和21世纪海上丝绸之路的愿景与行动》指出:"根据'一带一路'走向,陆上依托国际大通道,以沿线中心城市为支撑,以重点经贸产业园区为合作平台,探索投资合作新模式,鼓励合作建设境外经贸合作区、跨境经济合作区等各类产业园区,促进产业集群发展"。

2015年5月,国务院发布的《国务院关于推进国际产能和装备制造合作的指导意见》进一步明确:"要提高企业'走出去'能力和水平,鼓励企业积极参与境外产业集聚区、经贸合作区、工业园区、经济特区等合作园区建设,营造基础设施相对完善、法律政策配套的具有集聚和辐射效应的良好区域投资环境,引导国内企业抱团出海、集群式'走出去'。"显而易见,以中资企业为主体建设境外经贸合作区,已经是我国推动全球经贸合作战略布局的行之有效的方式之一,将成为中国政府倡导的"一带一路"建设和我国优势产业"走出去"的重要合作载体和运行模式。

表1　商务部确认的19家境外经贸合作区基本情况

序号	名称	所在国家	建园企业	园区产业
1	巴基斯坦海尔家电工业区	巴基斯坦	(山东)海尔集团	家电及配套产业和物流运输等
2	印尼中国沃诺吉利经贸合作区	印度尼西亚	(广西)广西农垦集团	建筑材料、化工、制药等
3	俄罗斯圣彼得堡波罗的海经贸合作区	俄罗斯	(上海)上海实业集团	房地产、商贸、办公、休闲、餐饮、娱乐等
4	俄罗斯乌苏里斯克经济贸易合作区	俄罗斯	(浙江)中国康吉国际投资有限公司	服装、鞋类、皮革、家电、木业等
5	俄中托木斯克木材工贸合作区	俄罗斯	(山东)烟台西北林业有限公司、中国国际海运集装箱股份有限公司	林地、采伐、木材深加工等
6	泰中罗勇工业区	泰国	(浙江)中国华立集团	汽车配件、机械、建筑材料、家电、电子等

序号	名称	所在国家	建园企业	园区产业
7	柬埔寨太湖国际经济合作区	柬埔寨	（江苏）红豆集团	轻纺服装、电子、机械、高新科技、物流等
8	越南中国(深圳)经济贸易合作区	越南	（深圳）中航集团、中深国际公司、海王集团	纺织轻工、医药生物、机械电子等
9	越南中国龙江经济贸易合作区	越南	（浙江）前江投资管理有限责任公司	机械电子、轻纺服装、建筑材料等
10	韩中工业园区	韩国	（重庆）中国东泰华安国际投资有限公司	汽车、船舶零件、生物科技、高科技、物流等
11	尼日利亚广东经济贸易合作区	尼日利亚	（广东）广东新广国际集团	家具、五金、建材、陶瓷等
12	尼日利亚莱基自由贸易区	尼日利亚	（江苏）江宁经济技术开发区和南京北亚集团	制造、进出口贸易、休闲旅游等
13	埃及苏伊士经贸合作区	埃及	（天津）天津泰达投资控股有限公司	轻纺服装、电器设备、通用工程产品等
14	埃塞俄比亚东方工业园	埃塞俄比亚	（江苏）江苏永钢集团有限公司	冶金、机械、建材等
15	阿尔及利亚中国江铃经贸合作区	阿尔及利亚	（江西）中鼎国际、江铃汽车集团	汽车制造、建筑材料等
16	赞比亚中国有色工业园	赞比亚	（北京）中国有色矿业集团有限公司	铜钴等有色金属开采、冶炼等
17	天利(毛里求斯)经济贸易合作区	毛里求斯	（山西）山西天利实业集团公司	生产加工、转口贸易、商务服务、度假娱乐等
18	委内瑞拉中国科技工贸区	委内瑞拉	（山东）山东浪潮集团	家电、农机、电子工业等
19	墨西哥中国吉利工业经济贸易合作区	墨西哥	（浙江）浙江吉利美日汽车有限公司	汽车生产、配套零件、商业贸易等

资料来源：根据商务部境外经贸合作区网站信息整理。

二、在澳大利亚的中资企业经贸合作区案例和
服务职能分析

中国与澳大利亚已经从战略伙伴关系提升为全面战略伙伴关系。中澳两国领导人正式宣布了中方"一带一路"倡议同澳方北部大开发、中国创新驱动发展战略同澳方"国家创新与科学议程"的对接。国家间的全方位战略合作为中资企业在澳大利亚产业集群化发展提供了前所未有的历史机遇。新形势下,中资企业在澳大利亚建设经贸合作区,能够高效率地助力企业集群化发展,推动产业转型升级,共同提高在全球价值链、产业链、物流链和创新链的地位。在经贸合作区内,中资企业不仅可以共享配套基础设施和各类标准化服务,还能因配套企业和合作企业的地理位置邻近而降低物流等交易成本,更能发挥集体效益,享受两国政府的优惠政策支持和便利制度安排,促进中澳两国形成新产业合作链条和产业合作集群,助力两国企业繁衍、发展和壮大,成为企业间互动和创新合作的发动机。

(一)在澳大利亚的中资企业经贸合作区案例分析

1. 新南威尔士大学火炬创新园区项目

(1)项目概述

澳大利亚新南威尔士大学创建于 1949 年,位于悉尼市,是亚太地区顶尖的研究密集型大学。2016 年 1 月,新南威尔士大学校长率团访问了科技部火炬中心,就在新南威尔士大学建设火炬创新园区与火炬中心达成了共识。火炬创新园将作为中澳科技产业合作的全新平台,重点围绕能源与环境、先进材料和生物技术等领域为中澳企业、科研专家、投资人及创业青年提供服务。

（2）项目进度

火炬创新园的建设将分两步走：一是新南威尔士大学将在其肯兴顿主校区内，提供 1000 平米的办公场所建设企业孵化器，用于吸引中国企业在澳设立研发场所或开展在澳业务；二是新南威尔士大学将使用悉尼校区内的 2 万余平米土地建设包括企业共享实验室、中试基地、创客空间和企业孵化器等众多创新平台的综合性科技产业创新区。

（3）中方因素

科技部火炬中心成立于 1989 年，隶属于国家科学技术部，以"发展高科技，实现产业化"为己任，大胆探索，不断创新，不断推动中国高新技术产业向前发展。该项目价值 1 亿澳元，将通过在新南威尔士大学新建科技园区，引导中资企业在澳大利亚科研领域加强合作。

（4）高访签约

2016 年 4 月，在李克强总理和来华访问的澳大利亚总理特恩布尔见证下，科技部火炬中心与澳大利亚新南威尔士大学签署了《关于在澳共建火炬创新园的谅解备忘录》，共同启动了新南威尔士大学火炬创新园项目建设工作。该项目首批合作伙伴包括富春江集团/杭州电缆股份有限公司、福州丹诺西诚电子科技有限公司、深圳凯豪达新能源有限公司、深圳市智能电力有限公司，以及一批在光伏能源领域具有优势的企业等。

2. 澳大利亚教育城项目

（1）项目概述

澳大利亚教育城项目位于墨尔本市区西南约 25 公里处，拟打造成南半球首个国际教育科研 CBD 和全球第一个"认知城市"，占地 5 平方公里，总建筑面积 604 万平方米，市中心面积 1.3 平方公里。澳大利亚教育城项目定位于打造国际级教育科研中央商务区，是澳大利亚过去 50 年最大的造城项目，将创造超过 10 万个就业机会，计划邀请中国、英国、美国和澳大利亚最好的研发型大学联合办学,加上澳大利亚最好的中学和技术培训学校的分校,将有超过 5 万名在读学生。

(2) 独特优势

澳大利亚科技水平高度发达,拥有十余位诺贝尔奖获得者,多项发明创造在全球享有较高的知名度,50% 的大学在学术和研究方面排名全球前 500 名,全球国际留学生数量排名第四。2016 年 5 月,澳大利亚政府颁布了首个国际教育规划,目标在未来 10 年把在澳留学生人数翻一番。墨尔本是公认的全球知识中心,拥有众多世界一流大学和研究机构,具有开发式合作办学理念。

(3) 中方因素

澳大利亚教育城项目由中资企业参与,计划邀请中国著名大学合作,为中国名校免费提供教学楼和其他教学设施,免租金 25 年,将协助中国名校在澳大利亚取得一切合法经营资质,按照学校要求在全球范围内招聘优秀教师,为学校提供行政管理和非教研类综合服务,并承诺确保澳大利亚本地学生和国际留学生的生源。

3. 丰盛综合产业园区项目

(1) 项目概述

丰盛综合产业园由南京丰盛产业控股集团有限公司独立开发,位于澳大利亚昆士兰州北部地区,占地面积约 30 平方公里,初步规划分为生态农业园区、教育培训园区、健康养生园区、体育运动园区、度假旅游园区和商业休闲园区。按现有规划,项目总建筑面积逾 80 万平方米,码头泊位约 860 个,住宅若干套,高尔夫球场 3 座,四星级酒店一座,五星级酒店一座,建成后可成为逾 1.5 万人长期居住的小城镇,总建设周期约 15—20 年。

(2) 项目进度

2016 年至 2023 年拟开展生态农业园区及配套基础设施一期项目,包括：农业园区的蓄水坝，灌溉系统和农作物采购、种植、采摘、储存、加工、运输；配套基础设施包括码头、小型私人及货运机场、体育公园、园区沟渠、道路、水、电、网络、排污系统、排水系统、变电站、储水站改造升级等。2017 年至 2024 年拟开展教育培训园区一期项目，拟推动国内大学和昆士兰的大学合作，设立农业、飞机游艇驾驶、医疗服务管理、酒店、高尔夫等的培训学校，包括前期规划审批、校舍建设、执照验证、运营管理、配套设施建设等。

（二）在澳大利亚的中资企业经贸合作区服务职能分析

作为产业集聚发展的重要平台，中资企业在澳大利亚建设经贸合作区，应当参考中国商务部等部委的产业服务指引，借鉴其他境外经贸合作区的成功经验，高度重视为入区企业提供高质量的综合服务。

1. 信息咨询服务，包括政策咨询、法律服务、产品推介等

经贸合作区可以为入区企业搭建与澳大利亚政府部门和有关机构沟通、协调的平台，提供包括投资、贸易、金融、产业等相关政策咨询服务，帮助入区企业了解澳大利亚法律，熟悉澳大利亚投资环境，寻找和委托澳大利亚的法律服务中介机构，协助入区企业参加澳大利亚举办的展览会、产品对接会、贸易洽谈会等，为入区企业在澳大利亚搭建本地化的合作平台。

2. 运营管理服务，包括企业注册、财税事务、海关申报、人力资源、金融服务、物流服务等

经贸合作区应当建立与澳大利亚外资管理部门或投资促进机构的沟通和联系机制，为入区企业提供在澳大利亚注册登记的相关咨询服务，协助

入区企业办理注册登记、投资项目环境影响评估和规划设计审批等相关手续，为入区企业提供澳大利亚相关财务和税收方面的政策咨询，并协助入区企业开展财务管理、商标注册、税收申报和缴纳等工作，为入区企业提供澳大利亚关于海关申报、进口设备清关、仓储运输、进出口手续、原产地证明及关税申报等相关咨询服务，为入区企业提供澳大利亚关于员工管理、人员签证等政策咨询服务，并协助入区企业办理员工培训、人员招聘、人才交流等人力资源事务，为入区企业提供投融资、保险等金融咨询服务，协助入区企业办理相关金融手续，建立入区企业和中国及澳大利亚金融机构联系的渠道，根据入区企业要求，提供必要的物流服务，如运输、存储、装卸、搬运、配送、信息处理等。

3. 物业管理服务，包括租赁服务、厂房建造、生产配套、生活配套、维修服务、医疗服务等

经贸合作区应当按照澳大利亚法律和商业惯例，为入区企业提供标准厂房、写字楼、仓库、展示厅、堆场等设施的租赁服务，在入区企业新建厂房时，提供必要支持，协助办理包括设计、施工招投标、建筑许可证、开工证以及验收执照等在内的相关手续，为入区企业提供供电、供水、供暖、通信、通气、安保、废水处理、垃圾处理、有毒废料处理等生产配套便利和服务，为入区企业提供生活配套设施服务，如员工宿舍、高级公寓、运动健身、文化娱乐，以及各式餐饮等，为入区企业提供专业、高效的维修服务，帮助入区企业解决生产和生活中遇到的维修困难，为入区企业员工提供简易医疗救治服务，与澳大利亚医院建立畅通的紧急救治通道等。

4. 突发事件应急服务

经贸合作区应当与澳大利亚政府管理机构紧密配合，做好突发事件应急预案，做到有效预防和应对火灾、水灾、罢工、破坏活动等突发事件，落实好灾后救援等突发事件保障工作，确保园区及入区企业的人身财产安全。

三、中资企业在澳大利亚建设经贸合作区的思路建议

（一）定位清晰，规划科学，坚持领先的国际竞争优势

在澳大利亚建设经贸合作区投资额度较大，回报周期较长，参与企业较多，不可预见的困难较复杂，如果定位不清晰，规划不科学，建区企业将会面临很大的投资风险。因此，建区企业应当找准产业定位，科学规划好产业集群化发展的各项条件，协调好政府和市场、建区企业和入区企业、园区小环境和澳大利亚大环境的关系，更好地发挥中资企业在对外投资中的竞争优势。近年来，基于中国改革开放以来的多年积累，中资企业积极探索高端制造业、技术和资本密集型的产业集群化发展方向，正在跳出发展中国家的以低成本、劳动密集型、中低端制造业为特点的产业集群化发展模式，将逐渐形成全新的中国特色的"国家比较竞争优势"。中资企业在澳大利亚建设经贸合作区，应当找准和坚持先进的国际产业竞争优势，因势利导形成具有中国特色的高端产业集群，在新的国际产业链分工中力争高附加值的上游地位。

（二）和当地经济优势互补，促进产业升级

科技创新始终是提高社会生产力和综合国力的重要战略支撑。科技革命源于社会需求的驱动，又将极大促进社会经济的大发展。在世界新科技革命

中抢得先机的国家，必将成为世界经济的领头羊。澳大利亚是资源、能源、农产品、健康产品等输出大国，中国是最大的消费市场和制造业大国。应该说，两国在先进制造业和科技创新领域具有极强的互补性和实用性。中澳两国企业的合作在全球化背景下具有很大的发展空间。中资企业和澳大利亚当地企业的经济优势互补发展，将有助于自身的产业升级，在更高层面上，还能共同领潮世界新科技革命。以高科技型产业发展为特色的经贸合作区作为世界新技术革命和知识经济时代的产物，能够高效率地实现"产学研"三位一体的发展目标，极大地推动科技创新和产业转型升级。成功的经贸合作区可以促进中澳两国企业形成新的产业合作链条和产业合作集群，助力中资企业繁衍、发展和壮大，成为中资企业创新创业的发动机。

(三) 强强联合，加强和国内一流产业园区的合作

中资企业在澳大利亚建设经贸合作区应当加强和国内一流产业园区的合作，强强联合，形成合力。北京的中关村产业园区、上海的张江产业园区、江苏的苏州工业园区等具有丰富的产业园区运作经验。2016 年 3 月，在国家"一带一路"办公室、科技部、外交部和中关村管委会的大力支持下，中关村"一带一路"产业促进会成立，将以"一带一路"建设为基础，围绕"一带一路"沿线国家基础设施互联互通、重点经贸产业园区建设及科技产业转移等内容，充分发挥中关村创新及高科技产业等优势，以市场运作的方式，建立企业"走出去"的合作共同体，打造最具全球影响力的国际合作服务平台，促进不同产业领域的企业、产业链上下游企业通过优势互补，抱团出海，有效应对企业独自"走出去"的挑战和风险，帮助企业拓展国际市场。2016 年 7 月，中关村"一带一路"产业促进会、国家开发银行上海市分行和南京丰盛产业控股集团有限公司签署了《开发性金融合作协议》，三方约定，发挥中关村的融智和企业服务平台优势，发挥

国开行的融资优势，支持丰盛集团在澳大利亚昆士兰州进行综合产业园区领域的开发和投资，推动园区建设项目成为"一带一路"和澳大利亚"北部大开发"战略对接的新领域和新方向。

参考文献：

胡怀邦：《以开发性金融服务"一带一路"战略》，《中国银行业》2015 年第 12 期。

Conway H.M., L.L.Liston, R.J.saul, *Industrial Park Growth: An Environmental Success Story*, Georgia: Conway Publicaitons, 1979.

澳大利亚中国总商会：《中资企业在澳大利亚》，中国人民大学出版社 2015 年版。

孟刚：《21 世纪海上丝绸之路南线四国融资合作研究》，《开发性金融研究》2016 年第 1 期。

孟刚：《中方对接澳大利亚创新驱动战略的路径和融资合作研究》，《全球化》2016 年第 7 期。

孟刚：《澳大利亚"北部大开发"为开发性金融带来战略新机遇》，《中国银行业》2016 年第 4 期。

孟刚：《澳大利亚基础设施公私合营（PPP）模式的经验与启示》，《海外投资与出口信贷》2016 年第 4 期。

孟刚：《中国在澳大利亚的国际产能合作研究》，《开发性金融研究》2016 年第 3 期。

Department of the Prime Minister and Cabinet, *Our North, Our Future: White Paper on Developing Northern Australia*, Australia, 2015.

National Innovation and Science Agenda, Australia commonwealth government.

Australian Bureau of Statistics, Australia.

肖雯：《中国境外经贸合作区的发展研究——以浙江省的境外合作区为例》，浙江大学硕士学位论文，2014 年。

关利欣：《中新境外工业园区比较及启示》，《国际经济合作》2012 年第 1 期。

余索：《中国企业境外产业园区开发的实践及体会》，《特区经济》2014 年第 1 期。

荀克宁：《"一带一路"时代背景下境外园区发展新契机》，《理论学刊》2015 年第 10 期。

李东红：《境外产业园区："一带一路"下产业抱团走出去》，《金融世界》2016 年第 1 期。

澳大利亚基础设施 PPP 模式的
经验和启示 *

一、澳大利亚基础设施 PPP 模式简介

（一）PPP 含义及全球基本状况

PPP（Public-Private Partnership），是公私合作合伙关系的简称，即政府和社会资本合作，为公众提供基础设施等公共产品的一种合作机制。英国是 PPP 模式的起源国。根据公私合作的复杂程度和合作程度，有些研究机构① 通过 PPP 模式融资的国家分成了三个梯队。英国和澳大利亚是第一梯队，被视为 PPP 模式发展最为成熟的国家。荷兰、意大利、新西兰、爱尔兰、法国、加拿大、美国、日本、德国等是第二梯队，PPP 市场成熟度相对较高。印度、俄罗斯、南非、巴西、匈牙利、捷克、比利时、丹麦以及我国是第三梯队，PPP 市场成熟度较低，有待进一步发展。根据著名的 PPP 研究机构 PWF（Public Works Financing）分析，1985—2011 年，

---

* 本文部分公开发表于《海外投资与出口信贷》2016 年第 4 期。

① 中债资信 PPP 系列专题研究之一：PPP 模式定义及在国内外发展情况概述，2015 年 1 月。

全球范围内的 PPP 项目总投资已达 7700 多亿美元，其中亚洲和澳大利亚合计占比 24.2%。

（二）基础设施 PPP 项目的基本特征

世界各国都高度重视本国的基础设施建设[①]。基础设施对于一国的社会经济及公众生活起到基础性的支撑作用。作为一个国际上通用的较为成熟的概念，各国的基础设施 PPP 基本上具有共同的特征：一是项目具有社会性和公益性特点，投资成本高，建设周期长，回报率较低，非竞争性和非排他性弱化，具有较强的公众参与性。二是政府通过让渡特许经营权和冠名权等项目权利的方式来吸引社会资本参与项目建设，政府担任项目发起人角色，社会投资主体担任项目投资人的角色。三是社会资本的参与有效缓解了政府的财政压力，能够转变政府职能，提高公共服务水平，增加基础设施建设活力。四是能够让政府和社会资本的双方合作实现优势互补，合理分担风险。

（三）澳大利亚基础设施 PPP 模式的基本类型

澳大利亚政府出台的政策指南将基础设施 PPP 模式分为两类。第一种类型称为"社会性基础设施 PPP"，是指偿还社会资本融资的主要收入来源或资金来源是政府支付的服务（或使用）费用。这种模式通常用于科

---

① 德勤在 2007 年提出了 PPP 的市场成熟度理论，列出了衡量各国 PPP 市场成熟度的九个要素：（1）对风险转移原则的理解程度；（2）公共部门运用 PPP 的经验；（3）私人部门运用 PPP 的经验；（4）公众与利益相关者的支持；（5）市场规模，（6）公共部门稳定、强力支持的氛围；（7）资金的可得性；（8）意识到并能够实现预期结果和创新；（9）法律框架和商业机构的状况。

研机构、学校、医院、文化设施、监狱等社会基础设施(即非创收型)。第二种类型称为"经济性基础设施 PPP",是指资金的主要来源是基础设施用户支付的费用,如收费公路的使用者缴纳的通行费,这种模式包括桥梁、公路、隧道、铁路、港口、码头、机场等交通设施,以及水电供应设施、排污设施、通信设施等。在澳大利亚,从项目数量上分析,这两类基础设施基本差不多;从项目总投资上分析,经济性基础设施项目占绝大多数比例。

(四) 澳大利亚社会资本参与基础设施 PPP 的方式

从社会资本的角度,在澳大利亚,最普遍的 PPP 运作模式是由几个投资者联合成立一个专门的 SPV 项目公司,由 SPV 公司和政府就项目设计、融资、建设和运营签订 PPP 项目协议,协议期限一般为 20—30 年。融资方对 SPV 公司的股东(投资者)一般为无追索权或者有限追索权。贷款采取子弹式还款方式,到期一次性还本。在贷款存续期间,融资方可以通过在金融市场上再融资的方式转让贷款份额。SPV 公司和政府还会就执行项目的各项任务和其他公司签署协议,确保这些公司能够按照约定履约,在出现履约失败风险的情况下,将按照合同约定的权利义务关系予以追究责任。SPV 公司被赋予了基础设施项目的长期特许经营权和收益权,因此也有足够的动力快速建设和高效运营。合同到期后,一般来说项目资产将会无偿转让给政府,也有可能经政府和投资者谈判后以合适的价格或最新的商务条件续签协议。

二、澳大利亚基础设施 PPP 模式的成功经验

（一）设立专门的 PPP 政府管理机构并公布政策指南

澳大利亚注重政府层面的协调。联邦政府成立了全国性的基础设施 PPP 管理部门，即澳大利亚基础设施和区域发展部（Department of Infrastructure and Regional Development）。该部负责统计全国各级政府基础设施建设需求并出台指引政策，业务不限于 PPP，但是推广 PPP 是其重要职能之一。2015 年 10 月，该部更新了 2008 年推出的澳大利亚全国的 PPP 政策框架，详细介绍了 PPP 项目的实施政策，包括 PPP 项目集中采购方法，投资者指南，社会性基础设施的商业原则，经济性基础设施的商业原则，政府操作指南，财务计算方法等。各级政府在此基础上制订了本地的框架指南，对 PPP 项目做了各自详细的规定。如维多利亚州就在 PPP 项目的信息披露上做了特殊规定，要求除了国有企业主导的项目，所有维多利亚州 PPP 中心参与的 PPP 项目合同，均需在融资方案完成后 3 个月内对外公布。

（二）确定 PPP 项目的"物有所值"准入原则

澳大利亚确定 PPP 项目准入的核心标准是"物有所值"（Value for Money, VFM）原则，即考察 PPP 模式是否比传统模式好，社会资本能够实现物有所值原则，即经济性上实现成本最低，效率上实现产出最大，效果上达到预期的期望。澳大利亚政府部门在立项阶段，会制订基础设施和公用事业发展规划，通过全面成本—效益分析法（Full Cost-benefit Analysis），考察项目建设的必要性和是否可以适用 PPP 模式，其基本原

理是运用技术经济、社会分析等方法,分别计算出特定基础设施项目在公共部门采购模式下和 PPP 采购模式下的成本和收益,并根据 VFM 原则和对比的方法,来决定此基础设施项目的最优采购方法。在 PPP 项目启动阶段,澳大利亚政府部门会采用公共部门比较因子法(Public Sector Comparator, PSC)比较 PPP 模式和传统模式的全寿命周期成本,如果 PPP 模式的投标价成本低于传统模式的成本,就体现出了物有所值原则。公共部门比较因子法(Public Sector Comparator, PSC)是在假设建设资金没有约束,与 PPP 项目建设运营期和产出标准相同,并考虑不同采购模式交易成本差别的前提条件下,基础设施项目采用传统的公共部门采购模式所需要的全部成本,主要包括建设运营净成本、可转移风险承担成本、自留风险承担成本、竞争性中立调整成本等。在量化比较得出 PPP 模式体现出了 VFM 最大化的基础上,澳大利亚政府部门将最终选择一个(或几个企业组成的联合体)最适合的企业授予其特许经营权。

(三)制订全流程绩效评估监督体系

澳大利亚政府强调制订全流程的绩效监管体系,通过产出和结果的绩效评估要求(Output and Outcome-based Performance Specification),促使社会资本确保所提供的产品或服务的质量并提高效率。澳大利亚政府监管的重点是产品或服务的质量和数量,而不是干涉社会资本通过什么方法来满足绩效要求,以利于发挥社会资本的能动性和创造性。具体而言,社会资本负责项目质量管理,制订管理计划,搜集监管数据,编写监管报告;政府部门负责对项目质量管理的审查,制定技术标准,审查社会资本的管理计划和监管报告,审计财务,实施评估和奖惩;第三方负责独立审计,数据搜集和争议处理;产品或者服务的用户则有权利向政府部门反馈使用情况并有途径举报自身权益受损情况。监管结果应当通过报告形式体现出来，监管费用一般要由政府和社会资本分担，但是如果结果不符合监管要求，需要再次检测的费用则由社会资本承担。

（四）强调保障社会资本的合理利益

在 PPP 项目中，保障社会资本的合理利益是社会资本积极参与的动力所在。澳大利亚政府推动的 PPP 项目一般有两种情况：一是项目自身收益，即使用者付费（Usage-based）或者政府付费（Availability-based）。使用者付费又称为特许经营权模式（Concession），通过向用户收费来实现合理的利润，如公路、桥梁、地铁等；政府付费是指项目在符合政府要求并建成投入运营后，政府按照约定一次性或定期向社会资本付费，无论项目的实际需求和利用情况如何；在现实中，使用者付费和政府付费往往结合使用，政府支付一定比例的费用，其余部分向用户收费；二是政府让利给社会资本，例如部分土地附加收益。在墨尔本皇家儿童医院 PPP 项目中，维多利亚州政府与社会资本在开始时谈好条件，新医院建成运营后，社会资本可以将原址的旧医院自行改造利用，开办超市或旅馆等，所得收入归社会资本所有，涉及税收项目可以享受优惠，但是最终的土地及所有不动产归政府所有。

（五）将保护公众利益作为推动 PPP 模式的前提条件

澳大利亚政府始终将保护公众利益作为推行 PPP 模式的前提条件。政府推行 PPP 项目有利于缓解政府财政约束、提高产品或服务质量、优化风险分担降低建设成本、促进经济增长与市场经济，最终体现为对澳大利亚所有纳税人的权益保护。在 PPP 模式下，社会资本得以更广泛地参与到设计、建造、融资、运营、维护等各个阶段，使其技术、经验、创造性得到充分发挥，政府部门则把重心放在综合协调、政策指引、质量控制、安全监督上来，以保障纳税人的权益为最终目标，最大限度上改进公共服务质量。与传统基础设施建设融资相比较，PPP 模式工期延长和预算超支风险转移给了社会资本，政府每年购买公共服务的支出固定化，从而使政府支出的确定性得到提高，进而提高了政府债务的可控性。由于 PPP 项目的运营和维护都由社会资本承担，因此社会资本会积极改进项目方案来控制风险和成本，且不会为赶工期而粗制滥造，这样就从整体上保障了公众的合法权益。

三、澳大利亚 PPP 模式的成功案例分析——普兰纳瑞集团

（一）公司简介

普兰纳瑞集团（Plenary Group）是澳大利亚基础设施 PPP 领域的领跑者，在澳大利亚 PPP 项目市场占据了 30% 左右的市场份额。自 2004 年成立起，该公司以 PPP 模式建设和运营着 37 个重大城市公共基础设施项目，金额达到 240 亿澳元，有超过 40% 的竞标成功率。该公司成功案例包括 12 亿澳元的澳大利亚国防 LEAP 项目，10 亿澳元的黄金海岸轻轨项目，14 亿澳元的墨尔本会议中心项目，17 亿澳元的图文巴市第二支线项目，12.7 亿澳元的维多利亚州癌症治疗中心项目，2.88 亿澳元的生化科研研究中心项目，1.2 亿澳元的 Casey 医院项目等。该公司曾经荣获全球发起人第二（所有 PPP 项目）、城市建设金奖、最佳项目发起人、年度全球 PPP 项目（悉尼铁路西北线）等多个荣誉奖项。

(二) 公司运营模式分析

在每个 PPP 项目中，普兰纳瑞集团均作为项目承办方、开发方、财务顾问、长期投资者和资产管理者，全程参与到设计、建设、融资和维护整个过程。在竞标阶段，一是作为发起人，与政府和项目伙伴紧密配合，组织并完成竞标计划，促进合同和融资的完成；二是作为财务和商务的安排人，协调政府、资金提供方和项目伙伴之间的关系，落实法律和商务谈判，建立财务模型和税务结构；三是作为股权投资者，吸收社会股权投资者参与，与项目伙伴结成同盟，持有项目股权。在施工和运营阶段，一是在施工和设计方面，设立 SPV 项目公司，搭建管理层机构；二是在服务提供方面，发挥好政府和资金提供者之间的角色，组织具体落实项目建设；三是在项目的母公司层面，做好公共关系和战略传媒，规范商务合同，指导项目运营，监督 SPV 项目公司的财务运营情况。

(三) 公司成功因素分析

普兰纳瑞集团取得成功主要有几个因素：一是公司的管理层自 20 世纪 90 年代初开始就具备丰富的 PPP 项目经验，完成了超过 40 个重大城建基础设施项目。二是公司在项目投融资领域有非常专业的团队，拥有大批金融和投资顾问，并且有商业、工程、设施运营和公共关系团队提供大力协助。三是在所有项目中公司都持有股权，尽力维护长期、活跃的股东关系，担任 PPP 项目起始的发起人、财务顾问、投资人和资产管理人。四是对 PPP 项目设计好长期的财务模式，体现"利益共享，风险共担"，提供更加精确的报价和更加高效的融资。五是对 PPP 项目可能出现的问题及时做好预案，提供最有效的解决方案。六是全球布局，在亚太和北美的重要市场取得巨大成功。

四、澳大利亚 PPP 模式的不足

（一）准入原则不好把握

澳大利亚 PPP 项目的物有所值原则是为了充分利用政府和社会资本各自优势。但是通过公共部门比较因子法计算 PPP 项目的物有所值原则是一个复杂的计算系统，应用难度较大。该计算方法重视定量计算和分析，特别是在缺乏真实准确数据资料的项目前期阶段，往往依靠投资、折现率、风险分担等方面的假设或者估值数据，容易出现偏差。因此，如何量化基础设施建设项目的经济效益和社会效益，充分利用政府和社会资本各自优势，把政府的社会责任、规划、协调机制和社会资本的资金支持、技术手段、管理效率和专业经验结合起来，实现物有所值原则，非常具有挑战性，较难把握。

（二）项目选择面上过窄

澳大利亚是 PPP 模式成熟度较高的国家，但在基础设施领域采用 PPP 模式运作的项目也不过百分之十几。虽然许多研究把 PPP 和私有化做了区分，PPP 仍然被认为是渐进私有化的特洛伊木马，由于私有化的担忧，PPP 的推广实施在一定程度上被制造了障碍。此外，在 PPP 模式下，由于政府要受到合同约束，就不能适应日新月异的经济社会发展速度的变化，不能进行灵活调整以适应公共需求的变化。因此，PPP 并不是在所有的领域都适用，也不能解决所有的问题，必须根据项目实际情况合理设计项目结构。

(三) 公私双方前期有效沟通难度较大

由于 PPP 模式比传统模式结构复杂，在立项阶段，澳大利亚政府和社会资本就需要进行深入的研究或咨询，产生了较高的交易成本和机会主义倾向。政府可能会为了吸引社会资本参与，先降低各项标准，在完成投招标后再修改条款。社会资本可能会为了获取项目，先开出优厚条件，待开工后再重新谈判。澳大利亚不少尚处于立项阶段的大型 PPP 项目，由于受到社会公众的关注和舆论监督的压力，政府和社会资本的沟通和谈判过程耗时相当漫长，项目甚至长达几年以上也不能进入实质性操作阶段。这些都可能成为 PPP 项目的潜在失败风险，不利于 PPP 模式的长期健康发展，不利于公众利益的真正保障。

(四) 融资支持力度不够

澳大利亚社会资本的融资成本显著高于政府举债成本。在澳大利亚金融市场上，PPP 项目的 2—3 年左右再融资安排的还款模式有些像"击鼓传花"游戏，5—7 年融资难问题比较突出。澳大利亚 PPP 项目中，社会资本的中长期融资渠道限制较多，有些项目不能得到稳定的中长期资金支持，不利于调动社会资本参与 PPP 项目的积极性。

五、对我国 PPP 模式的启示和建议

新形势下，中国政府面临"三期叠加"的挑战，一方面要消化前期刺激政策的不良影响，控制地方政府债务，另一方面又要解决就业和民生等问题，转变经济增长方式。党的十八届三中全会提出：使市场在资源配置

中起到决定性作用和更好发挥政府作用。PPP 模式受到了高度重视，成为促进市场和政府合作的方式之一。2015 年 5 月 19 日，国务院办公厅转发财政部、发改委、人民银行《关于在公共服务领域推广政府和社会资本合作模式的指导意见》（业界简称"42 号文"），明确要在能源、交通运输、水利、环境保护、农业、林业、科技、保障性安居工程、医疗、卫生、养老、教育、文化等公共服务领域广泛采用 PPP 模式，将 PPP 提升到了市场和政府合作的战略高度。通过对澳大利亚基础设施领域 PPP 模式经验和不足的系统研究，可以主要从以下几个方面对我国推广 PPP 模式提供借鉴。

（一）从国家战略层面加强顶层设计

澳大利亚非常重视 PPP 和国家增长与社会发展目标的联动。澳大利亚基础社会管理局（Infrastructure Australia）在给澳大利亚专门协调联邦、州和领地政府的澳大利亚政府委员会（The Council of Australia Governments）的报告中，多次强调需要更好地利用现有基础设施建设，为资本投资创造新的机会，消除阻碍澳大利亚经济社会增长的瓶颈和差距。中国推广和运用 PPP 模式，可以广泛引入社会资本参与公共产品和服务的投资建设，顺应了"大众创业、万众创新"的国家战略，是供给侧结构改革的重要内容。因此，中国应当从国家战略层面加强 PPP 模式的顶层设计，注意国家优先项目的实施，注意项目的经济效益、社会效益和环境效益等多方面因素，要在公共政策目标的实现和社会资本盈利目标之间达到一种均衡，通过 PPP 模式的公共性体现社会公众的利益，更好地促进公共政策目标的实现。

(二) 合理确定项目选择标准

中国是政府主导性的市场经济发展模式。因此，各级政府对公共服务需求的认定和评估比较粗放。在项目选择方面，地方政府领导的话语权较大，政绩需求有时会混淆公共服务需求，缺乏项目选择的相对客观标准。基于此考虑，建议可以借鉴澳大利亚 PPP 模式的经验，出台专门的项目物有所值 (Value for Money, VFM) 评估指引，将项目全生命周期内政府支出成本现值与公共部门比较值 (Public Sector Comparator, PSC) 进行客观比较，确保项目选择 PPP 模式是提升效率、降低成本的最优选择。

(三) 理顺政府职责

澳大利亚 PPP 模式的成功关键在于政府部门和社会资本的有效合作。为了落实好党中央、国务院的战略决策，各级政府部门应当切实统一思想，充分认识到 PPP 在提高公共服务供给质量、促进经济结构调整等方面的重要作用，主动转变自身职能定位，该管的管好，不该管的放手，该监督的要到位，特别是要提高 PPP 专业知识技能。此外，应当加强部委之间、中央和地方之间的协调统筹，建立跨部门的监管协调机制，避免主管重叠，防止监管缺位，改善政出多门、各行其是的政府部门条块分割现象。只有这样，政府部门和社会资本才能真正协同合作，适应 PPP 模式带来的从观念、治理结构、操作细节到有效监督落实的巨大挑战。

(四) 完善法律和政策体系

澳大利亚虽然属于英美法系，但是 PPP 模式经过长年的发展，也已经从法律和政策指引方面，建立了完整和有效的成文法保障体系，而不是仅仅限于通过案例法来规制。我国是大陆法系，更应当及时清理、修订、废止现存的、不适应当前 PPP 模式推广运用的法律、法规或地方性规章，争取尽早出台统一的 PPP 基础性法律，积极推动更高层次的系统化立法，解决现在严重制约 PPP 模式推广的法律、法规、部门规章、地方性规章、规范性文件等衔接不畅、相互冲突的突出问题。

（五）引入第三方建立系统的 PPP 项目监督评估机制

澳大利亚 PPP 全流程的绩效监管体系中，第三方监督评估具有非常重要的作用。通过政府、社会资本、独立第三方共同发挥作用的产出和结果的绩效评估（Output and Outcome-based Performance Specification），确保社会资本所提供的产品或服务的质量并提高效率。第三方监督评估并不是说不需要政府监管。政府监管的重点是制定技术标准，检查产品或服务的质量，审查社会资本的监管报告和财务等。第三方则是客观公正地负责独立审计，搜集数据和处理争议。通过建立系统的 PPP 项目监督评估机制，兼顾各利益相关方的利益诉求，加强信息披露和社会监督，增强 PPP 项目的透明度和公众度，防止可能出现的道德风险和暗箱操作。

参考文献：

Report on private investment in public infrastructure，www.partnerships.vic.gov.au，2012.

孟刚：《21 世纪海上丝绸之路南线四国融资合作研究》，《开发性金融研究》2016 年第 1 期。

Australian ministry of finance, *The policy principle about using the public-private partnership of Australian government*，2015.

Linda M.English，"Public Private Partnerships in Australia: An Overview of Their Nature，Purpose，Incidence and Oversight"，*UNSW Law Journal*，Volume 29（3）．

刘晓凯等：《全球视角下的 PPP：内涵、模式、实践与问题》，《国际经济评论》2015 年第 4 期。

吴守华等：《PPP 国内外现状和制约因素分析》，《开发性金融研究》2015 年第 1 期。

孟刚：《中国在澳大利亚的国际产能合作研究》，《开发性金融研究》2016 年第 3 期。

Miraftab F., "Public-Private Partnerships: The Trojan Horse of Neoliberal Development?", *Journal of Planning Education and Research*, Vol.24, No.1, pp.89-101, 2004.

Glendinning R., "The concept of value for money", *International journal of public sector management*, 2007, 01（01）.

莫小龙等：《澳大利亚发展公私合作伙伴关系的经验与启示》，《中国财政》2013 年第 6 期。

邢会强：《PPP 模式中的政府定位》，《法学》2015 年第 11 期。

于本瑞等：《PPP 模式的国内外实践及启示》，《现代管理科学》2014 年第 8 期。

孟刚：《中方对接澳大利亚科技创新战略的路径和融资合作研究》，《全球化》2016 年第 7 期。

戴正宗：《澳大利亚：PPP 完胜政府采购》，《中国政府采购报》2015 年 1 月 20 日。

梁晴雪：《国内外典型 PPP 项目案例研究及启示》，《建筑经济》2015 年第 8 期。

孟刚：《澳大利亚"北部大开发"为开发性金融带来战略新机遇》，《中国银行业》2016 年第 4 期。

推进中资企业在澳大利亚能矿领域
投资合作研究

一、中资企业投资能矿资源领域迎来周期性机遇

（一）能矿资源大宗商品价格出现新一轮"牛市"拐点

2008 年金融危机后，全球能矿资源等大宗商品价格跌幅惨烈，大步迈入"熊市"。2016 年以来，种种迹象表明，新一轮能矿资源大宗商品"牛市"行情正在摇摇晃晃中快步走来。首先，原油、铁矿石、煤炭、铜、铅锌、钢铁等价格出现大幅回升，大宗商品短期需求旺盛的特征非常明显。其次，从长期需求角度分析，全球经济稳中向好，美国等国家制造业重回兴旺，世界多个重要经济体的经济增速环比翻倍，中国供给侧结构性改革已初见成效，"一带一路"建设提振全球基础设施建设，大宗商品需求已然具备了旺盛增长的持续性动力。

（二）我国的战略性矿产资源对外依存度高

我国矿产资源对外依存度较高，早已成为经济社会发展的突出瓶颈。

为保障国家经济、国防安全和战略新兴产业发展的战略性需要，国务院于 2016 年 11 月批复通过《全国矿产资源规划(2016—2020 年)》(以下简称《规划》) 天然气等 24 种矿产列入战略性矿产目录。列入战略性矿产目录的 24 种矿产是：能源矿产石油、天然气、页岩气、煤炭、煤层气、铀；金属矿产铁、铬、铜、铝、金、镍、钨、锡、钼、锑、钴、锂、稀土、锆；非金属矿产磷、钾盐、晶质石墨、萤石。《规划》强调将列入战略性矿产目录的石油、天然气、煤炭、稀土、晶质石墨等 24 种矿产作为矿产资源宏观调控和监督管理的重点对象，系统开展国内外矿产品供需和资源形势分析，强化应对国际重大冲突资源安全预警能力，在资源配置、财政投入、重大项目、矿业用地等方面加强引导和差别化管理，提高资源安全供应能力和开发利用水平。

(三) 中资企业应当抓住能矿资源领域的周期性投资机遇

从某种意义上讲，全球大宗商品的定价权是由对资源的占有量最大的企业群体决定的。以铁矿石为例，全球海运铁矿石市场交易数量当前大约每年 13 亿吨，其中澳大利亚作为铁矿石出口大国每年出口约 8 亿吨，巴西出口近 4 亿吨，中国则进口约 10 亿吨。中国的铁矿石进口金额仅次于原油，位居单项大宗商品进口金额的第二位，但是却不拥有定价权，对外依存度极高。从历史走势分析，能矿资源大宗商品牛市行情具有市场价格持续性向上的特点，上升周期至少持续 5 年以上，在牛市初期投资风险较小。因此，在新一轮全球经济大发展的历史浪潮中，中资企业应当审时度势、顺势而为，抓住战略性时代机遇，在全球能矿资源市场上主动出击，从源头上取得主动地位，突破我国经济社会发展的能矿资源瓶颈。

二、新形势下中资企业投资澳大利亚能矿领域的 PEST 分析

(一) 共建"一带一路"是中澳政府合作框架下的新形势

2014 年 11 月，习近平主席在澳大利亚首都堪培拉发表演讲，提出南太地区是中方提出的 21 世纪海上丝绸之路的自然延伸，同时宣布中国与澳大利亚从战略伙伴关系提升为全面战略伙伴关系，热诚欢迎澳大利亚共同参与海上丝绸之路建设，推动经贸合作取得更大发展。2016 年 4 月，习近平主席、李克强总理和来访的澳大利亚特恩布尔总理正式宣布了中国"一带一路"倡议同澳大利亚"北部大开发"战略对接，中国的创新驱动发展战略和澳大利亚的"国家创新与科学议程"战略对接。

澳大利亚是中国对外能矿资源领域投资的重要合作国家，国土辽阔，人口较少，较早步入发达国家行列，2015 年 GDP 约为 1.598 万亿美元，人均 GDP 约为 6.658 万美元，是全球第 12 大经济体，政治和法律环境稳定，市场机制规范，产业结构合理，可投资领域较多，投资回报较为稳定，具有国际领先的技术和管理经验，是连接亚太地区和欧美发达国家的桥梁。在金属矿产领域，中资企业海外投资主要发生在大洋洲和北美洲，大洋洲的澳大利亚则是我国金属矿产类企业海外投资的主要目的地国。2005—2015 年，澳大利亚成为中国全球直接投资的第二大目的地国。2013—2015 年，中国成为澳大利亚第一大海外直接投资来源国。

表 1 2004 年、2009 年和 2014 年澳大利亚宏观经济数据

年份	GDP(亿美元)	经济增长率(%)	人口（万人）	人均 GDP(美元)
2004 年	6130	4.2	2013	30452
2009 年	9000	1.5	2169	41494
2014 年	14444	2.5	2349	61728

资料来源：IMF。

(二) 中资企业投资澳大利亚能矿领域的 PEST 分析

为了更好地把握新形势下中资企业投资澳大利亚能矿领域的宏观环境，笔者将从政治因素 (Political Factors)、经济因素 (Economic Factors)、社会因素 (Social Factors) 和技术因素 (Technological Factors) 等四个方面，分析研究中资企业在澳大利亚能矿资源领域投资的宏观环境和对战略目标制定的影响。

1. 政治因素：中澳全面战略合作为中资企业带来投资新机遇

在"一带一路"合作背景下，中澳两国领导人高度重视从政府层面构筑全面战略合作框架，保障企业投资利益最大化。在大洋洲地区，澳大利亚和新西兰是最早和中国建立全面战略伙伴关系的国家。中澳战略经济对话的内容在更高层面不断深化。中澳两国政府已经达成共识，要通过两国发展战略的对接进一步提升合作的领域和层次，特别是要巩固中澳在能矿资源领域的传统合作。2016 年 4 月，澳大利亚特恩布尔总理上任后不久就访问中国，和习近平主席、李克强总理深入探讨了中澳两国的经贸合作。可以说，中国"一带一路"倡议同澳大利亚"北部大开发"、中国创新驱动发展战略同澳大利亚的"国家创新与科学议程"的对接，是中澳能矿资源领域的传统合作打下的扎实基础。新形势下，中澳两国政府不断深

化的全方位战略对接，为中资企业加强在澳大利亚能矿资源领域的投资合作提供了前所未有的机遇。

2. 经济因素：签署自由贸易协定为中资企业带来投资新便利

2015 年 6 月，中澳两国政府签署了《自由贸易协定》。一是在货物领域，双方各有占出口贸易额 85.4% 的产品将在协定生效时立即零关税。过渡期后，澳大利亚最终实现零关税的税目占比和贸易额占比会达到 100%，中国实现零关税的税目占比和贸易额占比会分别达到 96.8% 和 97%，都远超过一般自贸协定中 90% 的降税水平。二是在服务领域，澳方承诺协定生效后对中方以负面清单方式开放服务部门，是世界上首个对中国以负面清单方式就服务贸易承诺的国家。中方会以正面清单方式向澳方开放服务部门。此外，澳方还对中方在假日工作机制等方面作出专门安排。三是在投资领域，双方自协定生效后相互给予最惠国待遇，澳方同时降低中国企业赴澳投资审查门槛，并给予便利化安排。四是协定还在 "21 世纪经贸议题" 的电子商务、政府采购、知识产权、竞争等十几个领域作了双方交流合作的推进规定。

3. 社会因素：多元移民文化为中资企业扎根发展创造新环境

澳大利亚建国之初就是移民国家，有很多外来民族、外来文化，如果不考虑少数西方不良政客制造出来的政治和意识形态因素，单就国家文化本身而言本质上不具有排斥性，具有鲜明的多元移民文化特点。澳大利亚没有以当地文化为中心的很狭隘的民族主义文化，相反非常融合开放，鼓励居民使用自己的语言、保持自身的文化。2016 年 9 月，澳大利亚在悉尼召开政坛种族多样化论坛，联邦少数族群社区委员会代理主席 Eugenia Grammatikakis 表示："当前，1/4 的澳大利亚人在海外出生，另有 1/4 的澳大利亚人父母至少有一人在海外出生。对此，澳大利亚所有政党必须付出更多努力，确保少数族裔的利益真正被代表。"此外，澳大利亚法律制度非常健全，从衣食住行到国家经济生活的各个方面基本做到了有法可依、有法必依、执法必严、违法必究，在投资经营、私有财产不受侵犯、消费者权益保护、刑事审判、民事纠纷、外商投资、交通管理、国家选举、行政管理、外交、保障妇女儿童权益等各个方面都有完善和公平透明的法律可以作为行事依据。澳大利亚多元的移民文化和健全的法律体系为中资企业扎根发展创造了和谐环境。因此，中资企业不会因为自己是亚洲中国面孔而受到排斥，可以通过沟通、融入和互动使得当地居民、当地政府充分理解投资意图是真诚和互利共赢的，是不带有威胁性和危害性的，进而营造出能够扎根长远发展的本土化经营环境。

4. 技术因素：科技创新对接为中澳企业技术合作营造新氛围

2016 年 4 月，习近平主席、李克强总理和来访的澳大利亚总理正式宣布了中国创新驱动发展战略同澳方"国家创新与科学议程"的对接。澳大利亚计划在中国上海、美国旧金山、以色列特拉维夫等海外地区设立 5 个创新中心（Landing Pad），以帮助澳大利亚初创企业在国际市场立足，并发展成为高增长、高回报企业。中国科技部火炬中心则与澳大利亚新南威尔士大学共同启动了新南威尔士大学火炬创新园项目。从历史上的几次全球化科技革命看，科技创新始终是提高社会生产力和综合国力的重要战略支撑。科技革命源于社会需求的驱动，又将极大促进社会经济的大发展。在世界新科技革命中抢得先机的国家，必将成为世界经济的领头羊。澳大利亚是资源、能源、农产品、健康产品等输出大国，中国是最大的消费市场和制造业大国。应该说，两国在科技创新领域的合作，具有极强的互补性和实用性。中澳两国企业的强强合作，是全球化背景下共同领潮世界新科技革命的必由之路。

三、澳大利亚能矿资源储量在全球占有突出地位

（一）澳大利亚能矿资源在全球地位

1. 澳大利亚多种能矿资源在全球排名前列

澳大利亚自然资源丰富，多种能矿资源储量居世界前列，是世界矿产资源人均占有量最高的国家之一，矿产品生产和出口全球领先。其中，铝土矿、氧化铝、金红石和锆英石的生产居世界首位，黄金、铁矿、铅、锂、锰矿、钨和锌的生产居世界第二，钛铁矿和铀的生产居世界第三，黑煤（也是最大出口国）、镍和银的生产居世界第四，铝、褐煤和铜的生产居世界第五。

就已经探明的有经济开采价值的矿产资源储量而言，澳大利亚的黄金、铁矿石、铅、镍、金红石、银、铀、锌和锆资源居世界首位，铝土矿、褐煤、钴、钛铁矿和钽资源居世界第二，铜和锂资源居世界第三，钍资源居世界第四，黑煤和锰矿资源居世界第五。其中，铝矾土约53亿吨，铁矿砂146亿吨，黑煤403亿吨，褐煤300亿吨，铅2290万吨，镍2260万吨，银4.14万吨，钽4.08万吨，锌4100万吨，黄金5570吨。此外，澳大利亚有约1600万平方公里的沉积盆地，沿海大陆架面积超过陆地面积两倍，海下油气资源储量也非常可观，原油已探明储量为11.08亿桶，可销售天然气89万亿立方英尺。

2. 澳大利亚能矿资源生产成本大多在全球处于低位

就生产成本而言，澳大利亚大型矿企的生产成本在全球都处于低位。以铁矿石为例，澳大利亚过去10年中品位保持在60%左右，开采成本较

低，远高于中国 33% 的平均水平。力拓、必和必拓等大型矿山开采成本在 30 美元 / 吨左右。FMG 公司等后期开发的企业，2013 年之前成本在 50 到 60 美元 / 吨，近两年经过大幅降本增效，目前开采成本也达到了近 30 美元 / 吨。与此相比，我国国内的铁矿石开采成本则在 130 美元 / 吨左右。

另以铅锌矿为例，澳大利亚铅锌矿品位较高，大多可露天开采，因此开采成本较低。例如昆士兰州西北部的 Cannington 矿，是世界上最大也是成本最低的银铅矿，铅品位 10.4%，锌品位 3.88%，银含量 455 克 / 吨，新南威尔士州布鲁肯山铅锌银矿，储量大（铅锌金属量 395.79 万吨）、品位高（锌品位 9.4%，铅品位 7.3%，白银品位 89 克 / 吨），易开采。但是，澳大利亚原油和 LNG 价格较高，全球而言没有竞争优势，成熟油田开发成本约 60—70 美元 /bbl，LNG 成本也几乎处于全球最高位，约为 12—16 美元 /MMBtu。

(二) 澳大利亚能矿资源分布情况

1. 西澳大利亚州

西澳大利亚州是澳大利亚的矿业之州，资源量大，分布广，埋藏浅，易开发，采矿业已经形成规模，设备大型化，自动化程度高。西澳大利亚州的铁矿产量占全球的四分之一，铝土矿产量约占全球的三分之一，铜和黄金占全澳的 70%，镍占全澳的 90%，原油和液化石油气分别占全澳的 66% 和 57%，天然气占全澳的 92%。西澳大利亚州矿区主要有 Pilbara、Koolyanobbing、Cockatoo、Koolanooka、Jack 等地区的铁矿，Jundee、Kalgoorlie、Kanowna、Plutonic、SunriseDam 和 YilgamSouth 等地区的金矿，Hollandaire、DeGrussa 等地区的铜矿，Yeelirrie 地区的铀矿，Mount

Weld 地区的稀土矿。西澳大利亚州的西北大陆架、Gorgon、Browse、Wheatstone 和 Pluto 等是全澳有影响力的液化天然气重大项目。

2. 昆士兰州

昆士兰州是澳大利亚最为重要的黑煤（冶金煤和动力煤）产地，拥有超过 300 亿吨黑煤，约占全澳的 59%。此外，昆士兰州还有三分之二的全澳锌矿资源，13% 的全澳铜矿资源等。昆士兰州矿区主要有鲍恩盆地、加利利盆地和苏拉特盆地的煤炭矿区，Cannington、NWBrooksRange、IberianPyriteBelt、GeorgeFisher、BlackStar 和 Hilton 等铅—锌—银矿区，Kalman、MountIsa 等铜—钼矿区，Weipa 铝土矿区。

3. 北领地

北领地有丰富的铀、铝矾土、锰和铅锌矿资源，有 12 处正在开采中的矿区，生产铀、铝矾土、锰、黄金、铁矿石、磷酸盐等。北领地矿区主要有世界第二大铀矿 Ranger，GrooteEylandt 和 BootuCreek 的全球领先的锰矿，全澳最大的黄金矿之一 Callie，全澳铅锌银储量最大的麦卡锡河矿，Gove 的大型铝土矿。

4. 南澳大利亚州

南澳大利亚州有丰富的铜和铀资源，铜储量大于 100 亿吨，铀储量占全澳的 80% 和全球的近 30%。南澳大利亚州矿区主要有世界排名第一的 OlympicDam、Beverley 和 Honeymoon 铀矿，世界排名第三的 OlympicDam 铜矿。

5. 新南威尔士州

新南威尔士州有金、银、铜、铅、锌等矿产，矿区主要有 Cadia 铜金矿，Northparkes 铜矿。新南威尔士州存在勘探机会的矿产品有：铜、金、锌—铅、银、锡—钨、镍、铁、金红石—锆石—钛铁矿等。此外，新南威尔士州 Sydney-Gunnedah 等盆地黑煤等煤炭资源较为丰富，有 60 多个小型运营矿山和 30 多个开发计划。

6. 维多利亚州

维多利亚州有丰富的金和铁、钢、铜、镍、铝、铅、锌、锡、钨等贱金属资源，矿区主要有 BCDResourcesNL 铜矿、JabiruMetalsLtd 铜—铅—锌矿、Stawell 金矿、Fosterville 金矿。

四、中资企业在澳大利亚能矿领域投资合作的案例分析

1980—2005 年，中资企业在澳大利亚开展了少量投资活动。这个阶段，中国在澳大利亚的投资合作尚不成规模，典型案例有中钢力拓洽那铁矿合营项目、中信集团投资波特兰铝厂等。2006—2012 年，中资企业开始大规模投资澳大利亚。这个阶段，中国的投资合作项目集中在能矿领域，累计投资总额的 73% 于矿业，18% 于天然气行业，包括五矿有色收购澳大利亚 OZ 公司、兖州煤业收购澳洲菲利克斯资源公司、中信泰富的西澳州铁矿石项目、中国海油的柯蒂斯 LNG 项目等。2013 年至今，中资企业在澳大利亚能矿资源领域处于投资低谷期和整理期。

（一）中钢力拓洽那铁矿合营项目

1973 年，世界三大矿业巨头之一的力拓有限公司成为第一家向中国出口铁矿石的外资企业。迄今为止，力拓累计向中国供应了超过 18 亿吨

的铁矿石产品,中国市场每年为力拓贡献 40% 的营业收入。中国中钢集团有限公司和力拓合作的洽那铁矿合营项目于 1987 年正式签署合作协议。中钢集团在合营企业项目中拥有 40% 股权,力拓占有 60% 股权。该项目位于西澳大利亚州皮尔巴拉地区,是中国企业在海外最早的矿业投资项目,也是中澳矿业合作时间最长的项目。

该项目是中资企业以合营且不控股的方式和全球矿业巨头成功合作的典型案例,一直是中钢集团旗下盈利最好的业务之一。合作伊始,该项目原定产量为 2 亿吨铁矿石,每年向中钢供应 1000 万吨,随后又扩产了 5000 万吨。2016 年 4 月,在李克强总理和澳大利亚特恩布尔总理的见证下,该项目再次续约至 2019 年末。根据协议,洽那铁矿项目总产量将再增加 3000 万吨。在此基础上,双方还签署了额外的包销协议,在 2016—2021 年,中钢将为力拓包销不超过 4000 万吨的铁矿石。

(二)五矿有色收购澳大利亚 OZ 公司

澳大利亚 OZ 矿业公司在 2008 年经过并购重组后新成立,是澳大利亚第三大矿业公司,也是世界上锌矿第二大生产商,拥有的锌资源相当于我国查明锌储量的 18.74%,拥有的铅资源相当于我国查明铅储量的 6.28%,此外还拥有较大产量的铜、金和银矿。2009 年 6 月,五矿有色经过艰难努力,在海外对中国投资并购不理解不支持的大背景下,打消了澳大利亚政府、企业股东、当地居民的疑虑,成功收购澳大利亚 OZ 矿业公司,并将目标公司整合为 MMG 公司,当年实现盈利 1.92 亿美元,次年实现利润 7.47 亿美元。这个项目是中资企业海外并购的经典案例,通过成功并购、整合、运营和管理,实现了并购双方互利共赢,成为中澳两国矿业领域投资合作的标志性桥梁。

这个项目的收购时间点,正好是中国公司在澳收购的密集期。华菱增持 FMG 股份、鞍钢投资 GINDALBIE、中铝注资力拓等几乎都在同时发生。中资企业的大规模并购激发了澳大利亚当地的民族主义情绪。澳大利亚反对党国家领袖率先在议会发难，呼吁"最好还是区分一下主要客户和拥有人"，由此引发了持续猛烈的反对浪潮，一些媒体大肆炒作"中国资源掠夺论"，将意识形态、政治因素等非经济因素纳入市场行为中。五矿管理团队严格秉承和遵守国际商业规则，低调表态，诚恳斡旋于澳洲政府、OZ 矿业董事会和高管层，拜访澳大利亚总工会，游说并获得反对党支持，致信外资投资审查委员会说明情况，最终赢得了澳方相关方面的支持，经 OZ 矿业公司年度股东大会投票，并购交易获得成功，赞成票比率高达 92%。

（三）兖州煤业收购菲利克斯资源公司

澳大利亚菲利克斯公司是一家主要从事煤炭开采和勘探的企业，产品主要包括动力煤、喷吹煤和焦煤，煤炭资产包括 4 个运营中的煤矿、2 个开发中的煤矿以及 4 个煤炭勘探项目，总资源量为 25 亿多吨，储量合计为 5 亿多吨，主要客户是亚洲、欧洲、美洲和澳大利亚本地的钢铁制造商、发电企业。兖州煤业股份有限公司由兖矿集团控股，1998 年分别在香港、纽约、上海上市，2008 年总资产 320 多亿元，是中国煤炭行业的领头羊之一，但煤炭资源短缺是制约兖州煤业发展的重大因素。对优质煤炭资源的强烈渴求是兖州煤业坚定地进行海外并购的内在动因。

在兖州煤业收购菲利克斯的过程中，澳大利亚各界对收购持支持态度。重要原因之一是兖州煤业领先的深层开采技术填补了当地的空白，提高了煤炭开采率。澳大利亚煤炭已经探明的储量中 6 米以上厚煤层占 58%，多采用露天开采，一般只开采到 4—6 米。厚煤层的回采率一般低于 50%，有的低于 30%，造成严重浪费。澳大利亚能源部采矿协会一直在积极推动井工开采，提高煤炭回收率。兖州煤业是我国向国外输出开采技术最多的企业之一，拥有国内外专利超过60项，"综采放顶煤液压支架"技术是综采放顶煤生产工艺的核心，解决了世界厚煤层开采的技术难题，是中厚煤层开采的首选技术。新技术可以使合作双方形成新的竞争优势。收购企业和被收购企业都希望从对方那里获得自己最渴望的资源。该并购交易成功后，兖州煤业和目标公司在技术、市场、专利、产品、管理、文化等方面实现了互补效应，极大增强了竞争实力。

（四）中国海油的柯蒂斯 LNG 项目

柯蒂斯项目位于澳大利亚昆士兰州，是全球第一个以煤层气为气源的世界级 LNG 项目。该项目探明和控制开采的煤层气源储量总计约 3500 亿立方米，液化处理后销售到中国、日本等亚太国家。英国天然气集团（BG集团）是该项目的第一大股东。中国海油下属的气电集团在该项目中拥有上游资产 25% 权益和中游液化厂第一条 LNG 生产线 50% 权益，是整个项目的第二大权益和投资方。柯蒂斯项目分两期开发，一期自 2011 年初开工至 2015 年中旬全部建成投产运营。二期于 2014 年 4 月开工，规划滚动开发至 2028 年。上游产出的煤层气经过长输管线输送到中游 LNG 厂液化、储存、外输。

柯蒂斯项目是中国首次参与海外 LNG 项目上中下游全产业链投资。中国海油和 BG 公司还达成了协议，从 BG 公司在澳大利亚的 LNG 项目每年购买 360 万吨 LNG 项目，为期 20 年。柯蒂斯项目将增强中国在 LNG 生产和分配领域的话语权，对保障我国能源安全、优化能源结构、提升 LNG 产业全球竞争力等方面具有重要意义。中国虽然不缺乏煤层气资源，但由于煤层气开采主体很多并非煤矿企业、煤层气与煤炭矿业权重叠等原因，煤层气的勘探和开发都异常缓慢。在全球获得具有竞争力的天然气资源，将会为发展中国天然气产业和保障中国清洁能源供应做出积极的贡献。

（五）中信泰富的西澳州铁矿石项目

中信泰富有限公司在西澳大利亚的 SINO IRON 铁矿石项目是中资企业在海外投资能矿资源领域遭遇到较大困难的一个项目。这个项目先期调研不充分，低估了澳大利亚磁铁矿开采的难度。作为项目 EPC 总承包商的中国中冶公司仓促施工，预算超支较大。项目建设工期延期，运营不顺利。汇率损失较大，衍生品交易受挫。项目的澳大利亚合作方帕尔默存在较大的道德风险，在接受采访的公开场合对中方合作方甚至中国表态很不友好，和中信泰富产生了诉讼纠纷。

SINO IRON 铁矿石项目倒逼中信泰富矿业公司提高技术水平和经营管理能力。中信泰富力争通过降本增效扭转被动局面。该项目于 2013 年底开始出口铁矿石精矿粉，供应给中信泰富在国内的特钢厂以及其他中国钢铁企业。目前，项目的六条生产线已经全部进入运营阶段。中信泰富的目标是尽快提升产量，以实现规模效益，成为全球成本最低的精矿粉生产商之一。显而易见，中资企业在海外投资不可能一帆风顺，但是可以通过总结失败经验教训，在压力下产生内生动力，进而提高自身综合能力。

五、推进中资企业在澳大利亚能矿领域投资合作的思路建议

（一）准确把握供给侧结构性改革的精髓，稳中求进

当前企业界有种说法，供给侧结构性改革的五大内容是"去产能，去

库存，去杠杆，降成本，补短板"，海外能矿资源投资项目应该暂缓推动。笔者认为，在一定程度上，这种观点曲解了"三去一降一补"的实质精髓，在全球能矿大宗商品价格触底反弹的背景下，将会贻误战机，错失抄底的绝佳机遇。简单地讲，"三去一降一补"的重点除了"三去"，还有降成本，补短板。中资企业在能矿大宗商品出现合适价格时果断出手，并购海外优质能矿资源，必将有效降低企业工业经济成本，弥补国民经济短板，甚至能够参与左右全球能矿资源大宗商品定价权。笔者 2012 年底至今在澳大利亚工作，见证了能矿大宗商品价格起伏波动的一个周期，目睹了能矿资源跨国集团为了应对周期波动，所采取的种种降本增效措施。以铁矿石价格为例，在 2012 年底达到 170 美元 / 吨左右，之后一路下跌至 2016 年初的 40 美元 / 吨左右。在铁矿石价格下跌过程中，力拓、必和必拓几大能矿跨国集团并没有消极等待，而是采取了一系列改进技术、调控产量、开拓市场等降本增效措施。铁矿石价格在盘整了较长一段时间后，2016 年年底已经反弹至 80 美元 / 吨左右。可以说，铁矿石等大宗商品价格在经历了雪山式崩塌的周期波动期间，几大跨国集团并没有被击垮，反而提高了经营管理和应对风险能力。更令人担忧的是，这几家跨国集团依旧控制着大量优质能矿资源。因此，能矿大宗商品价格的定价权仍然被牢牢掌握在这些控制供给端的跨国集团手中。

稳中求进，关键是稳，目的是进，方式则是统筹协调，有取有舍。笔者认为，对于中国对外依存度高、关系国计民生的重要能矿资源，应当由国家权威部门统筹协调，中资企业和科研机构广泛参与，明确参与各方的权利义务关系和统一决策及行动机制，主动观察和研究周期波动，多倾听一线能够听得见炮火的战士的声音，反复调研，科学论证，统一对外，果断出手，以合理价格控制境外优质能矿资源。毕竟，"抄底"的决策不可能一蹴而就，而是需要长期观察并把握规律后，才可能心中有数、毅然决策、果断出击。笔者曾经在 2015 年底撰文《21 世纪海上丝绸之路南线四国融资合作研究》，认为国际大宗商品价格的急剧下跌将给资源出口国带来更多问题，包括引发急剧的货币贬值、外汇短缺、通货膨胀或者削弱主权偿还外债能力等。但从另一个角度分析，当前全球能矿市场极其低迷，相当部分的能矿资源价值趋于理性甚至被严重低估。这为中资企业以"一带一路"战略为契机，参与全球能矿市场的合作与竞争，提供了难得的战略机遇期。建议设立能矿等大宗商品平稳基金，支持中资企业在互利共赢的前提下，以股权投资优先的模式开展商业合作，在帮助缓解大宗商品价格下跌对出口国经济崩盘式冲击的同时，增强中资企业在国际能矿等大宗商品定价方面的话语权甚至主导权。

（二）以参与和主导定价权为目标，形成合力

业内多数观点认为，铁矿石的公允价值应该在 40—50 美元（到岸价 fair value)，未来 2 至 3 年铁矿石将保持供过于求的趋势。以此为基础分析，虽然商品价格会在公允价值上下之间波动，短时间内价格偏离公允价值是正常的，但是目前铁矿石在持续供大于求的情况下价格还是大幅高于公允价值，并且上游铁矿石矿商等能矿资源跨国集团赚取超额利润而下游钢厂徘徊在亏损边缘，这种情况就非常不正常了。显然铁矿石的定价权机制本身不利于公平保护下游钢厂的利益。定价权一般是从商品生产方说的，指的是生产方在不影响需求数量情况下的提价能力。而作为买方，在一定采购数量下其降低采购价格或者获得更加优惠条件的能力则称为"议价能力"。因此从根本上讲，定价权是由占有优质能矿资源的企业决定的。

全球几大能矿资源跨国集团之间是一种竞争合作并存的关系。例如，淡水河谷和力拓之间达成交叉持股协议，目的很明确，就是为了控制定价权，从供给端获取不合理的垄断利润。中资企业对此要有清醒的忧患认识，争取铁矿石等能矿资源的定价权是最重要的目标。中资企业应当抱团

取暖，争取权益，在合适时机更是要果断出手，占有优质能矿资源，争取掌控定价权，至少提高话语权。在中资企业占有越来越高比例优质能矿资源的情况下，供给端会发生变化，倒逼几大能矿资源跨国集团改变不合理的定价权机制，促进能矿资源价格趋近于公允价值。总而言之，应当充分发挥我国政府主导型市场经济的优势，发挥政府部门协调能力和国有企业执行能力强的优势，司令部、参谋部、作战部队协同作战，规划先行、形成合力，最大限度上达到有效影响能矿资源定价权机制的预期目标。

（三）投资方案要切合实际，技术细节由专家团队把关

在投资澳大利亚能矿资源领域时，中资企业必须依靠专家团队，制订切合实际的投资方案，技术细节更是要由专家把关。

一是要对投资标的所在国和市场有深度的研究和把握。目的地国的投资环境决定了是否适合外国资本的进入。要深入研究目的地国的对外开放程度、政治格局、法律环境、行业准入门槛、外汇及劳工政策、宗教习俗、商业习惯、居民社区等相关情况。澳大利亚政治制度稳定，政权更迭合法有序，投资环境良好、经济高度发达，产业结构合理，但是中国威胁论在一定程度上影响着中澳两国关系。少数政客无根据地指责中国岛礁建设，对南海等问题指手画脚，甚至认为将关键资产出售给中资企业将引发民众的抵制情绪。因此，中资企业要注重和外资审查委员会等政府部门、主要党派、工会组织、社区居民等的充分沟通，避免前期投入较大成本后无功而返。

二是要高度重视前期的可行性研究报告。首先是充分了解拟并购的能矿资源情况，如矿产的禀赋大小、品位高低、可采与否。这需要技术团队做大量的信息收集、过滤、验证等工作，确保矿产资源禀赋和品位的真实可靠。其次是研究矿产开发项目运营所涉及的相关问题，如矿床所在地的

气候、水文、植被等地理环境，道路、码头、桥梁等基础设施条件是否适合项目实施，运输条件是否能够匹配产量。再次是要注重环境和劳工保护。一定要走绿色、友好、可持续的发展道路，高度重视生态效益和社会效益。植被复垦、污水处理、废渣堆放、环保成本核算、本地劳工是否充足、引进的技术工人的来源和签证等都要考虑，并要确保项目所在地居民生活不受开发行为影响。

三是要信任和依赖专家团队。能矿资源项目的特点是涉及的点面繁多，问题错综复杂，基础设施建设期投资较大且分阶段循序渐进，开发时间较长且突发事件有时不可预测，因此出现麻烦时不仅相互影响，而且牵一发而动全身。负责中资企业决策的高管层，职责是在综合考虑各方面因素后，最终拍板决定各项经营决策。决策层应该知人善用，拍板绝不能演变成拍脑袋。应当有一支强大的专家团队作为决策的智囊团，如技术专家、财务专家、法律专家、公关专家、谈判专家以及熟悉当地情况的中介服务机构等。整个项目的开发、投资、建设、运营、运输、销售等环节的方案设计都应当由专家团队广泛参与、反复论证，确保领导决策的科学性、准确性和严肃性。

(四) 搭建银企合作平台，避免资金错配，确保稳定现金流

矿产资源领域是典型的资金、技术、管理密集型行业，特别是需要大额长期稳定的资金支持。随着中国"走出去"战略的深化和"一带一路"战略的实施，国家开发银行、中国进出口银行、丝路基金等政策性金融机构以及各大商业银行也纷纷为中资企业投资海外矿产资源领域创新融资产品，为中资企业提供更为便捷的综合金融服务。中资企业应该把握国家对外开放政策和外资审批及支持政策的精髓，将鼓励政策用足用好，最大限度争取金融机构的大力支持。

中资企业投资海外能矿资源领域，项目建设期一定要避免资金错配，避免短贷长用，避免人为导致技术上的现金流紧张。澳大利亚资本市场高度发达，金融业占全国经济总量的比重最大，拥有亚太地区第二大股票市场，澳元在全球的交易量位居第五。中资企业在澳大利亚投资能矿资源领域，应当挥好中国的开发性金融、政策性金融，以及中澳两国商业性金融等各种金融形态的优势和作用，主动搭建银企合作平台，畅通投融资合作渠道。

国家开发银行是支持中资企业投资能矿资源领域的主力银行，具有保本微利的经营特点，可以投资、贷款、发债、租赁、证券等几个板块相结合，为中资企业提供全面的综合经营服务。自 2000 年左右至今，国家开发银行支持了大批在全球有影响力的能矿投资的大项目。这些项目的投资期较长，回报率虽然较大但是周期较长，利润率存在前低后高甚至上下波动的情况，易受到大宗商品价格周期变化的影响。国家开发银行在能矿资源领域有大批的行业专家，可以对中资企业提供专业的财务顾问服务，将能矿资源领域的各种投资风险较低到最低程度，并以自身的影响力，带动国内外商业银行以国际银团贷款的方式支持中资企业。国家开发银行是"一带一路"建设的主力银行，讲政治，顾大局，重视风险管控，重视尊重经济规律，可以为中资企业投资澳大利亚能矿资源领域率先提供支持，优化可持续发展的金融生态环境。

（五）加强经营管理，重视人才培养，促进可持续发展

境外能矿项目的经营管理是决定中资企业投资成败的重要因素之一。在不同国家、不同法律制度、不同文化及宗教习俗背景下，做好外派员工、属地员工、外籍员工的沟通管理协调工作，提高跨国思维转换能力和适应外部环境变化的应对能力，是中资企业境外能矿资源项目能够成功长期稳定运营的关键。根据澳大利亚的务工签证法律规定，外国公司在澳大

利亚投资，劳务工人等应当优先在本地公民或拥有长期居留证的居民中招聘，除非必须招募到企业发展需要的管理人才和特殊技术人才。因此，中资企业在澳大利亚的能矿资源项目中将有大量的本地工人。目前，五矿MMG 项目、兖煤澳洲项目、中信泰富西澳铁矿等项目、鞍钢卡拉拉铁矿项目等都是从国内委派较高层次的管理人员，中层和基层管理人员以及大量的工人基本上都是本地员工。这些大型中资企业的经营管理经验证明，这种模式是切实可行的，也取得了很好的经营管理效果，锻炼了国内外派的管理团队，培养了一批懂国际化经营管理的专家团队。

中资企业的项目管理人员如果大多从国内委派，由于文化差异等原因，确实很难达到理想的管理效果，如果和本地员工出现较大矛盾，更可能会酝酿成较大的运营风险和声誉风险。因此，国内中资企业外派的管理团队必须要少而精，能够承受很大的责任和压力，既要尽快适应环境，和本地员工打成一片，又要从管理沟通和运营经验上让本地员工信服。从一定意义上讲，整个国家和社会资源都在整合力量支持中资企业投资境外能矿资源项目。因此，中资企业要格外珍惜参与境外能矿资源项目投资和经营管理的机会，不仅要防范风险，确保经济效益最大化，更应当以国家长远利益最大化为己任，在实施海外矿产资源项目的过程中，高度重视软实力的提高，从培养较强的语言沟通能力、专业技术实力、开发和经营管理经验、跨文化管理能力等诸多方面，打造一支中国自己的高水平、复合型、精通经营管理的国际能矿资源项目人才队伍，在更高层面上，从更长远的角度，促进能矿资源企业自身和整个国民经济的可持续健康发展。

参考文献:

胡怀邦：《以开发性金融服务"一带一路"战略》，《中国银行业》2015 年第 12 期。

郑之杰：《抓住历史机遇，以开发性金融服务"一带一路"建设》，《人民日报》2016 年 8 月 4 日。

Department of the Prime Minister and Cabinet, *Our North, Our Future: White Paper on Developing Northern Australia*, Australia, 2015.

孟刚:《21世纪海上丝绸之路南线四国融资合作研究》,《开发性金融研究》2016年第1期。

杨爽:《对兖州煤业收购澳洲菲利克斯资源公司的思考》,《合作经济与科技》2011年第4期。

National Innovation and Science Agenda, Australia commonwealth government.

Department of the Prime Minister and Cabinet, *Green Paper on Developing Northern Australia*, Australia, 2014.

Australian Bureau of Statistics, Australia.

孟刚:《中澳创新驱动战略的对接路径和融资合作研究》,《全球化》2016年第6期。

何先虎:《中国五矿收购澳大利亚OZ矿业的思考》,首都经济贸易大学硕士论文2014年。

澳大利亚中国总商会:《中资企业在澳大利亚》,中国人民大学出版社2015年版。

靳颖妹:《中钢力拓洽那合营铁矿再次续约:中钢集团获利好》,《21世纪经济报道》2016年4月14日。

高薇:《国际直接投资理论的演变及其对中国的启示》,吉林大学博士学位论文2011年。

孟刚:《"一带一路"建设对接澳大利亚北部大开发的路径和融资合作研究》,《全球化》2016年第11期。

蒋群英:《中国企业对外直接投资现状与对策研究》,复旦大学博士学位论文2003年。

林莎:《中国企业绿地投资与跨国并购的差异——来自223家国内企业的经验分析》,《管理评论》2014年第9期。

卓丽洪:《一带一路战略下中外产能合作新格局研究》,《东岳论丛》2015年第10期。

武文卿:《中国制造追梦2025投资助推国际产能合作》,《中国招标》2015年第27期。

孟刚:《中国在澳大利亚国际产能合作研究》,《开发性金融研究》2016年第3期。

Forewords
Strategic Link with Other Countries for the
Belt & Road Construction

In September 2013, President Xi Jinping delivered a speech in Nazarbayev University, Kazakhstan. In the speech, President Xi reviewed the significant contribution made by the ancient Silk Road, and further advocated to build a modern "Silk Road Economic Belt" . He said that we can jointly build a Silk Road Economic Belt by innovative cooperation mode for more closely economic cooperation among European and Asian countries, more intensive cooperation and more significant growth. In October 2013, President Xi delivered a speech in Parliament of Indonesia. He addressed that Southeast Asia has since ancient times been an important hub along the Maritime Silk Road, China will strengthen maritime cooperation with ASEAN countries, and make good use of the China-ASEAN Maritime Cooperation Fund set up by the Chinese government and vigorously develop maritime partnership in a joint effort to build the Maritime Silk Road of the 21st century. As a new idea proposed by China's diplomacy, the Silk Road Economic Belt and Maritime Silk Road of 21st Century jointly constitute the significant the Belt & Road.

The Belt & Road proposal has been repeatedly mentioned in important conferences of the Party Central Committee, national policy documents and foreign affairs of leaders. In November 2013, *Decision of the Central Committee of the Communist Party of China on some Major Issues Concerning Comprehensively Deepening the Reform* was passed at the Third Plenary Session of the 18th CPC Central Committee, which clearly pointed out that accelerating the construction of infrastructure connecting China with neighboring countries and regions, boosting construction of the Silk Road Economic Belt and Maritime Silk Road, and forming a new pattern of all-around opening. At Boao Forum for Asia 2015 Annual Conference, President Xi Jinping called on all countries to actively participate in construction of the Belt & Road. Later, the China's Government issued *Vision and Actions on Jointly Building Silk Road Economic Belt and 21st-Century Maritime Silk Road*, which makes clear the joint construction principles, framework ideas, key of points cooperation and cooperation mechanisms of the Belt & Road.

In March 2016, the outline of the "13th Five-year Plan" was officially issued, there was a chapter focused on promoting the construcion of the Belt & Road. It means the Belt & Road would be the key emphasis and the strategic task for economic and social development in China. In next five years, China insists on the principle of joint discussion, construction and sharing to drive the strategic link with countries along the Belt & Road, and has signed the cooperative agreement of the Belt & Road with over 20 countries. China has preliminarily formed an international layout of capacity-cooperation, which has covered Asia, Africa, Latin America and Europe, driven joint development of China and other countries, and created a new cooperation mode between South-North and South-South. Under the background of the depressed global economy, the Belt & Road brings new hopes, opens new visions and injects new power for economic growth to Eurasia and even to the world.

In July 2014, President Xi Jinping lectured in Canberra, Australia. He officially raised the proposal of linking the Belt & Road with "Developing North Australia" . China and Australia set up a comprehensive strategic partnership. In April 2016, President Xi Jinping and Premier Li Keqiang respectively announced the decision of the link between the Belt & Road and "Developing North Australia" to Turnbull, Premier of Australia, in Beijing. The innovation-driven strategy between China and Australia is linked successfully.

China Development Bank (CDB) is the main bank for serving the Belt & Road construction. Since the the Belt & Road is proposed, CDB has been cooperating with "construction of the Belt & Road" actively. CDB provides financial supports for economic and social development of countries along the Silk Road. CDB focuses on the interconnectivity of the infrastructure and international capacity of the cooperation, supports China-funded enterprises and the advantageous capacity to go abroad and provides fund supports for the construction of key projects around infrastructure interconnectivity, energy resources cooperation and equipment manufactures and export in key fields of oil and gas, nuclear power, high-speed rail, equipments, ports and parks. It lays firm foundation of mutual political trusts for cooperative mechanism construction between mutual and bilateral governments.

The author of this book is a person who works for Australia Work Group of CDB, and takes charge of investment and financial cooperation between Chinese and Australian governments and enterprises with regard to the Belt & Road. This book summarizes the theoretical results of deveoping financial services in Australia. The author is greatly supported and helped by Chinese and Australian government departments, senior management of enterprises and friends from all sectors of the society when he is writing this book. This book, based on the analysis of historical and current status of China-funded enterprises' investment in Australia, largely covers hot fields of China-Australia the Belt & Road investment and financial cooperation, including: (1) research on investment and financial cooperation of 21st Century Maritime Silk Road in four South Pacific Countries; (2) research on China's strengthening international capacity cooperation in Australia; (3) research on the link route and financial cooperation between the Belt & Road and Developing North Australia; (4) research on route and financial cooperation of China's linking with Australia innovation-driven strategy; (5) research on investing and financial cooperation for China-funded enterprises to build economic and trade cooperation zone in Australia; (6) research on investment of China-funded enterprises in infrastructure fields of Australia; and (7) research on driving investing cooperation of China-funded enterprises in the field of energy and mining in Australia.

Australia is the second largest target country for global direct investment of China, and plays an important role of linking Asian-Pacific regions, developed countries in Europe and America. This book, uses China-Australia investing and financial cooperation for the Belt & Road as a framework, expounds the strategic significance for China to strengthen investment and financial cooperation with Australia under new situations in aspects of coping to global economy order restructuring by economic diplomacy, jointly ushering in new round global technology innovation reform, facilitating traditional cooperation in energy and resources fields to guarantee economy safety of China, and expanding "going abroad" cooperative space of China-funded enterprises, analyzes main fields of the Belt & Road strategy and international capacity cooperation between China and Australia, and proposes critical and practical suggestions on thinking to build a support system from the government level and explore investment and financing cooperation mode from the enterprise level. It is of theoretical guidance significances for China-funded enterprises to investing and financial practices in Australia and other countries.

The Belt & Road copes to general trends and public minds. It is necessary to summarize and study practical operative achievements for China and Australia, makes talents and ideas flow on the Belt & Road. It needs to make the Belt & Road sufficiently play the fundamental, leading and guiding role in the Belt & Road strategy and provide quality services, intellectual supports and talents guarantee for sustainable the development of the Belt & Road construction. According to the data released by the Commonwealth Government of Australia, only in 2016, over 50,000 Chinese students went to Australia for overseas study, increasing 23% on year-on-year basis. The Chinese students are important in the development of education export industry in Australia, and most of them majoring in business, finance, business administration and laws. Therefore, this book is suitable for Chinese scholars and overseas students to read as a specialized book, and helps them to know hot fields , developing direction of investment and financial cooperation between China and Australia regarding the Belt & Road, spreads the Belt & Road culture, and strengthen soft strength construction. It will lead and drive more excellent international talents to actively devote to theories and practices of the Belt & Road construction.

Research on Financial Cooperation of Four Countries along the Southern Route of the 21st Century Marine Silk Road

I. Australia, New Zealand, Papua New Guinea, Fiji: Key cooperative countries of development-oriented finance in South Pacific

The Southern Route of the 21st Century Maritime Silk Road is an important part of the Belt & Road strategy. As President Xi Jinping said in November 2014 during his visit in Australia, New Zealand and Fiji, the South Pacific is the natural extension of the 21st Century Maritime Silk Road proposed by China, and relevant countries are welcomed in construction of Maritime Silk Road to push great development of economic and trade cooperation. In the aspect of bilateral relations, the strategic partnership between China and Australia, New Zealand has been lifted to the comprehensive strategic partnership, and the bilateral relationship with South Pacific islands such as Papua New Guinea (PNG for short hereinafter) and Fiji has been upgraded to strategic partnership.

Currently, in addition to Australia and New Zealand there are a total of 14[①] independent countries in the South Pacific region, geographically located as part of Oceania and official members of the regional organization Pacific Islands Forum. Since these countries are mainly located to the south of Equatorial Pacific, they are generally referred to as the South Pacific Islands by the international society. In 2015, the total population of the South Pacific region (including Australia, New Zealand, PNG, Fiji and all other islands, regions) is 39.359 million, total land area is 8.95 million sq. km., and total ocean area is 46.62 million sq.km. In the South Pacific, Australia and New Zealand are developed countries, and their economic growth is far ahead of than other countries. PNG and Fiji are developing countries with powerful economic strength. According to IMF data, the total GDP of Australia, New Zealand, Papua New Guinea and Fiji in 2014 is USD 1.6584 trillion, accounting for over 99.99% of total GDP in South Pacific Region. The economic aggregate of other countries is small, and these countries mainly carry out international cooperation by inter-government development aids. For instance in Nauru, the smallest country, the land area is only 21sq. km. and population is 10,800. In 2014, its GDP is USD 48 million.

---

① By order of independence time:1. Australia (1901) ;2. New Zealand (1907) ;3.Samoa (1962) ;4.Nauru (1968) ;5.Tonga (1970) ; 6. Fiji (1970) ;7.Papua New Guinea (1975) ;8. Solomon Islands (1978) ;9.Tuvalu (1978) ;10.Kiribati (1979) ;11.Marshall Islands (1979) ;12.Vanuatu (1980) ;13.Palau (1994) ;14.Micronesia (1986) ;15.Cook Islands (1989) ;16.Niue (2006) , in which 10 countries have established diplomatic relations, respectively Australia, New Zealand, Fiji, Papua New Guinea, Micronesia, Samoa, Vanuatu, Tonga, Cook Islands and Niue.

Table 1   2014 GDP Global Rank of South Pacific Countries

Unit: Million Dollars

Country	Australia	New Zealand	Papua New Guinea	Fiji	Vanuatu	Microne-sia Fed	Palau	Kiribati
GDP	1,444,189	198,118	16,060	4,212	812	315	269	181
Rank	12	53	114	154	177	183	184	186

Data source: IMF.

The Belt & Road construction is a significant strategic decision made by the Central Party Committee and the State Council. The important support of the Belt & Road strategy is accommodation of funds. The support of development-oriented finance on significant projects shall particularly be strengthened. The development-oriented financial institutions in China mainly engaging in serving the Belt & Road strategy are Asian Infrastructure Investment Bank, Silk Road Fund and China Development Bank (hereinafter referred to as CDB) . As of the end of September 2015, the total assets of CDB exceeded over RMB 11 trillion, and balance of foreign exchange service exceeded USD 320 billion. It has supported over 400 financial projects for countries along the line of the Belt & Road. The loan balance is USD 107.3 billion, and CDB acquired favorable effect in supporting policy communication, road connection, smooth trade, currency circulation and citizen communication. Australia, New Zealand, Papua New Guinea and Fiji are of political influence in the South Pacific region, and meanwhile are the main forces of economic growth. With powerful infrastructure construction demand, abundant energy and mineral resources, high integrating degree with China, sturdy cooperative foundation, and strong cooperative willingness, these four countries are important for development-oriented financial institutions to participate in South

Pacific financing cooperation.

II. Analysis of economic advantages and disadvantages of the four countries

(i) Australia

1. Advantages

In the aspect of political environment, Australia implements the British Commonwealth system, and is divided into six states and two territories. The political system is stable, regime change is legal and ordered, and investment environment is favorable. The most important four bilateral partners are respectively USA, Japan, China and Indonesia. In the aspect of economic foundation, Australia has a highly developed economy and a reasonable industrial structure. It is the most developed country in the Southern Hemisphere and the 12th largest economy in the world. The per capita GDP is about USD 68,000. Service industry, manufacturing industry, mining industry and agriculture are its four leading industries. In the aspect of natural resources, the mineral products and agricultural resources in Australia are abundant, and the output of iron ore, coal, gold, Li, and Manganese ore ranks top globally. The export volume of various mineral products ranks world first; with high agricultural modernization and mechanization, Australia is the world fourth agricultural product exporter. In the aspect of its relation with China, Australia officially joined in the Asian Infrastructure Investment Bank in 2015, and signed bilateral FTA to reach consensus for linkage between "21ˢᵗ Century Maritime Silk Road" and "Developing Northern Australia" strategy.

2. Disadvantages

On one hand, China Threat Theory affects the relationship between two countries in certain degree. Firstly, minority politicians advocate "China Threat Theory", accuse China of island construction groundlessly, and interfere in South China Sea issues, against deepening of China-Australia bilateral trade relation; secondly, minority opposite factions believe the selling of key assets to state-owned enterprises of China will cause the public resistance. For instance, they forbid Chinese investors to purchase vast land, and are dissatisfied with the lease of Darwin Port to China. On the other hand, the price of bulk commodities such as iron ore and coal descends largely, in which, the price of iron ore slumped from USD 190 per ton in 2011 to USD 40 per ton in December 2015. The falling bulk commodities price stimulated continuous devaluation of AUD, and the exchange rate mean value is dropped to USD 0.71, creating the lowest record in six years. Meanwhile, the plummeting bulk community price affected government taxation. The predicted financial deficit during 2014-2015 is AUD 41.1 Billion. As of the end of the first quarter in 2015, the foreign debt of Australia has reached up to USD 955 Billion, accounting for 60% of GDP.

(ii) New Zealand

1. Advantages

In the aspect of political environment, the politics is stable and investment environment is favorable. New Zealand implements the British Commonwealth system, and is divided into 11 regions and five prefectures. The political system is stable, and regime change is legal and ordered. The Asian-Pacific region is its preferential field for foreign relations. In the aspect of economic foundation, New Zealand is a "small open economy" based on trade. The core of economic growth is export. Agricultural products are the largest export commodities. In the aspect of relation with China, both countries mutually trust in politics, and keep favorable communication and coordination in significant multilateral mechanism and important international and regional issues. China-New Zealand FTA is the first comprehensive FTA reached by China with other countries. New Zealand is the first developed country joining AIIB negotiation.

2. Disadvantages

On one hand, the natural disasters such as earthquake and drought affect economic growth. In New Zealand, earthquake takes place frequently. Two strong earthquakes took place in the South Island respectively in 2009 and 2010, and the second largest city, Christchurch, suffered from serious economic loss. In addition, since 2012, the North Island has suffered from droughts repeatedly, causing certain impact on development of pillar industries such as animal husbandry. On the other hand, New Zealand takes export market construction as primary target. The single economic structure is easily impacted by international market demand and price. In recent years, the domestic economy of New Zealand has declined, tax revenue has reduced, expenditure has increased and government financial resources have been weakened.

(iii) Papua New Guinea

1. Advantages

In the aspect of political environment, PNG implements the system of British Commonwealth Constitutional Monarchy, and is divided into 21 provinces and the capital territory. Since 2012, PNG has spent great efforts in pushing government reform, strived for party cooperation, and the political environment is relatively stable. In the aspect of economic foundation, since August 2002, PNG government has greatly pushed forward "economic recovery droven by export", strengthened exploration and development of mineral resources, and eased privatization reform so its economy grows sustainably and rapidly. The GDP growth speed in recent five years keeps at 5%-15%. The proportion of agriculture, industry and service is 1/3 respectively. As regulated by PNG laws, foreign debts shall not exceed 35% of GDP so as to effectively control financial risks. In the aspect of natural resources, the natural resources such as energy and mineral resources in PNG are abundant. It is the 10th largest copper producing country and the 11th largest gold producing country in the world. Moreover, the resources of fresh water, tropical rainforest and marine products are abundant.

2. Disadvantages

The disadvantages mainly contain (1) social security problem is prominent. The number of criminal cases, such as robbery, murder and armed confrontation, in metropolis increased year by year. The tribe disputes in highlands keep intensifying, and security expenses account a large proportion in investment cost; (2) infrastructure is outdated, and main transportation ways are air transportation and shipping (for cargo) .Also there are railway transportation, and no nationwide highway network. Its wharf capacity is insufficient, rural communication is under developed, and power supply capacity is low. There is no national power grid system, and electricity is available for only 15% population of the country; the electric power gap is large; (3) population quality is low. The computation capacity of youth is low, and literacy rate is lower than 70%. Most school-age children are inaccessible to education. Teachers are insufficient, and teaching quality is worse. Labor supply fails to meet demands of economic growth and sustainable social development; (4) land ownership management is irregular. PNG implements land privatization system. 97% lands are occupied by tribes. There is no clear land registration system. Land boundary is not distinct. Once developed, many land owners may claim for profits. The cooperative mechanism is uncertain greatly. Land resources are difficult to bring the superiority into full play and even become bottleneck restricting economic development.

(iv) Fiji

1. Advantages

In the aspect of political environment, the political environment of Fiji is relatively stable. Fiji became a member of the British Commonwealth after its independence in 1970; after the coup in 1987, it was renamed the Republic of Fiji, and broke away from the British Commonwealth. It is a country with active foreign diplomatic relation among Pacific islands. Since 2010, Fiji proposed the strategy of "Way up North", and actively developed relationship with Asian countries as well as African and American countries. In the aspect of economic foundation, Fiji is a relatively developed country among Pacific islands, and economy is in benign development. Since 2010, Fiji has realized stable growth for five consecutive years and kept a favorable development trend in construction, manufacture, wholesale and retail, finance, insurance, agriculture, communication, transportation and warehousing industry. Fiji contains numerous islands with abundant tourist resources. The government highly values tourism industry and has established a complete tourism development and management system.

2. Disadvantages

On one hand, due to global financial crisis, international market price falling and domestic industrial structure adjustment, the three traditional pillar industries including sugar industry, tourist industry and clothing industry are impacted in certain degree, and industrial structure should be further optimized. On the other hand, the land ownership problems restrict infrastructure construction. Only 10% of land in Fiji is freehold land, and the aborigines own over 88.37% land. For lease and use by any other people, relevant person shall firstly reach agreement with all tribes and use or lease the land under the supervision of NTLB. The land ownership problem of Fiji restricts infrastructure construction of power, road and port largely.

Table 2 Macro economic data of four countries in 2004,2009 and 2014

Year	Country	GDP (USD Billion)	Economic growth rate (%)	Population (million)	GDP Per capita (USD)
2004	Australia	613	4.2	20.13	30,452
	New Zealand	104	3.8	4.09	25,428
	Papua New Guinea	3.9	2.7	5.95	655
	Fiji	2.7	5.3	0.82	3,293
2009	Australia	900	1.5	21.69	41,494
	New Zealand	120	−0.47	4.30	27,907
	Papua New Guinea	8.1	5.5	6.70	1,209
	Fiji	2.8	−1.3	0.85	3,294
2014	Australia	1,444.4	2.5	23.49	61,728
	New Zealand	198.1	3.3	4.51	43,925
	Papua New Guinea	16.1	5.4	7.48	2,139
	Fiji	4.2	3.8	0.89	4,494

Data source: IMF.

III. Key financial cooperation fields

(i) Energy and mineral resource field

1. Current situation

Since 1997 when China started implementing the "going abroad" strategy of "two resources and two markets", the overseas investment in energy and mineral resources stepped into a peak period. However, since 2012, due to the plummeting price of bulk commodities, the overseas investment of China in energy and mineral resources tumbled to fall. In South Pacific region, the investment of China-funded enterprises in Australian energy and mineral resources is the largest. The influential projects contain iron ore projects of CITIC Pacific and Anshan Iron and Steel Group, and coal mine project of Yanzhou Coal Mining. Moreover, the Nickel Mine project of Metallurgical Corporation of China in PNG, and Mobil LNG project that Sinopec participated in also gained extensive attentions. The "going abroad" plan of China-funded enterprises in energy and mineral resource field in South Pacific is mainly centralized on the year between 2007 and 2008 few and lessons and costs are many.

2. Opportunities

Since the market is unpredictable, the international tycoons also made the same mistake. The mineral and energy crisis causes huge loss to many international energy and mineral companies. For instance, certain international mining tycoon bought an ore deposit at the price of USD 1 billion in 2011, which three years later was only sold at price of UAD 50 million. Currently, the global energy and mineral market is depressed, the price of quite a number of energy and mineral resources become rational and even is seriously underestimated. It provides an opportunity for China-funded enterprises to participate in cooperation and competition in global energy and mineral resource market by virtue of the Belt & Road strategy. China is the second largest economy in the world, and the largest energy and mineral resource demander. In the long run, it is the trend for China-funded enterprises to participate in global energy and mineral field largely. The South Pacific region is a place with strategic importance for China-funded enterprises to create internationally influential transnational energy and mineral resource groups.

3. Risks

The risks in energy and mineral resource fields of developed countries such as Australia and New Zealand are market risks and enterprise operation risks, leading to impact on investment return. In developing countries such as PNG and Fiji, the political risks and policy and laws risks are more prominent. Political risks refer to the uncertain factors with regard to sovereignty of the host country, such as unstable political situation, regime change, armed conflicts, social instability and policy instability.

(ii) Infrastructure

1. Current situation

The business that China-funded enterprises participate in infrastructure construction of Australia, New Zealand, Papua New Guinea and Fiji can be divided into international project contracting and overseas investment. Through development in the recent decade, the scope of business has been expanded from labor intensive field such as building, road and bridge construction to fund and technology intensive fields such as metallurgy and power; business mode has gradually developed from labor subcontracting and structure subcontracting to the mainstream general construction contract; the business scale has developed from the small construction projects of hundreds of thousands dollars to large-scale and super-large comprehensive project of over billions of dollars.

2. Opportunities

The infrastructures in Australia are complete, but many infrastructures have approached the service life. The new opportunities for cooperation in fields of port, road, machines and electric power come forth ceaselessly. By estimation, the gap of construction fund is over AUD 770 Billion. The economic volume in New Zealand is small, and demand scale of infrastructure is small. However, as affected by earthquakes, the infrastructure reconstruction gap in Christchurch and other regions will reach over USD 5 Billion. PNG and Fiji are developing economies with rapid growth. The demand for infrastructures such as electric power and roads is large. The low-cost advantages of China-funded enterprise are obvious. Although the scale of single project is limited, the quantity becomes larger.

3. Risks

In developed countries such as Australia and New Zealand, due to lack of project construction and operation experiences that developed countries own, it is difficult for China-funded enterprises to win bid and participate in infrastructure project independently. The access threshold is high. Moreover, constructors are difficult to acquire visas; environmental protection and aboriginal land right protection problems are prominent; labor cost is high, and difference between business and culture is large. In developing countries such as PNG and Fiji, the political risks, development risks (such as tender procedure, corruption, confidentiality regulations, and cut-throat competition), construction risks (such as environmental protection, whole-process approval documents acquisition), project operation risks after the construction is finished (such as relation with local community, and occupational health and security of local employees) and business risks shall be taken into account.

(iii) Agriculture

1. Current situation

According to historical cases, the investment in agriculture in the four countries shall face pressure from government review and public opinions. Moreover, most investment objects are medium and small family enterprises with limited scale operation ability, and less financial information for investors reference. The total investment of China-funded enterprises is small in agricultural field of Australia, New Zealand, Papua New Guinea and Fiji. The suitable agricultural projects are mainly farmland, forest land, fishery and a combination of large and medium-sized enterprise or Greenfield investment. Take Australia for example. The investment in agricultural field of Australia is the largest. Foreign companies own nearly 11.3% land in Australia, while Chinese companies may own less than 1%. Based on the investment higher than AUD 5 Million since 2006, there are only ten completed transactions for China-funded enterprises in agricultural fields in Australia, with a total investment of AUD 1 Billion.

2. Opportunities

According to the analysis on scale, and compared with investment in energy and mineral resource field, China's investment in agricultural field in Australia, New Zealand, Papua New Guinea and Fiji is still in the initial stage. China is not the major investment source of agricultural field in these four countries. However, China is a great agricultural product consumer. Therefore, a large international cooperation space is reserved in the agricultural fields of the four countries.

3. Risks

The early investment in costs of agriculture is large. It is necessary to get familiar with the local market, handle relationships with local communities especially aborigines, sufficiently know different weather conditions and other natural factors, and greatly invest in infrastructure construction such as water conservancy. Thus, the success of agricultural cooperation with the four countries greatly depends on whether early feasibility study of China-funded enterprises is sturdy, whether management and operation after intervention is efficient, and whether market expansion is smooth.

(iv) Equipment manufacture

1. Current situation

With the implementation of the Belt & Road strategy, China faces uncommon opportunity for the development of international capacity and equipment manufacture cooperation. In South Pacific Region, the key countries of cooperation are developing countries such as PNG and Fiji with greatly matching equipment and output, strong cooperation willing, and favorable cooperation conditions and foundation. Developed countries such as Australia and New Zealand are the markets to be actively expanded.

2. Opportunities

For Australia, New Zealand, Papua New Guinea and Fiji, the deep cooperation in the fields of energy and mineral resource, infrastructure and agriculture will undoubtedly drive cooperation for international capacity and equipment manufacture, and reach dot-to-plan effect. The four countries can, on that basis, further push the comprehensive cooperation between two countries in key industries including iron and steel, nonferrous metals, building materials, railway, electric power, chemical engineering, light textile, automobile, communication, engineering machinery, aerospace, ship and marine engineering.

3. Risks

The countries in South Pacific region are the key cooperation regions for developed European and American countries. In the aspect of equipment manufacture, the European and American transnational groups have the advantage as first movers. The four countries, especially Australia and New Zealand, have higher requirements for product standard and equipment quality. The customer loyalty is high, and consumption habits are difficult to change. The former failure cases are many. Therefore, in order to intervene in equipment manufacture field of the four countries, China-funded enterprises shall make comprehensive and meticulous preparation, and bring their comparative advantages into full play.

IV. Ideas and suggestions for development-oriented finance to participate in financing cooperation in South Pacific region

(i) Link with planning, and strengthen key project reserve

In Australia, New Zealand, Papua New Guinea and Fiji, the important approach to financing cooperation is planning first. For planning cooperation with the four countries, the development-oriented institution shall, closely around the overall strategic deployment of the Belt & Road, combine the strategy with significant economic development planning of the four countries, such as the "Developing Northern Australia" strategy and PNG "Infrastructure Construction" plan. While promoting overall planning cooperation, the development-oriented institution shall play the local advantages of social sectors such as well-known consulting companies, law firms, universities and scientific research institutions where the country locates in key fields, and deeply carry out special plans, including infrastructure, energy and resources, agriculture, business cooperation, industrial investment, financial cooperation, cultural exchange, ecological protection and offshore cooperation so as to realize combined strategic layout for planning cooperation. Based on overall planning, the devising of key projects and planning of financing plan in key fields shall be strengthened focusing on infrastructure, energy and mining resources, agriculture, equipment manufacture and international capacity cooperation.

(ii) With Australia as platform, play comprehensive operation advantage radiating countries in South Pacific

The total economy of Australia in South Pacific region is dominating, respectively as 8 times and 90 times as that of New Zealand which ranks the second and of PNG which ranks the third. The capital market of Australia is highly developed, and the proportion of financial industry to national economic aggregate is the largest, about 8.4% of GDP. Australia owns the second largest stock market in Asian-Pacific region, and the global trading volume of AUD ranks the fifth. Australia always, as the most important external factor, affects South Pacific islands countries[1], keeps close economy and trade cooperation with islands countries in South Pacific region, and possesses convenient traffic channels to most of the island countries. Therefore, by setting up operating branches in Australia, the development-oriented financial institutions can expand influence to the South Pacific island countries, and combine bilateral and multi-lateral cooperation, combine financial products such as investment

---

[1] After 2007, Australia strengthened aides to islands countries in the South Pacific region, and inputted large amount of fund in implementing South Pacific Partnership Plan. During 2006-2013, the bilateral aides of Australia in pacific region is as 6 times as that of China. The aids amount of Australia is USD 6.8 billion and of China is USD 1.06 billion.

and load to strengthen innovation of financial products and mode, explore new mode for investment and financing cooperation, comprehensively carry out project financing, trade financing, international settlement, financial consultant, offshore asset securitization and syndicated loan, and provide one-stop service to China-funded enterprises in the South Pacific region.

(iii) Combine government hot spots of four countries and actively participate in significant infrastructure project construction

Against the background of bulk commodity price plummeting, these four countries will strengthen infrastructure construction as new drive for economic growth, such as Developing Northern Australia, post-earthquake reconstruction of Christchurch in New Zealand, and power traffic in PNG and Fiji. Take the "Developing Northern Australia" as example. The Commonwealth Government sets infrastructure loan plan in the north with total amount of AUD 5 billion, attracts global investor by preferential interest rate loan to joint in the infrastructure construction of port, highway, pipeline, electric power and water conservancy, and directly invests about AUD 1 billion in early key infrastructure reconstruction. The development-oriented financial institutions shall combine the hot spots of governments of the four countries, lead the China-funded enterprises to explore multiple cooperation modes such as "EPC+F", PPP, BOT and PFI, actively participate in key infrastructure construction, and further promote international capacity cooperation and key equipment manufacture "going abroad".

(iv) Set bulk commodity stable fund, lay out equity in key energy and mining enterprises in the four countries

According to the analysis on short and mid-term trend, the price of bulk commodity such as energy and mineral resources could be lowered. The further rapid falling of international bulk commodity price will cause more problems including sharp currency depreciation, foreign exchange shortage, inflation or sovereignty and debt repayment ability reduction to resource-type exporters such as Australia and PNG. However, from another angle, this is a strategic opportunity for development-oriented finance to intervene in conversion period, and support China-funded enterprises to invest in overseas energy and mineral resource field. The development-oriented financial institution should explore the way to set up stable fund for bulk commodities such as energy and mining, aid the bulk commodity exports such as Australia and PNG in proper time, and support China-funded enterprises to, under premise of mutual benefits, carry out business cooperation by mode of equity investment priority so as to ease crash impact of bulk commodity price falling on economy of exporters in the short term, and enhance the right of speech and domination of China-funded enterprises in the pricing of international bulk commodities.

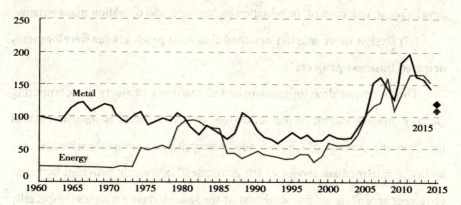

Fig.1 Price trend of international metal and energy bulk commodities （1960-2015）
Data source: IMF primary commodity price system; EIA; World Bank Global Economy Detection Database.

Note: Actual price index of certain commodity refers to the weighted average of global commodity trade at USD price, deflate according to manufacturing industry price index in developed countries and set the value in 2005 as 100.

(v) Strengthen inter-bank cooperation with four countries and jointly

support significant projects

The financial supervision laws in Australia are strict. The four commercial banks in Australia, Australia & New Zealand Banking Group, National Bank, Westpac Banking and Commonwealth Bank, set up branches in main south pacific island countries such as New Zealand, PNG and Fiji. The four banks are the main banks in South Pacific financial market with years of experience and powerful strength. The development-oriented financial institutions shall strengthen cooperation with local banks such as multilateral financial institutions, China-funded banks, four main commercial banks of Australia and South Pacific Bank of PNG, support significant project development and construction in the South Pacific region by means of syndicated loan, credit extension, and en-lending, and comprehensively improve overall operation ability and influence in the South Pacific region in the aspects of product development, risk control, information technology, and operation management.

(vi) Design more market-oriented financial products for development-oriented business projects

The overseas development-oriented business projects are competing fiercely, mainly shown as the following: firstly the fund is insufficient and the financing demand of China-funded enterprisers is comprehensive, and the ability of intermediate services such as financial consultant provided by banks is valued; secondly, the financial cost of the same industry overseas, especially foreign-funded banks, is low, financial decision is made faster, approval process is more efficient and loan currency is abundant, which can meet demands of clients for different financial products such as bullet repayment (repaying principle at lump sum upon maturity) . Therefore, the development-oriented financial institutions shall design different financial products for various development-oriented business projects, regulate different standards and requirements for risk preference, risk tolerance, credit structure, loan pricing, loan types and approval process of projects, establish long-acting cooperation mechanism, meet requirements of development-oriented financial institutions to support various development-oriented projects by market and commercial ways, and better sustainably serve the strategic demand for the Belt & Road construction.

References:

Hu Huaibang, "Serving the Belt & Road Strategy by Development-Oriented Finance", *China Banking Industry*, 2015（12）.

"Oceania 2015", Population Pyramids of the World from 1950 to 2100, http://populationpyramid.net/oceania/2015/.

Rom Crocombe, *The South Pacific*, IPS Publications: University of South Pacific,2008.

Yu Changsen, *The 21st Century Maritime Silk Road Southern Route Construction: Relationship between China and Oceania*, Oceania Development Report（2014-2015）, Beijing: Social Sciences Academic Press,2015.

Chen Jinghe, "Current Status and Future of Mining Industry in China under the New Normal Economy", *the 17th China Mining Conference*, October 2015.

Li Zheng, *International Project Contracting and Overseas Investment Business Financing*, Beijing: China Renmin University Press,2014.

CITI Group, Great Circle of Infrastructures in Australia,2008-06-20.

Australian Engineers Forum,2010 Report on Australian Infrastructure,2010.

Philippa Brant, *Lowy Institute for International Policy*, http://www.lowyinstitute.org/chinese-aid-map/.

Research on China's International Industrial Capacity Cooperation in Australia

International industrial capacity cooperation refers to the transfer of the industrial capacity among different countries or regions through international trade and investment etc so as to realize the allocation and combination of the factors of production across the globe. With external investment and trade, Germany in late nineteenth-century, the United States in 1950s and Japan in 1990s had transferred their industrial capacity in the global scope, resolved the domestic excess capacity, boosted the upgrading of the industrial structure, improved the trade conditions and exported domestic technologies and industry standards to other countries and then controlled the whole industry chain. In May,2015, the *Guiding Opinions of the State Council on Promoting the Cooperation between International Capacity and Equipment Manufacturing* was officially issued in China, emphasizing on seizing the historical opportunity of global infrastructure construction and industrial upgrading, taking 12 key industries of iron and steel, nonferrous metals, building materials, railway, power, chemicals, textiles, automotive, communications, engineering machinery, aerospace, shipbuilding and marine engineering as the key points of the international industrial capacity cooperation, which shall be categorized and implemented and promoted in order to build up the updated version of the overseas investment by Chinese-invested enterprises.

I. Analysis on the investment history and status quo of Chinese-invested enterprises in Australia

Having a vast territory and abundant natural resources, Australia has been into the rank of the developed countries comparatively early; with the GDP in 2015 at about $1.598 trillion and the per capita GDP at about $66,580, it is the twelfth largest economy in the world. Due to the stable political-legal environment, standardized market mechanism, reasonable industrial structure, more of the investable universe, relatively stable return on investment and with the world-class technologies and management experiences, Australia has become a bridge connecting the Asia Pacific regions and Euramerican developed countries. Australia became the second largest destination country of Chinese direct investment in the world from 2005 to 2015 and China became the largest source country of foreign direct investment for Australia from 2013 to 2015. Chinese-invested enterprises have so many years of their exploration and practice in the foreign investment and experienced the process of the gradual changes in the investment field in Australia.

(1) 1980—2005: Start-up Stage

Chinese-invested enterprises made a small amount of investment activities in Australia. During this stage, Chinese investment in and cooperation with Australia did not yet work at the scale with the typical cases of CITIC Group investing in Portland Aluminium Smelter, Sinosteel Corp investing in Channar Mine operated by Rio Tinto, COSCO Group establishing a Sino-Australian joint venture—Five Star Shipping & Agency Company Pty. Ltd, Chinatex Corp investing in the cotton industry and Bank of China recovered its business in Australia.

(2) 2006—2012: Fields of Energy and Mineral Resources

Chinese-invested enterprises began a large-scale investment in Australia, during which the Chinese investment cooperation projects concentrated on the energy and mining sectors, resulting in 73% of the total cumulative investment in mining and 18% in natural gas industry, focusing primarily on Western Australia and Queensland, including CNOOC's A $25-billion LNG project, CITIC Pacific's $9.9 billion iron ore project, the $6 billion project of Yanzhou Coal and the $2 billion acquisition project by China Minmetals. Many of such cases involved in large-scale investment because of much of the investment made in the energy and mining sectors. The direct investment of Chinese-invested enterprises in Australia had jumped from $1.54 billion in 2007 to $16.2 billion in 2008. The investment of Chinese-invested enterprises in Australia 2012 was $10.1 billion, of which more than half of the investment projects worth more than $200 million.

(3) 2013—present: Trend of Diversity

The trend of diversity has begun to take on for Chinese-invested enterprises to invest in Australia. During this stage, in addition to the sectors of energy and mining, the investment projects made by Chinese-invested enterprises in Australia included the infrastructure, agriculture, manufacturing, high-end food, leisure, retail and logistics etc, having the typical cases of China Communications Construction Company (CCCC) buying Australian construction firm John Holland for A$1.15 billion, China Merchants Group Ltd obtaining a 99-year lease for the port of Newcastle for A$875 million, Shandong

Landbridge Group obtaining a 99-year lease for the port of Darwin for A$506 million, the State Grid acquiring the equity of a local power grid company, Shanghai Zhongfu Group acquiring the framing land in the Northern Territory, the New Hope Group investing in the dairy farms and dairy processing plants, several well-known and leading real estate companies such as Greenland Group investing in the commercial real estates, Wanda Cinema Line Corporation acquiring Australian cinemas, Lenovo Group investing in the seafood industry, and Alibaba's layout of e-commerce Platforms.

(4) Analysis on Status Quo

From 2006 to 2012, 2/3 of the total Chinese investment was made in the sectors of energy and mining resources in Western Australia and Queensland. In 2013, the direct investment of Chinese-invested enterprises made in Australia was $9.19 billion; according to the analysis on the proportion of the total investment, it was 40% in power transmission, 24% in mining, 21% in natural gas, 14% in real estate and 1% in agriculture, where 48% of the Chinese total investment was accounted for by Vitoria, 36% by Queensland and 11% by New South Wales. In 2014, the direct investment of Chinese-invested enterprises made in Australia was $8.35 billion, of which the investment made by the private enterprises in Australia exceeded that made by the state-own enterprises for the first time in terms of the number of transactions (accounting for 85%) and the aggregate investment (accounting for 66%) ; according to the analysis on the proportion of the total investment, it was 46% in real estate, 21% in infrastructure, 12% in the leisure and retail industries, 11% in mining, 7% in oil and gas, 2% in manufacturing, and 1% in agriculture; New South Wales has become the first choice of Chinese direct investment, accounting for 72% of the total investment. In 2015, the direct investment of Chinese-invested enterprises made in Australia was $10.11 billion; according to the analysis on the proportion of the total investment, it was 45% in real estate,20% in new energy,17% in health care,9% in mining,3% in oil and natural gas,3% in infrastructure, and 3% in agriculture; there were 12 agricultural projects with a total investment of $375 million; then number of transactions by private enterprises accounted for 78%; New South Wales kept the first to attract Chinese direct investment, accounted for 49.3% of the total investment, Victoria came next, accounted for 34%.

II. The significance for China to strengthen the international industrial capacity cooperation in Australia under the new situation

(1) Coping with the global economic order reconstruction by the economic diplomacy

After the financial crisis, the United States launched a new round of global economic and trade rules featured by high standards and exclusiveness, such as the Trans-Pacific Economic Partnership Agreement (TPP) and Transatlantic Trade and Investment Partnership (TTIP) . Such agreements are very exclusive and will seriously affect China, the emerging markets and the developing countries. Faced with this situation, while holding an open attitude to TPP, China has proposed the Belt & Road initiative, with emphasis on building up a development platform connecting to Asia Pacific Economic Circle and the European Economic Circle by the investment output and capital output rather than commodity output. As a developed country with strong influence on the politics and economy in the Asia-Pacific Region and a founding member of the Asian Infrastructure Investment Bank, Australia has been positively in response to the construction of the Belt & Road and signed officially the Sino-Australia Free Trade Agreement with China in June 2015, it is an important cooperating country for China to adapt initiatively to the new situation of the economic globalization. To deepen the international industrial capacity cooperation in Australia has important strategic significance for China to cope with the reconstruction of the global economic order by economic diplomacy.

(2) Jointly greeting the new round of the revolution of the global technological innovation

In June 2015, China promulgated the *Opinions of the State Council on Several Policies and Measures for Vigorously Advancing the Popular Entrepreneurship and Innovation*, which stresses that that innovation is the primary driving force for development and the top priority must be given to it in overall national development to implement deeply the strategy of the innovation-driven development. In December 2015, Australia published the *"National Innovation and Science Agenda"* to comprehensively promote the innovation-driven strategy. Seen from several global science-tech revolutions in the history, the scientific and technological innovation has always been an important strategic support to improve the social productive forces and the overall national strength. Those countries that take the preemptive opportunities in the new scientific and technological revolution will surely become the leader of the world economy. Since Australia is an important exporting country in terms of the resources, energy, agricultural products and health products while China is a consumption power and manufacturing power, the bilateral cooperation between China and Australia in the field of science and technology innovation is highly complementary, which is the only way for both countries to jointly greet a new round of the revolution of global science-tech innovation.

(3) Consolidating the traditional cooperation in the sectors of energy and resources to guarantee the economic security in China

Australia has abundant mineral resources and agricultural resources with the output of the iron ore, coal, gold, uranium, zinc, lead, bauxite, manganese, petroleum, natural gas and shale gas etc coming on top of the world; with highly agricultural mechanization and modernization, it is the fourth largest exporter of agricultural products in the world. The proven iron ore resources in Australia are about 16 billion tons with more mature exploration and development, Australia is one of the key countries for the leading miners in the world such as Rio Tinto, BHP Billiton and FMG as well as Chinese-invested enterprises to invest in the iron ore resources. Australia is the world's largest exporter of coal, having about 57.5 billion tons of black coal geological reserves (industrial economic reserves of 39.7 billion tons), ranking the sixth in the world, having about 41.8 billion tons of lignite geological reserves (industrial economic reserves of 37.6 billion tons), accounting for 20% of global lignite reserves, ranking the second in the world. To strengthen the international industrial capacity with Australia has important strategic significance for China to guarantee the security of the energy and resources as needed by the economic development.

(4) Widening the cooperative space for Chinese enterprises to "go abroad"

In the past, the way for Chinese-invested enterprises to "go abroad" depended mainly on trade, namely the product output, exporting the products made in China via trade. Under the new situation of economic globalization, the core for China to promote international industrial capacity and the equipment manufacturing cooperation is to upgrade the product trade and product output of

Chinese-invested enterprises to industry output and capacity output, to transfer from exporting the low-end products to high-end manufacturing products and to realize the new external economic cooperation mode that is changing from the trade-driven mode to the investment-driven and finance-driven modes. The diversified investment carried out by Chinese-invested enterprises in Australia is either the opportunity or the challenge, which, if successful, can not only transfer domestic advantageous industries into Australia to obtain a stable return on investment, but also acquire the internationally advanced technologies and management experiences to lay a solid foundation to become the transnational corporations with global influence.

III. The theoretical basis of China's international industrial capacity cooperation in Australia

Based on summing up lots of practical cases and the in-depth study, the experts and scholars of various countries have formulated a great deal of theories with regard to the transfer of international industrial capacity, which has very useful indications for China to carry out international industrial capacity in Australia in a better manner.

(1) Product Life Cycle Theory

The product life cycle theory is a famous theory to explain the strategic choice of the finished products trade and the foreign direct investment by enterprises. Not considering the issue from the point of view that the natural attribute of a product is gradually disappearing, this theory analyzes the decisions on the foreign direct investment made by the enterprise from three stages of the product innovation, product development and maturity, and standardization of product. At the stage of product innovation, the market demand is mainly in domestic, and an innovation country meets the demand from other countries mainly through export rather than direct investment. During the stage of product development and maturity, the markets of the innovation country become increasingly competitive, and transnational production is gradually emerging in order to avoid the trade barriers such as the importing countries' customs tariffs, therefore, the cost factors become the main means of market competition, and the direct investment begins to be made in other countries with the similar market structures, the similar consumer preference and relatively lower cost. During the stage of product standardization, the competition is more and more intense and the enterprise begins to seek for the place with the lowest production costs in the world, at this point, the country with rich natural resources and the low-cost advantages becomes the best choice for enterprises to invest abroad.

(2) Theory of Investment-Induced Factors Portfolio

The theory of Investment-Induced Factors Portfolio was formed in the late 1980s. According to this theory, the international direct investment in any form occurs under the composite effect of the direct and indirect induced factors. Direct induced factors refer to the various elements of production, including natural resources, labor force, capital, production technology, knowledge information and management skills, inducing the foreign direct investment made by the investing country. The indirect induced factors refer to other factors in addition to the direct induced factors, of which the first is the induced factors of the investing country, such as the State encouraging enterprises to invest overseas top sign cooperation agreements with the host country; the second is the induced factors of the host country, such as the superior investment environment, preferential policies to attract foreign investment, and sound laws and regulations; and the third is the globally induced factors, such as economic globalization, technological innovation and so on.

(3) National Comparative Advantage Theory

The theory of national comparative advantage is the latest research result regarding the theory of international direct investment, in which how an enterprise forms and maintains a sustainable competitive advantage is analyzed. This theory divides the development of the national economy into the stages driven by the production factors, driven by investment, driven by technology innovation and driven by wealth, and subdivides the main factors that may affect the international competitiveness of a country into four points: the first one is the natural resources, capital resources, knowledge resources, human resources, infrastructure and so on; the second one is the domestic demand that is easier to form the scale economy, the higher demand levels and of an obvious advance; the third is the industrial factors with the supply from the upstream raw materials and the support from downstream sales channels; the fourth is the conditions to support the creation, strategic planning, organization and management of the enterprises. This theory acknowledges that domestic fierce competition will lead to the occurrence of foreign direct investment and the enterprise must obtain the full competitive advantages in order to ensure the success of foreign direct investment.

(4) The Theory of Global Strategy of Multinational Corporation

The theory of global strategy of Multinational Corporation means that the multinational corporation fully integrates and uses the comparative advantages of the investment country and the host country, rationally allocates the resources for the production and marketing and seeks for the maximum benefits under the background of economic globalization. This theory points out that the objectives of the global strategy of the MNCs shall not be limited to the host country, but shall seek to maximize the profits worldwide, emphasizing globalization, integrity and collaboration, coordinating and managing all kinds of resources in all the countries through the rational allocation, achieving the integration of all the links of the procurement, production, marketing, R&D, and finance to truly realize the specialization of production and enhance the international competitiveness and risk prevention capacity of the enterprise.

IV. The major Sectors of China's international industrial capacity cooperation in Australia

(1) Sector of energy and mineral resources

Since the "going abroad" strategy that makes full use of "two resources and two markets" carried out in our country in 1997, the overseas investment in energy and mineral resources has been gradually entering a peak period. However, since 2012, China's overseas investment in energy and mineral resources has suffered a cliff-like drop due to the sharp fall in commodity prices. There have been fewer successful cases but more lessons and costs since it was at the moment of higher market bubble that Chinese-invested enterprises invested in the energy and mineral resources in Australia. At present, the global market of the energy and mineral resources has taken on the trend to hit the bottom and rebound, the value of a considerable part of the energy and mineral resources tends to be rationalized and even has been seriously underestimated, which affords a rare chance for Chinese-invested enterprises to participate in the cooperation and competition within the global market of energy and mineral resources by taking the Belt & Road strategy as the opportunity. As the second largest economy in the world, China is the largest demand market for the energy and mineral resources in the world. In the long run, it is a general tendency for Chinese-invested enterprises to participate in the competition in the sector of global energy and mineral resources to a greater extent, and therefore, Australia is an important strategic cooperative country for Chinese-invested enterprises to build up the multinational corporations in the sector of energy and mineral resources with a strong international influence.

(2) Infrastructure Sector

The Australian Government officially announced the Australian Infrastructure Plan in February 2016, which puts forward emphatically the Infrastructure Priority List for 93 projects aiming at the demands and challenges confronted with the infrastructure sector in Australia for the next 15 years together with 78 proposals for the governments at all levels to develop infrastructure with the contents covering the expansion of the rail transportation in the capital cities such as Sydney and Melbourne, the redevelopment and renovation of the old cities such as Hobart, the development of the toll roads, the expansion of large airport hubs, the reform of the financing and operation modes in the fields of electric power, water supply, and broadband. While the infrastructure in Australia is relatively perfect, much of the infrastructure has been nearing the end of their projected life-spans, so, the new opportunities for cooperation in the aspects of the ports, roads, machinery and electric power are constantly emerging, and it is estimated that the construction fund gap may be more than A$770 billion. Due to lack of the experiences in the project construction and operation in the developed countries, it is very difficult for Chinese-invested enterprises to win the bidding independently and participate in the infrastructure projects in Australia; on the other hand, the barriers to entry are much higher, and it is much harder for domestic construction personnel to get the visas, the issues regarding the environmental protection and the protection of the indigenous people's rights and interests on land are particularly outstanding along with the higher labor costs and greater differences in commerce and culture.

(3) Agricultural Sector

Analyzing from the perspective of the scale, compared with the investment in the sector of the energy and mineral resources, Chinese investment in Australia in the sector of agriculture is still in its infancy, and China is not a major source country of investment in the sector of agriculture, but a big consuming power of agricultural products. Therefore, the agricultural sector in Australia contains larger space for the international industrial capacity cooperation. Due to larger pre-project investment costs, it is necessary to be familiar with the local market, get on well with local communities, especially the indigenous people, fully understand the natural factors such as climatic conditions that are different with those in our country, and heavily invest in the construction of water conservancy infrastructure. The success in the agricultural cooperation in Australia also depends on many factors such as whether the feasibility study conducted by Chinese-invested enterprises at the earlier stage is well-knit or not, whether the management and operation after taking over are put in place or not, whether it is smooth to develop the market. The agricultural investment projects in Australia that are suitable for Chinese-invested enterprises mainly include the livestock farms and breeding farms, the processing of dairy and animal products, fishing industry and trade, the plantation, processing and trade of the food crops, the plantation, processing and trade of the fruits as well as the forestry.

(4) Sector of equipment manufacturing

Due to higher economic fit, the strong desire for cooperation, and better cooperative conditions and foundation between China and Australia, with the implementation of the Belt & Road strategy, Australia ought to be a market in the developed countries for Chinese-invested enterprises to actively carve out the cooperation in the equipment manufacturing industry, through which to expand to the neighboring countries. To deepen the cooperation in the sectors of energy and mineral resources, infrastructure and agriculture will undoubtedly drive the cooperation in equipment manufacturing to result in the effect to use the experiences from this to promote our work in the entire area, based on which the Chinese-invested enterprises can further promote the all-round cooperation between both parties in the key industries of iron and steel, nonferrous metals, building materials, railway, electric power, chemical industry, light textile, automobile, communications, engineering machinery, aerospace, ship-making and marine engineering. Traditionally, the Euramerican developed countries have cooperated widely with Australia in equipment manufacturing with the first-mover advantages. Australia has a higher requirement on the product standards and quality of the equipment manufacturing. The customer loyalty of the Australian enterprises is much higher, and it is difficult for them to change the consumption habits. Therefore, before involving in the sector of Australia equipment manufacturing, Chinese-invested enterprises need to do a full range of careful preparations, so as to give full play to their own comparative advantages.

V. Constructing the supporting system for China's international industrial capacity cooperation in Australia at the government level

(1) Taking the opportunity of strategic alignment between the Governments of both countries

In November 2014, the governments of both China and Australia agreed to push forward their strategic partnership into a comprehensive strategic partnership. In August 2015, the second round of China-Australia Strategic and Economic Dialogue was held in Canberra and both sides reached a consensus to further enhance the scope and the level of the cooperation through aligning the development strategies of the two countries. In February 2016, the ministerial talk between China and Australia further clarified the specific contents of the synergy between the development strategies of both countries. In April 2016, President Xi Jinping, Premier Li Keqiang, together with visiting Australian Prime Minister officially announced to synergize the Belt and Road Initiative of the Chinese side and the Vision for Developing North Australia of the Australian side as well as the innovation-driven development strategy of the Chinese side and the National Innovation and Science Agenda of Australian side. On April 19,2016, Daniel Andrew, Premier of Australian State of Vitoria, declared the Strategic Plan for China of the State, which emphasizes that the first is to strengthen the exchanges with the central government and the provincial governments of China to make it clear the direction and goals to carry out such work and to lay the foundation for broader Sino-Australian cooperation; the second is to promote Vitoria to become an excellence center in Australia with deep understanding of Asia and the capabilities to deal with Asian affairs; the third is to establish connections and build up the new platform for people-to-people exchanges through cultural exchanges and cooperation; the fourth is to attract investment for the large governmental infrastructure projects, and provide support for the continued growth of the economy in Vitoria; the fifth is to provide support for the success of the business exchanges between Australia and China; the sixth is to carry out trade activities pointedly based on Vitoria's competitive advantages and China-specific market opportunities. The all-round strategic alignment between the two governments of China and Australia has provided the unprecedented opportunity for Chinese-invested enterprises to carry out international industrial capacity cooperation in Australia.

(2) Taking the free trade agreement between the two countries as the guarantee

In June 2015, the Free Trade Agreement was signed by the two governments of China and Australia. First, in terms of commodities, zero tariffs shall immediately apply to the products accounting for 85.4% of the export trade volume of both sides upon the entry into force of the Agreement. After the transition period, the proportion of the tax items and the proportion of the trade volume to which Australia eventually apply zero tariff will reach 100%, while those applied to by China will be 96.8% and 97% respectively, whose tariff reducing level is far more than 90% in ordinary trade agreements. Second, as for the service sector, Australia commits to open its service sector to China after the entry into force of the agreement by way of the negative list, being the first country in the world to make the commitment on service trades to China by way of the negative list. And China will open up the service sector to Australia by way of the positive list. In addition, Australia has also made special arrangement on the working mechanism on holiday for China. Third, in terms of investment, the two sides will grant each other the most-favored-nation trading status after the agreement into effect; at the same time, Australia will reduce the reviewing threshold for Chinese enterprises to invest in Australia and provide facilitation arrangements. Fourth, the promoting provisions on the exchanges and cooperation of both sides have been made in the agreement for more than a dozen areas such as the E-commerce, government procurement, intellectual property, and competition etc. under the Topics regarding Economy and Trade in 21st Century.

(3) Taking the Policies on Industrial Support of both countries as the Guidance

The international industrial capacity cooperation as a development model promoted jointly by the governments of two countries can not completely rely on the market and to certain extent, the governments guidance are consciously required. The governments of China and Australia should play the roles to guide and promote through their policies on industrial support, build up the information platform of the international industrial capacity cooperation, serve as a bridge for aligning with the projects, and solve the issues that can not be addressed by market regulation such as asymmetric information, larger trade costs and higher investment risks. The governments of China and Australia should establish a guidance platform of the policies on industrial support for the international industrial capacity cooperation to form a network system for the information on policy and guidance, find out the status of supply and demand of the international industrial capacity cooperation from the enterprises, and release the information on the supply and demand and the survey analysis reports regarding the projects of industrial cooperation from time to time. The embassy or consulate, the news agency, or the associations, chambers of commerce, or the financial institutions of China in foreign countries should actively communicate and coordinate with the relevant government departments of Australia, so as to obtain the policies on industrial support of Australian government and the information on development of major projects, and assist Chinese-invested enterprises positively follow up the projects and establish the aligning and cooperative relations.

VI. Exploring the basic path of China's international industrial capacity cooperation in Australia at the enterprise level

(1) Chinese-invested enterprises being the main bodies of China's international industrial capacity cooperation in Australia

The *Guiding Opinions of the State Council on Promoting the Cooperation between International Capacity and Equipment Manufacturing* puts forwards the basic principles of "enterprises serving as the main player and government as the facilitator, giving prominence to the key points, proceeding in an orderly manner, emphasizing practical results, mutual benefit and shared profit, actively yet prudently and prevention and control of risk". The enterprises as the most dynamic economies should play the most important role in Sino-Australian international industrial capacity cooperation. Only taking the enterprises as the main bodies, can the market orientation be insisted on and the market demand can be reflected. Whether the position of the enterprises as the main body can be established or whether the leading role can be played predetermines to a large extent the success of the international industrial capacity cooperation between China and Australia. The Chinese-invested enterprises can obtain the high-end elements of production such as the design, R & D, marketing, service, and re-innovation ability through carrying out the international industrial capacity cooperation in Australia and gradually increase their positions among the global value chain, industrial chain, logistics chain and innovation chain.

Chinese-invested enterprises can form their own strategic objectives from different angles, such as: combined with Australian infrastructure market demand, promote the international cooperation with the advantages of industrial capacity in the industries of the iron and steel, nonferrous metals and building materials; combined with the HSR construction that may be carried forward in Australia, accelerate to expand the international market of the rail transportation equipment; develop and implement the overseas electric power projects in Australia; continue to promote the overseas investment in the key sectors such as the energy and mineral resources; increase the level of the international cooperation in agricultural industry; improve the international competitiveness of the information communication industry; promote the overall distribution of the manufacturing enterprises such as the engineering machinery in Australia to improve the global business network; promote the export of aerospace equipment to Australia; develop the high-end market of the shipping and marine engineering equipment in Australia. When carrying out the international industrial capacity cooperation in Australia, the Chinese-invested enterprises shall even more respect the laws of the market to accelerate the enterprises to enter the international market through the overseas acquisitions in Australia. The governments of China and Australia should also give the necessary policy guidance and supports, should make overall plans by taking the enterprise as the main body to build the platform for the enterprises of the two countries to carry out the international industrial capacity cooperation and promote and support the major economic cooperation projects of the enterprises of the two countries.

(2) Taking Planning First as the forerunner to carry out the international industrial capacity cooperation in Australia

Planning first is an important handhold for Chinese-invested enterprises to carry out the international industrial capacity cooperation in Australia, which can be promoted jointly by three aspects of the banks, governments and enterprises. To carry out the planning and cooperation with regard to international industrial capacity by Chinese-invested enterprises in Australia should closely encircle the overall strategic arrangement of the Belt and Road construction, fully aligning with the major economic development strategies of Australia's own. At the same time when promoting the cooperation of the overall planning, Chinese-invested enterprises shall make full use of the localized advantages of the social forces from the well-known consulting companies, law firms, colleges and universities and scientific research institutions with focus on the key areas, carry out in-depth planning for special projects, take the industries of the infrastructure, energy and mineral resources, agriculture, equipment manufacturing as the keys and strengthen the reserves of the major projects in international industrial capacity cooperation.

Taking the development of Northern Territory of Australia as an example, the Australian Government has set up a total of A\$5 billion Special Loan Program for the infrastructure projects in Northern Territory of Australia to attract global investors to join in the constriction of the infrastructures such as the ports, highways, pipelines, electricity, water conservancy in this region with the loans at preferential rates; in addition, the energy and mineral resources within Northern Territory of Australia are extremely rich, mainly including iron ore, coal, gold, uranium, zinc, lead, bauxite, manganese, petroleum, natural gas and shale gas etc. there are eight major mines under operation in the Northern Territory with the mining industry value more than A\$3.2 billion in 2014-2015; the annual production capacity of LNG is 12 million tons; the investment in oil exploration in 2014 reached A\$550 million; and the potential of shale gas resource is more than 200 trillion cubic feet; and 17 mature projects are looking for investment opportunities; Australia attaches great importance to the cooperation with China in agriculture; the cooperation in agriculture has been involved comprehensively in the China-Australia Free Trade Agreement formally implemented in December 2015; every year, the governments of Western Australia, Queensland and the Northern Territory will organize the entrepreneurs of the two countries to participate in the forums and symposia with focus on the cooperation in agriculture, publicizing, introducing and aligning with the cooperation projects, of which the animal husbandry, crop plantation, fisheries and forestry etc are suitable for the investment and development by Chinese-invested enterprises.

(3) Jointly constructing the industrial parks for the international industrial capacity cooperation to serve the demands of the industrial clusters

Under the new situation, to build up the industrial parks jointly is an important way for the international industrial capacity cooperation between China and Australia. As the creature of the new technology revolution in the world and the era of knowledge economy, the new industrial parks shall be mainly in the form of science and technology innovation, able to effectively realize the development objective combined by production, study and research of the international industrial capacity cooperation and vigorously promote industrial transformation and upgrade. To build up the industrial parks jointly by China and Australia, it is necessary to coordinate appropriately the relationship between the two governments and the relationship among the government and the market and enterprise, bring the roles of the research-based universities in technological innovation into full play, establish the perfect support system of innovation, and create a cultural atmosphere in favor of the international industrial capacity cooperation among then enterprises.

Within the industrial parks, Chinese-invested enterprises can not only share the supporting infrastructures and various types of the standardized services, but also reduce the logistics transaction costs due to the geographical proximity to the supporting enterprises and the cooperative enterprises and can even give full play to collective efficiency to enjoy the support from the preferential policies and the arrangement of the simplification system by the two governments. The successful industrial parks can promote the two countries to form the new industrial cooperation chain and the industrial cooperation clusters for the international industrial capacity cooperation to help the enterprises of two countries multiply, develop and grow sturdy, becoming the engine for the interaction and innovative cooperation among the enterprises.

As for jointly constructing the industrial parks for the international industrial capacity cooperation by China and Australia, special attention shall be paid to the differences in terms of the culture, the legal systems, the cooperative modes within the region and the capital investment. First, the borders of the enterprises within the industrial parks for the international industrial capacity cooperation shall not be too clear, or else, not conducive to communications and cooperation among the enterprises, or not conducive to the future in-depth development of the industrial clusters. Second, the cooperative forces of both Chinese and Australian enterprises in the international industrial capacity cooperation shall not be too scattered and it is necessary to increase the incubation efficiency of the production resources and take the high-tech and innovation as the main power for Chinese and Australian enterprises in the international industrial capacity cooperation, otherwise, the characteristics of the labor-intensive and low added value low-end industries would be formed. Third, it is required to integrate the financial resources to provide sophisticated financial products for Chinese and Australian enterprises in the international industrial capacity cooperation so as to better promote the sustainable development of the industrial parks for the international industrial capacity cooperation.

(4) Building up financial platform to support the projects of international industrial capacity cooperation between China and Australia

The capital market is highly developed in Australia, the proportion of the financial sector within the total economy is the largest, accounting for 8.4% in GDP, with the second largest stock market in the Asia Pacific Region, and the transaction volume of the Australian dollar ranks as the fifth in the world. It is necessary to build up the platform in Australia to support the financial cooperation for the international industrial capacity cooperation between China and Australia, bring into full play of the advantages and functions of various financial forms such as the development finance, policy finance and commercial finance, strengthen the cooperation with the local banks such as ANZ Bank, National Bank, Westpac and Commonwealth Bank, and the financial institutions such as the industrial investment funds, the insurance companies and venture capital, keep the channels of cooperation in investment and financing smooth, totally enhance the comprehensive management and operation ability and the influence of its own in the aspects of the product development, risk control, information technology and operation and management, carry out the comprehensive financing services such as the project financing, trade financing, international settlement, financial adviser, offshore asset securitization and syndicated loans in an all-round way, provide all-round and one-stop services for Chinese-invested enterprises, and jointly support the development and construction of major projects in the international industrial capacity cooperation between China and Australia.

In particular, it should be pointed out that, different from the commercial finance, not targeting with profit maximization, the development finance may take the lead into the sectors with relatively lower margin in the international industrial capacity cooperation between China and Australia at the early stage and be the forerunner and pioneer in China's international industrial capacity cooperation in Australia. At the initial stage of the international industrial capacity cooperation between China and Australia, the major projects are featured by longer payback period, lower profit rate and larger funding gap, in which the commercial finance is difficult to participate. Therefore, the development finance can provide the pre-project support and guarantee for the entry of other forms of financial forms based on its own experiences, influence and capital investment. Centered on the hot fields in the international industrial capacity cooperation between China and Australia, the development of financial institutions can guide Chinese-invested enterprises to explore a variety of modes of cooperation such as EPC+F (Engineering, Procurement and Construction plus financing), PPP (public-private partnership), BOT (build - operate - transfer) and PFI (private finance initiative) etc. first of all, participate actively in the construction of related major infrastructures, create a good market environment and the rules of the market for commercial finance to gradually enter into and optimize the ecological environment of the financial support in the international industrial capacity cooperation between China and Australia.

References :

Hu Huaibang, "With the Development Finance to Serve 'The Belt and Road' strategy",

China Banking, 2015 (12).

Zhang Yansheng, "Strategic Background and Practice Opportunities of the Belt and Road", *Tsinghua Financial Review*, 2015 (9).

Bai Chunli, "Taking 'Four Comprehensiveness' to Guide the Development Driven by innovation", *People's Daily*, 2015.3.19.

Meng Gang, "The Research on financing cooperation by four countries along 21st Maritime Silk Road", *Study in Developmental Finance*, 2016 (1).

Department of the Prime Minister and Cabinet, *"Our North, Our Future: White Paper on Developing Northern Australia"*, Australia, 2015.6.

National Innovation and Science Agenda, Australia Commonwealth Government.

Department of the Prime Minister and Cabinet, Green Paper on Developing Northern Australia. Australia,2014.6.

Australian Bureau of Statistics, Australia.

Meng Gang, "Research on the Docking Path and Financing Cooperation of the innovation driven strategy between China and Australia", *Globalization*, 2016 (6).

Xia Xianliang, "The Institutional mechanism and policy system to build up Belt and Road International Industrial Capacity Cooperation", *International Trade*, 2015 (11).

China Chamber of Commerce in Australia, *Chinese-invested Enterprises in Australia*, Beijing: China Renmin University Press.2015 (12).

Yan Jun, "International Industrial Capacity Cooperation: The Paradigm of Utilitarianism in Global Economic Governance", *State Governance*, 2015 (42).

Gao Wei, *The Evolution of the International Direct Investment Theory and Its Enlightenment to China*, Doctoral Dissertation of Jilin University,2011 (12).

Meng Gang, "The Great Development of Northern Australia Bringing New Strategic Opportunities for Developmental Finance", *China Banking*, 2016 (4).

Jiang Qunying, *Research on the Present Situation and Counter Measures of Chinese Enterprises' Foreign Direct Investment*, Doctoral dissertation of Fudan University,2003 (4).

Lin Sha, "the Difference between Green Land Investment and Cross-Border M & A of Chinese Enterprises—An Empirical Analysis on 223 Domestic Enterprises", *Management Review*, 2014 (9).

Zhuo Lihong, "Research on the New Pattern of Chinese and Foreign Industrial Capacity Cooperation Under the Belt and Road Strategy", *Dongyue Tribune*, 2015 (10).

Wu Wenqing, "Made in China 2025 Investment Promoting International Industrial Capacity Cooperation", *China Tendering*, 2015（27）.

Li Jin, "the Seven Points Shall be grasped by the Central Enterprises to Participate in the Belt and Road Initiative", China Maritime, 2015（8）.

Research on the Linkage between the Belt & Road and Developing Northern Australia with Development-oriented Finance

I. Linkage of two strategies is an important economic cooperation in South Pacific area

The 21st Century Marine Silk Road is an important part of the Belt & Road strategy and mainly covers two routes. The first is from coastal port of China to the Indian Ocean via the South China Sea, and extends to Europe; the second is from coastal port of China to the South Pacific Ocean via the South China Sea. In November 2014, President Xi Jinping delivered an important speech themed as "Jointly Pursue Dream of Development for China and Australia and Realize Prosperity and Stability in Our Region" . Xi pointed out that the South Pacific Region is a natural extension of the ancient Maritime Silk Road, and showed open-mind for Australia's participating in the construction of the 21st Century Marine Silk Road. Xi said China will support the strategy of "Developing Northern Australia" . Both parties should consolidate traditional cooperation on energies, accelerate to develop new cooperation growth points of infrastructure construction and agriculture, and realize diversified trading ties between the two countries. This speech points out the way for linkage between the Belt & Road strategy and "Developing Northern Australia" strategy.

Australia is of political influence in the South Pacific Region, and meanwhile is the main power of economic growth. It highly integrates with the Chinese economy, cooperates with China sturdily and intensively. The bilateral relation between China and Australia is advanced to the comprehensive strategic partnership from common partnership. In June 2014, the Commonwealth Government of Australia issued a green paper and announced the "Developing Northern Australia" strategy. In June 2015, the Commonwealth Government of Australia officially released the whitepaper of "Northern Australia, Our Future – Conception for Developing Northern Australia" to comprehensively formulate the Developing Northern Australia plan, and propose development prospect and blueprint of Northern Australia in the next 20 years. The regions covered by Developing Northern Australia strategy contain north zone upper south regression line of Western Australia and Queensland, as well as the entire Northern Territory. The area is about 3 million square kilometers, accounting for 40% of total area of Australia; its population is about 1.2 million, accounting for 5% of the total Australian population. Based on statistics in 2012-2013,55% of export volume exits from ports in northern Australia by sea. The energy and mineral resources in Northern Australia are rich; agricultural potential is vast, infrastructure construction demand is great; and it is near to Asian countries such as China. Particularly the main ports such as Port Darwin are the portals of Maritime Silk Road to the South Pacific Region.

In August 2015, in the second Australia-China Strategic Economic Dialogue held in Canberra, both parties reached consensus that the proposal of the Belt & Road and international capacity cooperation share many common ideas with the Developing Northern Australia strategy and international infrastructure development plan. Both countries should further improve fields and level of cooperation by linking development strategies in China and Australia. In February 2016 when met the press, the Ministers of Foreign Affairs of China and Australia agreed to promote linkage of development strategies of the two countries, and mainly promote the linkage between the Belt & Road and "Developing Northern Australia" . In April 2016, President Xi Jinping, when met in Beijing with Turnbull, the Prime Minister of Australia, reaffirmed the wish that both sides conduct good linkage between the Belt & Road and "Developing Northern Australia" and between innovation-driven development strategy and "National Innovation and Science Agenda" , implement China-Australia FTA, and discuss on more practical cooperation projects. It is foreseeable that the optimal linkage point between the Belt & Roadstrategy and key development planning of Australian government will be the northern Australia. The linkage between the Belt & Road and "Developing Northern Australia" will undoubtedly become one of the important symbolic cooperation content in the south Pacific region.

II. Key construction field of linkage between the Belt & Road and "Developing Northern Australia"

The implementation of the Belt & Road strategy will promote free, convenient and integrated trade cooperation between countries and regions along the line, drive infrastructure construction and industry development along the line, promote ordered and free flow of global economic elements, efficient resource configuration and in-depth market integration, and realize the win-win strategic target. By participating in construction of the Belt & Road and cooperation for international industrial chain, China-funded enterprises can enhance international capacity and equipment manufacturing cooperation ability in energy resource, infrastructure and agriculture, and the structural transformation of economy in China is pushed forward greatly. The 21st Maritime Silk Road firstly promotes construction of infrastructure interconnection, industrial and financial cooperation and mechanism platform, and strengthens economic and business cooperation between countries and regions along the line orientating at policy communication, facility interconnection, smooth transaction, financial integration and public communication. The Commonwealth government of Australia takes agricultural food, energy and mining, tourism, overseas education, and medical care for the aged as five pillar industries supporting the development of Northern Australia, and emphasizes that strengthening infrastructure construction is the precondition and key point to implement Development Northern Australia. In terms of linkage between the Belt & Road strategy and Developing Northern Australia, the cooperation in the following fields can be focused on.

(i) Infrastructure

The infrastructure interconnection is the prior field of the Belt & Road construction. The Belt & Road strategy advocates that countries shall strengthen cooperation in infrastructure construction, control key channel, key node and key project of traffic infrastructure, and jointly promote construction of international backbone channels such as ports and realize convenient international transportations. Due to less population in Northern Australia, the development of infrastructure is weak. The Australian Government mainly plays the role of macro-management such as formulating planning, implementing policies, marketing and investment in infrastructure field such as highway, railway, port, airport and pipeline, rather than directly participate in investment and construction of infrastructure project. In order to promote and implement the Developing Northern Australia plan, in 2014, the Australian Government broke fresh ground to particularly set AUD 5 billion Special Northern Australia Infrastructure Loan to attract global investors to join in infrastructure construction such as port, highway, pipeline, power and water conservancy, and directly input AUD 1 billion in key infrastructure reconstruction, in which AUD 200 million is used in water resource development engineering, AUD 100 million is used in construction of live cattle transportation channel, and AUD 600 million in highway reconstruction project including Great Northern Highway; in 2015, the whitepaper proposed an investment plan with amount of AUD 1.2 billion as the supplement for the former AUD 5 billion investment in infrastructure.

(ii) Energy and mineral resources

The Belt & Road strategy advocates that countries shall strengthen cooperation in exploration and development of traditional energy resources such as coal, oil, gas and metal ores, strengthen cooperation in energy resource deep processing technology, equipment and engineering service, actively promote the cooperation in clean and renewable energies such as hydropower and solar power, and form integrated international cooperation industrial chain for energy resource cooperation. The energy and mining resources in Northern Australia are abundant, mainly containing iron ore, coal, gold, uranium, Zn-Pb, alumina, Mg, Petroleum, natural gas and shale gas. About 90% of proved iron ore resource in Australia is centralized in Western Australia, accounting for over half trades of global iron ore. The exploration and development has been mature. It is the key region that world top mining business such as Rio Tinto, BHP, FMG and enterprises from various countries invest in. The black coal resources in Queensland are abundant, mainly open-pit mines. The proved industrial economy reserves account for 62% of that in the entire Australia, with high coal quality, high heat value, and low content of sulfur, nitrogen and ash. The export of black coals such as coke and steam coal is about a quarter of total ore and energy export in Australia[①]. The energy and mining resources in Northern Territory are mainly gold, uranium, Zn-Pb, alumina, Mg, Petroleum, natural gas and shale gas. Currently eight mines are under operation. During 2014-2015, the output of mining exceeded AUD 3.2 billion, and annual capacity of LNG reached 12 million tons; in 2014, the investment in petroleum exploration and investment reached AUD 550 million, and potential capacity of shale gas exceeded over 20 billion c.f.. Totally 17 mature projects are seeking for investment opportunity.

(iii) Agriculture

The Belt & Road strategy advocates that countries shall carry out in-depth cooperation in fields such as agriculture, animal husbandry and fishery, agricultural machinery and agricultural product production and processing, and actively promote cooperation in fields of sea-culture, deep-sea fishing, and aquatic product processing. The countries along the line, by deepening cooperation in agriculture field, can focus on agricultural products with high foreign-trade dependence, improve safety guarantee capacity of important agricultural products, and help promote agricultural export of partner countries. The soil and weather in Northern Australia is suitable for the production of

---

① Australia is the world largest coal exporter. The geological reserve of black coal is 57.5 billion ton, (39.7 billion tons industrial economy reserve), ranking the sixth in the world; the geological reserve of lignite is about 41.8 billion ton, (37.6 billion tons industrial economy reserve), accounting for 20% of global lignite reserve, and ranking the second in the world.

multiple agricultural crops. The agricultural development mainly depends on animal husbandry, planting industry, fishery and forestry, and agricultural products are mainly export-oriented. The largest export markets are Northeast Asia, ASEAN, and the Middle East. The agricultural products, by order of output value, are respectively wheat, rape, barley, wool, beef, vegetables, sheep and lamb, fruits and nuts, hay, milk, oat, gardening, seedling, eggs, and avocado. The total area of Queensland is 1.73 million square meters, and agricultural land area is about 1.47 million kilometers, accounting for 85%. About 68% of the area is used for pasture in natural forest and grassland. The total area of Western Australia is 2.52 million square meters, and agriculturalland area is about 1.09 million kilometers, accounting for 43%. Due to large area of desert,37% of the state is covered by rarely used land. The total area of Northern Territory is 1.35 million square meters, and agricultural land area is about 670,000 kilometers, accounting for 50%. The main type of land use is natural pasture, accounting for 50%. Australia attaches high importance to cooperation with China in agriculture. In the China-Australia FTA which officially implements from December 2015, the agricultural field is involved the most largest and comprehensive aspects. The governments of Western Australia, Queensland and Northern Territory organize entrepreneurs of China and Australia to participate in the forum and workshops for agricultural cooperation, promote, introduce and link cooperation projects. Currently, the agricultural projects suitable for China-funded enterprises in Northern Australia are mainly dairy and animal products processing in livestock breeding farm, fishing and trade, grain crop planting, processing and trade, fruit planting, processing and trade, gardening and forestry.

(iv) Industrial parks

The Belt & Road strategy advocates that countries shall develop comparative advantages, explore new mode for investment cooperation, jointly build various industrial parks such as overseas economic trade and cooperation zone and cross-border economic cooperation zone, and promote development of industry cluster. By jointly building overseas industry clusters and promoting local industrial system construction, countries can expand cooperation in fields of education, technology, culture, tourism, health and environmental protection. Northern Australia has various industrial parks, which are although different from the Chinese mode, have the same function as industrial cluster, and the same target to promote local industrial system construction such as education, technology, medical care, agriculture and tourism. China-funded enterprises can play the comparative advantages of industrial park construction, explore new mode for investment and cooperation with Western Australia, Queensland and Northern Territory, and cooperate with local Australian enterprises and other cross-border enterprises to build various industrial parks such as trade, economy and high technology cooperation zone so as to promote the industrial cluster development in Northern Australia, jointly expand cooperation space in the fields of education, technology, culture, tourism, health and environmental protection, and deepen the industrial system cooperation between China and Australia for international capacity and equipment manufacturing industry.

III. Main contents of Developing Northern Australia

Australia sets up the Northern Australia Strategic Partnership Forum, which is comprised of Prime Minister and Vice Prime Minister of the Commonwealth Government, and governors of Western Australia, Queensland and the Northern Territory, to jointly lead, coordinate and implement the Developing Northern Australia strategy by common efforts of various levels of government. In 2015, the Commonwealth Government of Australia released development plan of Developing Northern Australia for the next 20 years (2015-2035) , and established Developing Northern Australia Office led by Minister of Ministry of Industry, Innovation and Technology to push the implementation of Developing Northern Australia plan from the following six aspects.

(i) Formulate simpler land policy to support investment

The Australian Government will sort out the principles of animal husbandry reform in 2-5 years, and provide more supports for land right management of aborigines. The COAG submitted report about land management and usage situations of aborigines, and consulted the public for the new mode of aborigine land development; established business land ownership information data in Northern Australia, and introduced new results-based appropriation mode in aborigine land management; carried out land investigation and made progress, studied the exclusive use land for business land and made progress. On that basis, The Australian Government summarized experiences in land ownership management in the northern pilots, consulted for long-term lease of rural land in the Northern Territory, reduced regulations and requirements in pasture lease management, and adopted a simpler management method for aboriginal land owned individually. In the next 10-20 years, the Australian Government will relieve all pasture lease regulations and requirements, and strive to realize exclusive aboriginal land right lease so that the agricultural potential information of aboriginal land and pasture land is easy to acquire.

In that way they can attract investor, finish affirmation of existing aboriginal land, make sure more land with confirmed ownership can be used in investment and development, and bring more opportunities to Australian aborigines in the aspect of land.

(ii) Developing water resource of Northern Australia

The Australian Government will invest AUD 200 million to set up water resource infrastructure development fund in 2-5 years, carry out and finish water resource appraisal in Mitchell of Queensland, Fitzroyreservoir of Western Australia and Darwin of the Northern Territory, finish feasibility study of Nullinga Damproject in Queensland and the Oder River Project Phase III of Western Australia (promoting the two projects based on feasibility study results), and launch sustainable plan of the Great Artesian Basin Phase IV to control the formation of cavity in this region, confirm key projects in Northern Australia supported by water resource infrastructure development fund, decide the maximum water consumption of key reservoirs, make great progress in repairing the cavity of the Great Artesian Basin, promote water source transaction market by means of water license auction in key reservoirs, and appraise water resource in more reservoirs with industrial utilization potential. In the next 10-20 years, the Australian Government will finish the review of statutory water resource plan in the Northern Territory, Queensland and Western Australia, build more water resource infrastructures as required, help investors know water resource position, realize distinct and legally approved water right system in the North to make water resource utilization in the northern area more convenient, and build effective water resource transaction system in reservoir and aquifer.

(iii) Playing the role of the north entrance, and promote cooperation with Asia-Pacific countries for economy, trade and investment

The Australian Government will release price appraisal information of mature project proposals for investment in the North in the next 2-5 years, carry out investigation, confirm simplified management system of fishery and aquaculture, push cooperation between scientific research institutions in Northern Australia and local partners on health problems of tropics, carry out new tropical research and commercial application project, help consulters enter business operation in Northern Australia, extend validity period of environment license for low risk fishery to 10 years, consult historical heritage protection and management system with aborigines and commercial enterprises, build new Developing Northern Australia Cooperation and Research Center and put into operation, open new border port in Darwin, open online application for tourist visa in China and India, carry out pilot fast channel service, strengthen bio-safety management in Northern Australia, make special insurance team of Northern Australia provide recommended programs and more aborigines serve as bio-safety inspector, release fishery and aquaculture appraisal report, introduce multiple-entry visa in 10 years and carry out pilot of simplified Chinese visa application process, release aquaculture management authority from the Commonwealth to each state and territory, operate new fishery joint management window for Northern Australia, and simplify the export management measures for crocodile product trade, aboriginal art made by protected animals, kangaroos and Australian ostrich. After consultation, the Australian Government considers to revise aboriginal heritage legislation of the Commonwealth, reduce repeated contents, increase corresponding protection, prolong the export permit of fishery companies with favorable management situations to 10 years, and appraise entry and exit port of the Northern Territory and add ports in Queensland and Western Australia. In 10-20 years, the Australian Government will urge scientific research institutions and foreign partners to acquire industrial-oriented results by powerful cooperation, commercialize research findings of tropical health problems, make Northern Australia the world leading Tropical Health Research Center and closely contact with APEC and ASEAN countries. Australia will establish a growing and profitable agricultural industry with large scale by the world-class research and development and district and low-cost supervision system so as to support elastic business development, and generate more investment projects in more extensive industries.

(iv) Accelerate promoting infrastructure project in Northern Australia orderly

The Australian Government will release Northern Australia infrastructure audit report in 2-5 years; set up a Special Loan for Northern Australia Infrastructure with total amount of AUD 5 billion; establish a business group to make preparation for improving air transportation in Northern areas start a four-year plan for regional air transportation and remote area airport upgrading; improve productivity of cattle raising industry supply chain in Northern Australia; increase input of immigration control and bio-safety facilities in order to cope with the newly increased international passengers in Townsville Airport; announce road package plan with total investment of AUD 600 million; release and ceaselessly update new Northern infrastructure construction plan; announce beef transportation road appropriation project; start pre-feasibility study for railway from Mount Isa to Tennant Creek; consider reducing costs of inspection and tick treatment announcing the commencement time of road package plan project;

finish preparing plan improving air transportation of Northern Australia; relieve the current shipping management framework along the coast, promote efficient development of coastal shipping, and strive to make great progress for projects supported by special loan of northern infrastructure; promote expected improvement of road package plan on roads under pivot development; improve key roads for beef transportation road appropriation project, and build shorter and more direct transportation lines. In 10-20 years, the Australian Government will improve conditions of remote airports, provide higher quality information to support vigorous development of Northern Australia infrastructure, and build more roads for heavy beef transportation trucks; the productivity of beef production will be more powerful and stable and northern infrastructure can be better used. The government and business industry will jointly invest to support more modern and efficient infrastructures.

(v) Improving labor quantity and quality in Northern Australia

The Australian Government will launch new national employment promotion service in 2-5 years; carry out fixed-point immigration agreement in Northern Australia including Northern Territory and make progress; expand and simplify seasonable labor service projects to cover more agricultural and accommodation industry; allow working holiday visa holders to work longer time in required area; launch low-skill labor pilot plan facing residents of Pacific islands; strengthen support of Northern business cycle in the aspect of industrial skill appropriation; support the Northern Australia to simplify work skill license process; complete the aborigines employment policy prepared for highway construction project; submit seasonal labor pilot program for tourist industry, release report on immigration labors in Australia, release framework report of labor relationship, expand applicable range for automatic affirmation of occupational skill license simplification in the Northern Territory, and appraise influence of working holiday visa on domestic labor market; implement fixed-point immigration agreement in Northern Queensland after discussion with Queensland State Government, business cycle and community, and appraise implementation situation of low-skill labor pilot plan facing residents of Pacific islands. Within 10-20 years, the Australian Government will employ more Australians to work in the north. The aboriginal community will be provided with more employment opportunities, and the business circle in the north will hire more working holiday labors so that the labor demand of Northern Australia can be satisfied largely. The skillful domestic labor can be supplemented by low-cost and efficient foreign labor service projects.

(vi) Strengthen construction of common governance structure such as government and non-government organs

The Prime Minister of Australia will keep strategic partnership with Chief Executive of Queensland, Western Australia and Northern Territory, seek for support from Australian Parliament, set Northern Joint Commission of Parliament as permanent commission, and continuously carry out "national map open data action" in Northern Australia. The government secondment project will be launched. For the first time, the Vice Prime Minister will report Northern Australia Development to the parliament, and the project will be carried out every year. The proportion of content regarding Northern Australia will be increased in annual national defense whitepaper, and the Northern Australia Office will be moved to the northern area. The Australian Government will strengthen bio-safety management in the north, allocate more front-line law enforcement personnel, reduce excessive official documents with topics of Northern Australia, release the Commonwealth reform whitepaper, set up a new cooperation and research center to study Developing Northern Australia, and build an entry-exit port in Darwin. The Northern Joint Commission of Parliament will submit annual report to the Parliament, and extend leadership by strategic cooperation. Based on key national defense investment projects confirmed in the annual national defense whitepaper and by improving government organ work ability by temporary personnel transfer, the governments of various levels shall set up more optimal joint conferences and powerful cooperation to jointly build Northern Australia.

IV. Suggestions on ideas to support linkage of two strategies by development-oriented finance

The important support of the Belt & Road strategy is the accommodation of funds. The support of development-oriented finance on significant projects shall particularly be strengthened. For the development-oriented finance which targets at long-term economic growth and government intention one or multiple countries establish a financial institution with national credit to provide medium and long-term credit to specific demander, build market and system, and lead social capital to input in specific projects with large-amount medium and long-term investment and financing as carriers so as to finally realize national strategy. The development-oriented financial institutions in China which dominantly engage in serving the Belt & Road strategy are Asian Infrastructure Investment Bank, Silk Road Fund and China Development Bank. The China Development Bank is currently the largest development-oriented financial institutions and foreign-oriented investment and financing bank in the world. In the third plenary session of the 18th CPC central committee, the CPC central committee files for the first time put forward the concept of "development-oriented financial institution" . In March 2015, the State Council officially approved to clarify the orientation of the China development Bank as development-oriented financial institutions. In recent years, the China Development Bank actively plays the role as the finance engine and leader, greatly expands international cooperation service by means of marketization, spares no efforts in serving the Belt & Road strategy, and establishes favorable foundation for cooperation with countries and regions along the Maritime Silk Road. In view of linkage between the Belt & Road construction and Developing Northern Australia, the development-oriented financial institutions can play the role of supporter from many aspects.

(i) Cooperating with bilateral government to carry out project linkage by planning

The development-oriented financial institutions will deploy closely around the overall strategy of the Belt & Road, and sufficiently link with the Developing Northern Australia plan by planned cooperations. While pushing overall planning cooperation, the development-oriented financial institutions, centered key fields, play the local advantages of local social forces such as consulting companies, law firms, universities and research institutions to deeply carry out special planning, including infrastructure, energy and resources, agriculture, business cooperation, industrial investment, financial cooperation, cultural exchange, ecological protection and offshore cooperation so as to realize combined strategic layout for planning cooperation. Based on overall planning, the devising of key projects and planning of financing plans in key fields shall be strengthened focusing on infrastructure, energy and mining resources, agriculture, equipment manufacture and international capacity cooperation.

(ii) Playing the demonstrative role and siphon effect of mature regions

The linkage of the Belt & Road strategy and Developing Northern Australia strategy can emphasize on mature regions, and develop and support significant project cooperation. In June 2016, the Consulate General of China in Brisbane held Developing Northern Queensland forum for the Belt & Road linkage in Brisbane. Over 200 people from government departments and enterprises of Queensland and representatives form Australia-based Chinese enterprises and banks, and domestic enterprises in Jiangsu, Shandong and Shaanxi attended the forum. Under witness of Jacky Strand, the Vice Governor of Queensland and Zhao Yongchen, the Consul General of China in Brisbane, the director general of Trade and Investment Bureau of Queensland, business consul of the Consulate General of China in Brisbane, and the China Development Bank jointly signed the minute of investment opportunity and cooperation conference for linkage between the Belt & Road and "Developing Northern Queensland" to clarify that all three parties jointly support linkage of the two strategies, and strengthen planning and cooperation in fields of infrastructure, energy and resources, agriculture and industrial parks. Trade and Investment Bureau of Queensland and the Consulate General of China in Brisbane will, within the range of government ability, provide maximum convenience for Chinese investors. The China Development Bank will support investment made by Chinese enterprises when complying with internal credit approval management systems, and provide financing support so as to jointly promote investment and realize win-win situation. All three sides will, according to requirements, irregularly exchange opinions, communicate about business plan, and properly carry out planning and cooperation in distinctive fields; support agricultural industrial park, wharf and airport reconstruction and expansion, health and medical care industrial park and other comprehensive industrial park of Full Share Group in Northern Queensland driven by the Queensland Government to play the demonstrative role and siphon effect of key project.

(iii) Build inter-bank cooperation platform and improve comprehensive service ability

The development-oriented financial institution shall play advantages and roles of various financial modes such as policy finance and commercial finance, strengthen cooperation with international financial institutions, and local banks, industrial investment fund, insurance company and risk capital financial institutions such as Australia & New Zealand Banking Group, National Bank, Westpac Banking and Commonwealth Bank to improve comprehensive financial service ability, carry out financial services such as project finance, trade finance, international settlement, financial consultant, offshore assets securitization and syndicated loan, create financial cooperation platform, smoothen channels for investment and financing cooperation, and comprehensively improve own overall operation ability and influence in product development, risk control, information technology, operation and management. The development-oriented financial institution can set operating offices in Australia to combine with local financial institutions by means of syndicated loans, direct credit granting and en-lending to jointly support the development and construction of key projects in Northern Australia, provide one-stop services to China-funded enterprises participating in Developing Northern Australia plan, lead the China-funded enterprises to explore multiple cooperation modes such as "EPC+F", PPP, BOT and PFI, actively participate in key infrastructure construction, and further promote international capacity cooperation and key equipment manufacture "going abroad".

(iv) Innovating financial products and establish long-acting cooperative mechanism

Australia is a maturely developed market economy. Many development projects in Developing Northern Australia plan are operated by market and commercial mode. The competition in financial field is fierce, mainly shown as follow: firstly, the legal system of Australia for investment and financing is complex, involving labor protection, environmental protection, aborigines protection, land and water sources; the financing demand of China-funded enterprisers is comprehensive and values the service ability of intermediate services such as financial consultant provided by banks; secondly, the financial cost of the same industry overseas, especially foreign-funded banks is low; financial decision is made faster; approval process is more efficient and loan currency is abundant, which can meet demands of clients for different financial products such as bullet repayment (repaying principle at lump sum upon maturity). The development-oriented financial institutions shall combine financial products such as investment and loans, strengthen innovation of financial products, explore new modes for investment and financing cooperation, design different financial products for development-oriented business projects, regulate different standards and requirements for risk preference, risk tolerance, credit structure, loan pricing, loan types and approval process of projects, establish long-acting cooperation mechanism, meet requirements of development-oriented financial institutions to support various development-oriented projects by market and commercial ways, and better sustainably serve the strategic demand for linkage between the Belt & Road and Developing Northern Australia.

References:

Hu Huaibang, "Serving "One Belt One Road" Strategy by Development-Oriented Finance", *China Banking Industry*, 2015 (12).

Department of the Prime Minister and Cabinet, "Our North,Our Future: White Paper on Developing Northern Australia", *Australia*, 2015.6.

Meng Gang, "Research on Financial Cooperation of Four Countries along the South Routine of the 21st Century Marine Silk Road", *Journal of Development-Oriented Finance Research*, 2016 (1).

Department of the Prime Minister and Cabinet, "*Green Paper on Developing Northern Australia*", Australia, 2014.6.

Australian Bureau of Statistics, Australia.

Meng Gang, "Australia Northern Development Strategy Brings New Opportunity for Development-oriented Finance", *China Banking Industry*, 2016 (4).

Meng Gang, "Study on International Capacity Cooperation of China in Australia", *Journal of Development-Oriented Finance Research*, 2016 (3).

Meng Gang, "Approach of Australia Science and Technology Innovation Strategy Integrating to China and Financing Cooperation", *Globalization*, 2016 (7).

Research on Linking Pathways and Financing Cooperation Possibilities in China and Australia's Innovation-Driven Strategies

I. Cooperation in innovation-driven strategy is a focal point of Chinese-Australian collaboration

On 11 November 2014, President Xi Jinping delivered a key speech in Australia's capital, Canberra, where he stated that the strategic partnership between China and Australia had moved up to the level of a comprehensive strategic partnership, and he emphasized that both parties, China and Australia, should strengthen such traditional and major areas of cooperation as energy resources and so on, and expedite the nurturing of new growth points in cooperation. In August 2015, the second round of Chinese Australian strategic economic talks was held in Canberra, and the two parties reached a common understanding that both the areas and levels of cooperation would be further boosted by the linking brought about by the strategic development of both countries. In February 2016, the foreign ministers of the two countries went further in spelling out the cooperative goals of such comprehensive linkages and innovation driven strategic development.

Going forward, the world's major countries have been gradually placing technological innovation at the core of national development strategies in order to better meet the challenges being brought about by the new technological revolution[①], and they have been progressively promulgating strategies for innovation and action programs. On 11 June 2015, the State Council of China published the "Opinions on Several Policy Measures for Vigorously Promoting Public Entrepreneurship and Innovation" . This was a systematic and inclusive policy document promoting public entrepreneurship and innovation, and, more particularly, a systematic document to expedite the implementation of innovation-driven development strategies. On 5 March 2016, in the "Report on the Work of the Government" Premier Li Keqiang emphasised more strongly

---

① It is the view of Bai Chunli, President of CASS, that there are two kinds of drivers for world-wide technological revolution: one is the driver arising from the needs of society, one is an internal driver from within the knowledge and technological systems. Up until now, the world has undergone five scientific and technological revolutions (two of them scientific, three technological) . The first occurred between the sixteenth century and seventeenth centuries, represented by scientists such as Galileo, Copernicus, Newton and so on, bringing the first technological revolution in such domains as astronomy, physics and so on. This technologi-cal revolution, spanning 144 years from start to finish, is a notable milestone in the birth of modern science. The second was in the mid-to-late eighteenth century, with the invention of the steam engine and textile machinery as well as with machine labour starting to replace manual labour, ushering in the second technological revolution. This was also the world's first industrial revolution, with the broad use of steam engines propelling England's industrial revolution and modernisation forward. The third occurred in the mid-to-late nineteenth cen-tury, mainly marked by the invention of electrical technologies and the internal combustion engine, pushing forward the rapid development of such industries as in steel, oil, locomotion, and plane flight, etc. The fourth occurred between the mid-to-late nineteenth and the mid twentieth centuries, represented by such scientific breakthroughs as the theory of evolution, the theory of relativity, quantum theory and so on bringing about a fourth technological revo-lution and also a fundamental revolution in theories of natural science. The fifth occurred in the mid-to-late twentieth century, marked by the appearance of electronic computing and the Internet and bringing about a fifth technological revolution. Until now, the development pro-cess of technological revolution is ongoing.

that innovation is the primary driver leading development and must be placed in a core position in the national overall development, deeply becoming part of the implementation of innovation driven development strategies. Australia's science and technology decision-making management system is a diverse and decentralised system of the Commonwealth government possessing guiding influence. The Commonwealth government lays out national science and technology policies and major science and technology development initiatives, subsidises research and development organisations, universities, cooperative research centres and major industrial science and technology programs. The state governments administer and subsidise the science and technical work of the states in the agricultural, health, environmental and energy domains. The current Australian Commonwealth government, for this term, is placing high emphasis on driving innovation-placing innovation and science as a core strategy for the government. In December 2015, the Australian Commonwealth government published the "National Innovation and Science Agenda" for public consumption, a strategy for comprehensively promoting its innovation driven strategies over several areas from culture and capital, collaboration, talent and skills to government as an exemplar and so on.

II. The plan for the implementation of Australia's innovation-driven strategy

From 2013 until today, the Australian government has already put ten major innovative measures in place[①]: the first is the establishment of

---

① Australian science and technology enjoys great international prestige and their technologies in such areas as agriculture, biotech, geoscience, astronomy, and medicine are at a leading, world-class level. Preliminary research and applied preliminary research is done at a high industry growth centres in such key sectors of competitive advantages as advanced manufacturing, food and agribusiness, medical technologies and pharmaceuticals, mining equipment, technology and services, and oil, gas and energy resources; the second is the delivery of an Entrepreneurs' Programme to help entrepreneurs be successful in the initial stages; the third is a reformation of the employee share system, to make it easier for start-up companies to attract outstanding staff from all over the world; the fourth is the implementation of a tax concession policy through a $5 billion small business and jobs package; the fifth is the provision of support for the teaching of computer coding across school levels; the sixth is the reformation of the Australian curriculum to provide teachers with more class time for science, maths and English; the seventh is a requirement for new primary school teachers to be proficient in a specialised subject with priority given to science, technology, engineering and maths (STEM) ; the eighth is the establishment of a regulatory system for crowd-sourced equity funding; the ninth is the signing of three historically significant free trade agreements with China, Japan and South Korea, including a Trans-Pacific Partnership; and the tenth is an improvement of regulatory systems and the adoption of international standards where possible in the innovative and entrepreneurial domains. From 2015 to 2019, on the historical basis of successful past practice, the Australian government will promote comprehensive implementation of innovation and science drivenstrategies in the

---

standard, with quite strong research teams and world-class universities and national research and development organisations, having contributed seven Nobel Prize winners in the scientific and medical areas. However, there is a long-term issue with Australian science and technology being dislocated from the economy, with relatively weak corporate research and development capabilities and not particularly strong capabilities with respect to the commercialisation of research gains.

four areas of culture and capital, collaboration, talent and skills and government as an exemplar.

(i) Culture and capital

The Australian government hopes to promote a change in entrepreneurial culture, emphasising that innovation is the product of a strong and vibrant entrepreneurial culture and promoting an attitude of greater tolerance towards entrepreneurial failure and for having had courage in making the attempt, to provide more sources of funding for start-ups, boosting the power of research support, and providing comprehensive support to innovative companies. It is the view of the Australian government that the period between the initial funding investments to the point where revenue is generated is an innovative start-up company's "valley of death", and that during this period it is extremely easy for the company to experience cash flow difficulties. As a result, a culture of entrepreneurship and innovation must be established and adjustments made to the taxation system and company law.

In terms of taxes: first of all, new tax breaks will be provided to early stage investors in innovative start-up companies. In accordance with the amount of their investment, the investor will receive a twenty percent non-refundable tax offset, as well as a capital gains tax exemption. In addition, there will be a ten percent non-refundable tax offset based on the amount of capital invested for Early Stage Venture Capital Limited Partnerships (ESVCLPs), and the cap on committed capital in new ESVCLPs will go from $100 million to $200 million. Secondly, a more flexible "predominantly similar business test" will be introduced, relaxing the requirements of the "same business test". According to the "same business test", a company's operating earnings post a change in its business activities cannot be used to offset previous tax losses. In accordance with the new requirements, a start-up company can bring in an equity partner and secure new business opportunities without needing to worry about a "tax penalty". Thirdly, limits on statutory life depreciation deductions for some intangible assets (such as patents) will be removed, replaced with new rules that allow them to be depreciated over their economic life.

In terms of the regulatory system: there will, first, be a reformation of insolvency laws. Current insolvency laws overemphasise penalising failed businesses or force them to carry the burden of being a credit risk due to their failure. As a result, the reformed insolvency law will reduce the default bankruptcy period from three years to one year and introduce a "safe harbour" for directors from personal liability due to the bankruptcy, with a pre-requisite being that the director must appoint a professional restructuring advisor to develop a revitalising program for a company in financial difficulty; contract provisions of an "ipso facto" nature will be banned, that is, if the company is undertaking a restructure, terminating an agreement solely due to an insolvency event will not be permitted. Secondly, the existing Employee Share Scheme (ESS) will be modified in a friendlier fashion, to make it easier for promising companies to hire and retain top staff. The new system will allow companies to offer shares to their employees without having to reveal commercially sensitive information to their competitors. These changes are built on recently undertaken reforms to ESS, including the deferring of the tax start date for employees, and the introduction of an additional tax concession to the employees of start-up companies.

In terms of capital investments: the first is the establishment of a new 200 million dollar CSIRO innovation fund to co-invest in new spin-off companies and existing start-ups, that will develop technology from CSIRO and other publicly funded organisations and universities. The second is the establishment of a new biomedical translation fund to co-invest $250 million with the private sector for the commercialisation of medical research. The third is the provision of support for small businesses and start-ups to assist in their smooth formation and development. The fourth is the support of "incubators" which plays a crucial role in the innovation ecosystem, ensuring that start-up companies can access to the resources, information and networks that they need, to help them transform their ideas into new, globally scalable industries.

(ii) Collaboration

First of all, world-class national research infrastructure will be established. Stable long-term funding will be provided to cutting-edge, national research infrastructure and facilities to ensure that research projects and jobs stay in Australia and that they stay consistently at the level of being at the forefront of global discoveries. In the next ten years, the Australian government is going to provide funds of $520 million for the Australian Synchrotron,$294 million for the Square Kilometre Array, and $1.5 billion for the National Collaborative Research Infrastructure Strategy (NCRIS) . In 2016, Australia's Chief Scientist will begin a process of identifying the various needs of the national research infrastructure, in order to determine in what areas funding will be required over the future.

Secondly, there will be greater and strengthened collaboration between universities and businesses. The Australian government will arrange for the apportionment of greater research and development funding subsidies through their reforms, encouraging collaboration between researchers and industry, providing an additional $127 million outside of estimates to research and development grants and subsidies. When assessing university research work, more clear and transparent measures will be adopted, introducing for the first time non-academic impact and industry engagement. This measure will be piloted through the Australian Research Council in 2017 and fully implemented by 2018, and will connect more small and medium-sized businesses with researchers expanding and launching the Innovation Connections program and so on, opening up Australian Research Council Linkage Projects to continuous applications to fast track decisions, with a new application round for the Cooperative Research Centre Program starting in February 2016.

The third component is linking to the world. Linkages will be strengthened with global key economies, ensuring that Australia will be able to make progress in such areas as research, commercialisation and business performance, and can fully access to international supply chains and the global market. This will include providing Australian entrepreneurs with science and innovation centres in Silicon Valley, Tel Aviv, Shanghai and two other locations, making full use of the expertise of the Australian diaspora in key national markets, while also providing funding for Australian collaborations with international research industry clusters.

The fourth concerns investment in the future information technology. A new Cyber Security Growth Centre will be established to create growth opportunities for Australian businesses in these key sectors, investing $26 million in building a silicon quantum circuit, boosting Australia's quantum computing capabilities to a world-class level while creating new job opportunities and innovative business models.

(iii) Talent and skills

The first component here is to nurture a new generation of young people, ensuring that they are equipped with skills in innovation and can use digital technologies. In order to help young people make adequate preparation for the jobs of the future, the Australian government is investing $51 million in boosting the abilities of teachers to implement a digital curriculum through online learning activities and expert help, bringing in a collaborative partnerships program of scientists and Information Communication Technology (hereby abbreviated to ICT) professionals in science, technology, engineering, and mathematics (hereby abbreviated to STEM) .

The second is expanding opportunities for women in STEM. The Australian government is investing over $13 million to support more girls and women to participate in the research sector in STEM industries, start-up companies and entrepreneurial firms, with the setting up of STEM sector female role models and the establishment of programs and networks that are helpful for bringing about workplace gender equality, such as the Science in Australia Gender Equity (SAGE) pilot program.

The third is improvements in visa arrangements. A new type of Entrepreneur Visa will be provided, which will actively seek and encourage talented individuals to come to Australia using existing government overseas networks, and enhancing pathways to permanent residency for high quality STEM and ICT post-graduate students.

The fourth is the encouragement of strong STEM literacy skills. To inspire the next generation's strong STEM skills,$48 million will be invested over the entirety of their schooling: encouraging school students to participate in and achieve in science and maths, supporting student participation in international competitions, and by introducing youth prizes in the prestigious Prime Minister's Prizes for Science; for fun experiments and play-based apps to be designed for pre-schoolers based on STEM concepts; to support science activities in our communities, such as National Science Week, inspiring interest in learning more about STEM fields of knowledge for young people.

(iv) Government as an exemplar

The first component here is the establishment of a new independent statutory board:"Innovation and Science Australia". This board will be supported by a chief executive officer, being coordinator for national scientific, research and innovation policy and economic strategies. The board will help to coordinate policies that affect innovation so that Australia can establish a stronger, more entrepreneurial economy. One of the board's first responsibilities will be to review current R&D tax incentives to improve their effectiveness and integrity, by strengthening encouragement and review of additional research and development spending.

The second is the encouragement of innovation through government procurement. The Australian government will set up a Digital Marketplace, standardising ICT products and services, breaking down barriers to technology procurement, making government more accessible to start-up companies and small and medium-sized start-up businesses, trialling a new approach to government procurement through the Business Research and Innovation Initiative, requiring small to medium-sized enterprises to deliver innovative solutions, rather than directly tendering for an existing product. Businesses will find it easier to compete for the $5 billion that the government spends annually on ICT through the new Digital Marketplace.

The third is for the government to join the data revolution. To promote innovation and make full use of vast quantities of public data, the Australian government will remove the barriers between many different data holdings across government departments. Non-sensitive data will be made publicly available by default on the gov.au website to facilitate its use and reuse by the private sector to create new innovative products, processes, services and business models.

Diagram: Overview of Australia's Innovation and Science Agenda
and Government Investment Funds Program

Unit: AUD Million（*denotes unquantifiable）

	Classification	2015-2016	2016-2017	2017-2018	2018-2019	Sub-total	Total
Culture and Capital	Tax incentives for angel investors	0	3	51	51	106	
	New arrangements for venture capital investment	0	0	*	*	*	
	Access to company losses	0	*	*	*	*	
	Intangible asset depreciation	0	0	20	60	80	
	CSIRO Innovation Fund*	0	5	5	5	15	
	Biomedical Translation Fund*	2	6	1	1	10	
	Incubator Support Programme	0	3	3	3	8	
	Improve bankruptcy and insolvency laws	0	0	0	0	0	
	Employee Share Schemes	0	0	0	0	0	
Collaboration	Critical research infrastructure	0	15	198	245	459	
	Sharper incentives for engagement	0	25	51	52	127	
	Global Innovation Strategy	0	7	9	10	26	
	Cyber Security Growth Centre	0	4	7	11	22	
	Innovation Connections programme	0	3	7	8	18	
	Quantum computing	0	5	5	5	15	
	Measuring impact and engagement in university research						
	ARC Linkage Projects Scheme	0	0	0	0	0	

Tal-ent and Skills	Inspiring all Australians in digital literacy and STEM	0	26	25	33	84
	Support for innova-tion through visas	1	1	0	0	1
Govern-ment as an Exam-plar	Data	0	25	25	25	75
	Business Research and In-novation Initiative	0	4	10	5	19
	Digital marketplace	3	5	4	4	15
	Innovation and Sci-ence Australia	1	2	3	2	8
	Public data strategy	0	0	0	0	0
Overall Australian Government Investment Funds in the Innovation and Science Agenda						1,097

Source: The Commonwealth Government of Australia.

III. An analysis of pathways linking with Australia's innovation-driven strategies

(i) Actively Meeting the Needs of Collaboration in the New Technological Revolution for Both Countries

Looking at the several globalised technological revolutions that have occurred throughout history, technological innovation has consistently been an important strategic pillar for raising the productive forces of a society and overall national capabilities. Technological revolution arises from the driving impetus of social needs, and further greatly promotes the significant development of a society's economy. Those countries able to seize the advantage in the new worldwide technological revolution are bound to become leaders of the worldwide economy. Scientists in China and Australia have forecasted areas in which a new round of technological revolution might take place; the first is in our understanding of the evolution of universe, the structure of matter, the nature of consciousness and such other basic scientific questions, e.g. new breakthroughs in understanding the quantum world or in thinking robots and so on; the second would be in post-fossil fuel energy sources and renewable resources; the third would be in internet information technologies; the fourth in the making of advanced materials and in manufacturing; the fifth in agriculture; and the sixth in population health. A major, original, innovative breakthrough in any of the previous six major fields mentioned would open up opportunities for a new technological revolution. Australia is a major exporter of resources, energy, agricultural products, health products and so on, and China has the largest consumer market and is the biggest manufacturer. It should be said that there is enormous complementary potential and practicality in cooperation between the two countries in areas of scientific and technological innovation. Very strong cooperation between China and Australia is a necessity for them to lead the worldwide new technological revolution together under the backdrop of a globalized world.

(ii) The establishment of the Belt & Road and the free trade agreement between the two countries a significant opportunity

The outline of China's "13th Five Year Plan" clearly points to a commanding role being played in the establishment of the Belt & Road, with great efforts being put into the formation of a backdrop for mutually beneficial cooperation with a deep degree of integration, initiating a new, external and open layout. Australia possesses significant influence in political and economic affairs in the South Pacific region, and is a key cooperating country in the establishment of the 21st Century Maritime Silk Road. A deepening of innovation-driving strategic cooperation will greatly propel forward communication in policy, infrastructure linkages, trade freedom, financial facilitation and people-to-people exchanges between the two countries, and will have a key impact when it comes to our country's successful promotion of the establishment of the Belt & Road in the

South Pacific Region. In addition, Australia is a major exporter worldwide of agricultural products, energy and mineral products, and is a major developed economy with a relatively large total economic output, a mature market and economy as well as a corresponding legal system and model of governance. In the next several years, we will see a continual strengthening of the mutually complementary nature of the economies of China and Australia. In June 2015, the governments of China and Australia signed their "Free Trade Agreement". Firstly, in the area of goods, products account for 85.4% of export trade and will immediately see zero tariffs on the agreement taking effect. At the end of the transitional period, Australia's zero tariff categories and terms of trade proportions will reach 100%, China's zero tariff categories and volume of trade proportions will reach 96.8% and 97% respectively, far exceeding the 90% tariff reduction typical of free trade agreements. Secondly, in terms of the service sector, after Australia's commitment agreement takes effect, it will open up the service sector to China by a negative list approach, making it the first country in the world to make a commitment for services trade to China using a negative list approach. China will open up the service sector to Australia using a positive list approach. In addition, Australia will make special arrangements towards China in such areas as the working holiday system and so on. Thirdly, in the area of investment, the two parties shall treat each other as a "most favoured nation" from the time the agreement takes effect, while at the same time Australia will lower the review thresholds for Chinese enterprises seeking to invest in Australia, while also providing more convenient arrangements. Fourthly, the agreement has also implemented progressive provisions for exchange and collaboration for both parties in dozens of "21st century economic and trade issues" such as in e-commerce, government procurement, intellectual copyright, competition and so on.

(iii) Business as the principle player in the promotion of an innovation-driven strategy linking China and Australia

According to the definition from UNESCO, international cooperation in science and technology refers to "exchange in knowledge undertaken by the organisations, businesses or individuals of two or more than two countries after the reaching of a cooperative agreement". The sharing of knowledge in science and technology often serves as a mainstay or pillar deepening economic cooperation and trade, but it is only by having businesses serve as the principle actors that one can sustain a market orientation and reflect the needs of the market. It is businesses that are the economic entities with the greatest vitality, and occupy the central role in the promotion of science and technology and the close integration of innovation and the economy[①] as well as in terms of international cooperation. In every area of innovation in science and technology, businesses can choose from multiple formats in regard to international cooperation, such as establishing new infrastructure and facilities as well as strengthening internet services, data storage, cloud services and so on, setting up R&D organisations abroad, forming technological innovation partnerships with each other, acquiring R&D companies, pooling together international talent and so on. Economic globalisation has expanded the breadth and the depth of scientific and technological innovation as well as international cooperation with businesses at the centre. The degree to which the central role for businesses in innovation can be established and to which they can exert a guiding effect will decide, to a

---

① The five hundred largest multinationals from developed Western countries collectively control more than 90 percent of this country's production technology and 95 percent of its technological trade.

great extent, the success or failure of cooperation between China and Australia in an innovation-driven strategy. As a result, China and Australia should organise arrangements with businesses at the centre, setting up a collaborative science and technology innovation and industry-university transformation platform for businesses, promoting and supporting significant economic and trade cooperation for businesses in areas of scientific and technological innovation.

(iv) The Co-Creation of Innovative Centres for Science and Technology with a Global Reach

China has designated Beijing and Shanghai, among other cities, as national centres for scientific and technological innovation, closely following the national innovation-driven development strategy, which are being planned with a global vision in mind, where independent innovation is being promoted from a superior starting point with the distribution of major national science and technology projects as well as the establishment of key science and technology infrastructure actively served, with an expansion in opening up and cooperation in science and technology. Independent capabilities for innovation will be strengthened, boosting capabilities in original, integrated and "re-creation by learning and improving", laying out a set of cutting edge and investigative technology research and development, creating a set of noteworthy or even revolutionary technologies, moving from being a "technology follower" to being a technology "co-creator" or "leader" to create the most active centre possible for science and technology worldwide, striving greatly to become the leader in the new globalised revolution in science and technology innovation. Australia plans to set up five innovation centres (Landing Pads) in California, Tel Aviv, Shanghai and other overseas regions in order to help Australian start-up companies find their footing in international markets, and to develop into high growth, high-return businesses. These five regions will become meeting places for innovative companies worldwide, and the setting up of these innovation centres will provide more space for jointly handling businesses as well as more market opportunities for Australian science and tech companies, being of assistance to Australian enterprises in their integration into international trading circles and for reaching out to more entrepreneurial talent and investors.

(v) Servicing the Needs of Innovation-Driven Industry Clusters with an Industry Park Platform

As distinct from the positioning of mature and developed cities as "centres for innovation in science and technology" , the definition for an industry park could be "the development of a large block of land after subdivision providing to the use of enterprises at one time, in order to provide a benefit to the enterprises in terms of their geographical proximity and mutual enjoyment of the infrastructure and facilities" [①]. High-tech industry parks are products of the new worldwide technological revolution and the age of the knowledge economy. They are able to realise three-in-one "industry-diversity-research" development goals to a high degree of efficiency, greatly promoting global

---

①   Peddle MT. ,"Planned Industrial and Commercial Developments in the United States: A Review of the History, Literature and Empirical Evidence Regarding Industry Parks", *Economic Development Quarterly*, 1993, (1) :107-124.

technological innovation and expediting industry transformation[①]. For China and Australia to establish an industry park together would serve well to coordinate relationships between the two countries' governments as well as between the governments, markets and businesses, effectively maximising the efficiency of research universities in technological innovation, forming a more complete system for supporting innovation, and creating a cultural environment beneficial for business innovation and start-ups. Businesses would not only be able to together enjoy a supporting set of infrastructure and facilities as well as various kinds of standardised services, they would also be able to reduce such transaction costs as in logistics and so on due to the geographical proximity and position of the supporting and collaborating enterprises, bringing out greater collective benefits and the enjoyment of the innovative and entrepreneurial arrangements of both countries' systems. Successful industry parks can help both countries form new industry partnership chains and industry cooperation clusters, being of assistance in the multiplication, development and growth of both countries' businesses, becoming an engine for inter-business interaction, innovation and entrepreneurship.

For the co-creation of industry parks between China and Australia, cultural

---

① For the world's earliest high-tech industry parks one can look back to the 1940s in the twentieth century in England and America. When England started to establish and cultivate independent satellite towns with life-work balance around particularly large cities, it was an embryonic form of integrated industry-city development. On the other hand, America founded the world's first high-tech park in 1951– the Stanford Science Park, that is, the famous "Silicon Valley" . From the 1970s there were great strides in the development of industry parks globally and many countries would see the emergence of a numerous variety of "parks" and "areas" (Industry Parks, Business Parks, Office Parks, Science and Research Parks, Biotechnology Parks, Eco-industrial Parks, Creative Parks; Export Processing Zones, Free-trade Zones, Enterprise Zones) .

differences, differences in industry, university, and research systems, differences in technological innovation within an area, differences in the independent creativity and entrepreneurship of technical personnel, and differences in venture capital investment all deserve special attention. First of all, the demarcation between enterprises within the industry park cannot be too clearly defined, or it will prove unhelpful for enterprise dialogues and cooperations and for the future deeper development of industry clusters. Secondly, research capabilities cannot be overly dispersed, or this will prove unhelpful for the boosting of incubative efficiencies in intellectual and productive resources. Thirdly, key technologies and core technologies are to become the new main drivers for enterprise innovation, otherwise we will see the characteristics of low-level industries such as being labour-intensive and low value-adding. Fourthly, there needs to be a smooth road for the transformation of fruitful outcomes in science and technology, otherwise it will prove a setback to the independent and spirited entrepreneurship of high-level tech talent. Fifthly, high-level technology is a capital-intensive industry, and financial resources should be brought together to provide mature financial products for business innovation and entrepreneurship, better promoting the sustainable development of high-tech industries and industry parks.

IV. Recommendations for Chinese-funded enterprises with financing support in linking to Australia's innovation-driven strategy

(i) Follow the lead of planning in linking with China-Australia innovation-driven strategic partnerships

High-tech and innovative industries follow a labour-intensive development model, which is to say that financial investment is essential, as well as policy-related financial backing, and more particularly that market funds operate at high volume and with high efficiency, which can enable high-level science or technology to transform into a final product or innovation and entrepreneurship into a mature business model. All the innovation-driven strategies supported in the world's nations will closely integrate several methods of financial funding such as fiscal, credit and securities financing. As a result, the governments of China and Australia should strengthen their top-level design via planning in order to manage effectively the relationship between government and the market, and release holistic programs for innovation-driving strategic cooperation that encompass financing within, giving the market relatively stable policy forecasts. In terms of the prior release of funding programs: firstly, key domains for innovation-driven cooperation for the two countries should be integrated, laying out a holistic and collaborative backdrop for industry-finance integration. Secondly, the need for the creation of a cooperative platform for enterprises must be met, and finance funding models of various types integrated, supporting the centre for innovation in science and technology, industry parks and such other places of collaboration as well as the establishment of infrastructure and facilities as in Internet, data storage, cloud services and so on. Thirdly, funds must be led to focus their support on major cooperative projects in accordance with the specific characteristics defining industry cooperation for both countries, where they will strive to make notable breakthroughs, realising "role model" type follow-on effects. Fourthly, it is on the basis of a stable growth mechanism for financial investment that diverse and multi-level market financing channels will be founded, leading and inspiring Chinese-funded enterprises to participate in the two countries' strategic linking.

(ii) Development financing as the main force backing the participation of Chinese-funded enterprises in major projects

The objective of development orientated finance is to realise long-term economic growth as well as the intentions of the government, and through a financial organisation established by one or more countries possessing sovereign credit,[①] to provide medium to long-term credit for those specially requiring such, to establish a market and system, and with the carrier being the investment of capital in large amounts and for medium to long term duration, bringing about the investment of society's funds into specific projects and ultimately achieving national strategies. As distinct from commercial financing, development financing does not have as its objective the maximisation of profit, and can take the lead at an early stage in entering relatively low-profit areas such as for the Belt & Road and "science and technology innovation" strategies, being the forerunners and pioneers in financial and industrial integration. Infrastructure particularly needed in scientific and technological innovation cooperation between China and Australia are centres of scientific and technological innovation, industry parks and other such spaces for cooperation as well as the prior establishment of major infrastructure projects such as for the Internet, data storage, cloud services and so on. As these projects have a relatively long-term time frames for return on investment, their

---

① China's National Development Bank is currently the world's largest development finance organisation and externally directed capital finance investment bank. At the Third Plenary Session of the 18th Central Committee, the paper from the Chinese Communist Party's Central Committee raised for the first time the idea of a "development financial organisation". In March 2015, the State Council formally gave approval for the position of the National Development Bank and formally clarified the position of the National Development Bank as a development financial organisation.

202

profitability is relatively low, the funding gap sizeable, and it is difficult for commercial investing to get involved at an early stage. Hence, development finance is a major force supporting Chinese-Australian innovation-driven strategic cooperation, and may contribute its own experience, impact and capital investments for other forms of finance providing support and protection in an early period. Development finance organisations can integrate hotspots together in innovation-driven strategic cooperation for the Chinese and Australian governments, leading Chinese-funded enterprises to explore the "EPC+F" (Engineering Procurement Construction Plus Finance), PPP (Public Private Partnership), BOT (Build-Operate-Transfer), PFI (Private Finance Initiative) and such other collaborative models, to actively participate in the establishment of related major infrastructure, and to create a healthy market environment and market norms for the gradual entry of commercial finance, optimising the financial ecosystem for Chinese-Australian innovation-driven strategic cooperation.

(iii) The provision of comprehensive financial services by a platform of same industry banking partnerships

A deepening of cooperation in the same industry cooperation between Chinese and Australian banks is a key success factor for innovation-driven strategic cooperation for the countries. Until January 2016, the scale of total assets for Australia's financial markets was roughly $6.37 trillion Australian dollars, with the four major commercial banks, National Australia Bank, Commonwealth Bank, ANZ Bank, and Westpac taking approximately an 80% share. These four major commercial banks have seen outstanding performance in such areas as product development, risk control, information technology and business management; they have very strong capabilities and are the main banks in Australia's financial marketplace. Chinese-funded banks should strengthen their cooperation with Australia's main four commercial banks as well as with multilateral financial institutions, comprehensively raising their overall business capabilities and influence in Australia, and supporting the development and establishment of major projects in Chinese-Australian innovation driven strategic cooperation by methods such as syndicated loans and the provision of direct credit and refinancing. At present, many Chinese-funded enterprises that go abroad to invest have ample capital of their own and complex financing needs, where they value more the service capabilities of intermediaries such as a bank's financial consulting arm. Cooperation between Chinese and Australian banks brings about mutually complementary advantages, can mean the tailoring and design of different financial products for Chinese-funded enterprises, formulating those which are able to meet the standards and requirements of regulatory provisions in project risk preferences, risk appetite, credit structure, loan pricing, loan types, the approval process and so on, providing more convenient comprehensive financial services in Chinese-Australian innovation-driven strategic cooperation.

(iv) Perfecting the long-term mechanism for financing support with risk management and control at the core

Risk management and control for centres of innovation in science and technology, industry parks and such other bases for cooperation as well as such major infrastructure projects as Internet services, data storage, cloud services and so on are key to the success of cooperation between the two countries, and are also basic safeguards for a vibrant long-term mechanism of financial support. In addition, from a global point of view, small-to-medium tech enterprises are the main effectors of technological innovation and certain to be the main force in Chinese-Australian innovation-driven strategic cooperation. In sum, technology companies are characteristically capital light, high-risk, high-growth, information asymmetric, and such like. When selecting business clients, financial organisations will normally pay attention to four kinds of repayment sources: the first being cash flow, the second collateral, the third the guarantors, and the fourth their ability to refinance. Hence, technology companies often encounter quite stringent financing constraints. When finance-backed, Chinese-funded tech enterprises participate in China-Australia strategic linking and a vibrant risk management model must be equipped when carrying out risky loans and/or equity business. Financial organisations and enterprises should all seek to perfect their internal risk control mechanisms, establish early warning systems, and holistically distinguish, oversee and control financing risk procedures and models. Technology companies must strive to raise the commercialisation rate of their technologies, maintain an excellent credit record, and thus obtain an excellent credit record for receiving long-term financial capital support.

References:

Hu Huaibang, "Servicing the Belt & Road Strategy by Development Orientated Finance", *China Banking*, 2015 (12).

Hu Huaibang, "An Initiation of Development Finance Servicing National Strategy and the New Picture", *The People's Daily*, 2015.1.20.

National Innovation and Science Agenda, The Commonwealth Government of Australia.

Bai Chunli, "Worldwide Technological Innovation Trends and Discoveries", *Scientific Development*, 2014 (3).

"Commanding Innovation-Driven Development by the 'Four Comprehensives'", *The*

People's Daily, 2015.3.19.

"The Strategic Background and Opportunities in Practice for the Belt & Road, *Tsinghua Financial Review*, 2015（9）.

Conway H. M., L. L. Liston, R. J. Saul, *Industrial Park Growth: An Environmental Success Story*, Georgia: Conway Publications,1979.

Du Yanyan, Shu Langen, "A Look at Tech Finance in China through American Venture Loans", *New Finance*, 2013（7）.

Wang Lijun, "Promoting the Belt & Road International Science and Technology Cooperation with Enterprises at the Core", *Reform & Opening*, 2015（23）.

Zhou Yinghao, "A Comparison and Discoveries in the Development Models for Chinese and American High Tech Parks – A Case Study of Silicon Valley and Zhongguancun", *Enterprise Economy*, 2013（3）.

Meng Gang, "Research into Financing Cooperation for Four Southern Route Countries on the 21st Century Maritime Silk Road", *Journal of Development-Oriented Finance Research*, 2016（1）.

Meng Gang, "Significant Development in Northern Australia Brings New Strategic Opportunities for Development Finance", *China Banking*, 2016（8）.

Research on Economic and Trade Cooperation Zone Construction in Australia by China-invested Enterprises

I. Basic situation of overseas economic and trade cooperation zone construction by China-invested enterprises

(i) Basic connotation for China-invested enterprises to build overseas economic and trade cooperation zone

The overseas economic and trade cooperation zone refers to various economic and trade cooperation zones built in foreign countries by China-invested enterprises, participated by multiple enterprises to be stationed in the zone, and operated by commercial mode with perfect infrastructure facilities, complete industrial chain and strong radiation and driving ability. They can be named as agricultural park, processing and manufacturing park, science and technology industrial park, and comprehensive industrial park, etc.[①].

1. In terms of countries: the overseas economic and trade cooperation

---

① The earliest high-tech industrial parks can be traced back to UK and USA in 1940s. UK started building and developing independent satellite cities with balanced life and work around megalopolis, which became the prototype of industry-city integrated development; USA built the world first high-tech park, Stanford science and industry park, i.e. the world famous "sili zones initiated by China-invested enterprises are mostly in developing countries such as Pakistan, Cambodia and Thailand. With the comprehensive industrial capacity of China increases, the overseas economic and trade cooperation zones built in developed countries in recent years start emerging.

2. In terms of industries: the overseas economic and trade cooperation zones initiated by China-invested enterprises are mostly for manufacturing industries with outstanding capacity advantages in China, such as mineral resources, light textile, household appliances, machinery, electronics, and auto parts. The high-tech overseas cooperation zones are few. With the comprehensive national strength of China increases and per capita income improves greatly, the overseas parks for biotechnology, education and tourism and health and medical care start emerging.

3. In terms of functions: The overseas economic and trade cooperation zone initiated by China-invested enterprises can be further subdivided into market expansion type, export-oriented type, resource development type, technical research and development type, and comprehensive industry type. When the Chinese government greatly implements the "going abroad" strategy, the investment and operation modes of overseas economic and trade zones keep innovating, and the industrial cluster "going abroad" strategy of China has made great progress.

---

con valley", in 1951. From 1970s, the global industrial parks and zones developed greatly. Various parks and zones emerged in many countries. (Industrial Parks, Business Parks, Office Parks, Science and Research Parks, Bio-technology Parks, Eco-industrial Parks, Creative Parks; Export Processing Zones, Free-trade Zones, Enterprise Zones)

(ii) History of overseas economic and trade cooperation zones built by China-invested enterprises

From the beginning of reform and opening up in 1978, China mainly introduced foreign fund. In the 1990s, the China-invested enterprises started exploring way of overseas investment. In 2000, the Chinese Government officially proposed the national strategy of "going abroad", and clarified in the Report at the 16th Party Congress to combine "investment attraction" and "going abroad" and ceaselessly improve opening up level of China. In the end of 2005, upon approval of the State Council, the Ministry of Commerce officially launched construction mechanism for overseas economic and trade cooperation zone, and the Chinese government leads and supports clustered "going abroad" of China-invested enterprises. After overseas economic and trade cooperation zone operates maturely and complies with certain conditions, the Ministry of Commerce of China will confirm and offer policy support to greater degree. From June 2006 to July 2007, the Ministry of Commerce confirmed 19 overseas economic and trade zones in 15 countries by two batches. Through accumulation and development for nearly a decade, the Chinese overseas economic and trade cooperation zone construction mechanism has made great achievements.

In accordance with statistics from the Ministry of Commerce, as of September 2015, totally 69 China-invested projects in 33 countries with nature of overseas economic and trade cooperation zone are under construction. The constructing enterprises of the 69 cooperation zones have accumulatively finished investment of USD 6.76 billion, in which the investment in infrastructure is USD 3.42 billion, and totally 376.6km^2 lands are leveled. Totally 1088 enterprises are stationed in the cooperation zones, of which 688 are China-invested holding enterprises, and accumulated paid-in investment is USD 9.92 billion; the total accumulated output in cooperation zones is USD 40.21 billion, and total tax paid to host countries is USD 1.29 billion; local employment for 149,000 people is solved. The 48 overseas economic and trade cooperation zones built in countries along the Belt & Road are distributed in 18 countries.

(iii) Policy support for China-invested enterprises to build overseas economic and trade cooperation zone

After China officially launched construction of overseas economic and trade cooperation zone, relevant ministries and commissions such as the State Council, Ministry of Commerce and Ministry of Finance, as well as China Development Bank and China Export & Credit Insurance Corporation successively issued multiple supporting policies and measures including *Basic Requirements and Application Procedures for Chinese Overseas Economic and Trade Cooperation Zone, Confirmation Assessment and Annual Assessment Management Measures forOverseas Economic and Trade Cooperation Zone,Opinions on Overseas Economic and Trade Cooperation Zone Construction Promotion, and Notice on Strengthening Risk Prevention of Overseas Economic and Trade Cooperation Zone*, and offered policy support for the construction of overseas economic and trade cooperation zone in aspects of development fund, credit, tax, approval, customs clearance, safety, insurance and training.

In 2013, the Ministry of Commerce and China Development Bank jointly released the Notice on Supporting Construction and Development of Overseas Economic and Trade Cooperation Zone to provide policy support to implemented enterprises and stationed enterprises in conforming cooperation zone in aspects of investment and financing. The specific measures are: firstly, the Ministry of Commerce provides macroscopic guidance to the cooperation zone invested and built by enterprises, and provides support in aspects of country and industrial guidance, capital investment convenience, and overseas investment guarantee; secondly, China Development Bank, according to demands of national external development strategy, supports the domestic enterprise cluster to "go abroad", and provides financing service the construction of cooperation zone; thirdly, the Ministry of Commerce and China Development Bank will support or jointly carry out research in cooperation zone layout and development planning; fourthly, the Ministry of Commerce and China Development Bank will establish information sharing mechanism for relevant cooperation zones, strengthen information communication, notify progress of cooperation zone confirmation assessment, annual assessment and investment and financing, and lead enterprises to invest and operate in the cooperation zone in order; fifthly, the Ministry of Commerce and China Development Bank, according to cooperation zone promotion, irregularly coordinate important problems in cooperation zone project financing.

(iv) Development prospect of overseas economic and trade cooperation zone built by China-invested enterprises

Under the new situation, the overseas economic and trade zone is given new missions. In March 2015, the *Vision and Actions on Jointly Building Silk Road Economic Belt and 21st-Century Maritime Silk Road* jointly released by National Development and Reform Commission, Ministry of Foreign Affairs, and Ministry of Commerce in March 2015 pointed out that "take advantage of international transport routes, rely on core cities along the Belt and Road, and use key economic industrial parks as cooperation platforms on land according to the direction of the Belt & Road to explore new investment and cooperation mode, encourage the building of various industrial parks and zones such as overseas economic and trade cooperation zone and cross-border economic cooperation zones, and promote industry cluster development".

In May 2015, *the Guiding Opinion on Promoting International Capacity and Equipment Manufacture Cooperation* released by the State Council further clarified to "improve the going abroad capacity and level of enterprises, encourage enterprises to actively participate in construction of cooperation parks and zones such as overseas industry cluster district, economic and trade cooperation zone, industrial park, and special economic zone, create favorable regional investment environment with perfect infrastructure, supporting laws and policies and aggregation and radiation effect, and lead domestic enterprises to go abroad by clusters". It is obvious that the overseas economic and cooperation zone built mainly by China-invested enterprises has become one of the effective means to promote global economic and trade cooperation strategic layout of China, and will become an important cooperation carrier and operation mode for the Belt & Road construction and advantageous industry "going abroad" strategy advocated by the Chinese government.

Table 1　Profile of 19 Overseas Economic and Trade Cooperation Zones Confirmed by the Ministry of Commerce

No.	Name	County	Constructing Enterprise	Industry
1	Pakistan Hair Household Appliances Industrial Zone	Pakistan	(Shandong) Hair Group	Home appliances, supporting industry and logistics transportation
2	Indonesia-China Wonogiri Economic and Trade Cooperation Zone	Indonesia	(Guangxi) Guangxi State Farm Group	Building materials, chemical engineering and pharmaceuticals
3	Russia St. Petersburg Baltic Sea Economic and Trade Cooperation Zone	Russia	(Shanghai) Shanghai Industrial Investment (Holding) Co., Ltd.	Real estate, business, office, leisure, catering, entertainment
4	Russia Ussuriysk Economic and Trade Cooperation Zone	Russia	(Zhejiang) China Kangji International Investment Co., Ltd.	Clothes, shoes, leather, household appliances, and wood industry
5	Russia-China Tomsk Timber Industry Trade Cooperation Zone	Russia	(Shandong) Yantai Northwest Forestry Co., Ltd., China International Marine Containers (Group) Ltd.	Forest land, logging, and timber deep processing
6	Thailand-China Rayong Industrial Zone	Thailand	(Zhejiang) China Holley Group	Auto parts, machinery, building materials, home appliances and electronics
7	Cambodia Taihu International Economic and Trade Cooperation Zone	Cambodia	(Jiangsu) Hongdou Group	Light textile, clothes, electronics, machinery, high and new tech, and logistics
8	Vietnam China (Shenzhen) Economic and Trade Cooperation Zone	Vietnam	(Shenzhen) China National Aviation Corp, Zhongshen International Logistics Co., Ltd., Neptune Group	Textile, light industry, medicine, biology, machinery and electronics

9	Vietnam China Longjiang Economic and Trade Cooperaiton Zone	Vietnam	(Zhejiang) Qianjiang Investment Management Co., Ltd.	Machinery, electronics, light textile, clothes, and building materials
10	Korea-China Industrial Park	Korea	(Chongqing) China Dongtai Huaan International Investment Co., Ltd.	Auto, ship parts, biotechnology, high technology, and logistics
11	Nigeria Guangdong Economic and Trade Cooperaiton Zone	Nigeria	(Guangdong) Guangdong Guangxin International Group	Furniture, hardware, building materials and ceramics
12	Nigeria Lekki Free Trade Zone	Nigeria	(Jiangsu) Jiangning Economic and Technology Development Zone, Nanjing Beiya Group	Manufacture, import & export trade, leisure and tourism
13	Egypt Suez Economic and Trade Cooperation Zone	Egypt	(Tianjin) Teda Investment Holding Co., Ltd.	Light textile, clothes, electrical equipment, and common engineering products
14	Ethiopia Orient Industrial Park	Ethiopia	(Jiangsu) Jiangsu Yonggang Group Co., Ltd.	Metallurgy, machinery, building materials
15	Algeria China JMC Economic and Trade Cooperaiton Zone	Algeria	(Jiangxi) Zhongding International, JMCG	Automobile manufacture, and building materials
16	Zambia China Nonferrous Industrial Park	Zambia	(Beijing) China Nonferrous Metal Mining (Group) Co., Ltd.	Nonferrous metal mining and smelting such as copper-cobalt
17	Tianli (Mauritius) Economic and Trade Cooperation Zone	Mauritius	(Shanxi) Shanxi Tianli Enterprise Group	Production, processing, carrying trade, commercial service, holiday and entertainment
18	Venezuela China Science and Technology Industry and Trade Zone	Venezuela	(Shandong) Shandong Inspur Group	Household appliances, agricultural machinery and electronic industry
19	Mexico China Geely Industry, Economic and Trade Cooperation Zone	Mexico	(Zhejiang) Zhejiang Geely Merrie Auto Co., Ltd.	Auto production, supporting parts and commercialbusiness

Data source: website of overseas economic and trade cooperation zone of Ministry of Commerce.

II. Trend and opportunities for industrial investment of China-invested enterprises in Australia

With vast land and abundantnatural resources, Australia became a developed country earlier. In 2015, its GDP is about USD 1.598 trillion, and per capita GDP is about USD 66,580. As the world 12th economy in the world, Australia has stable political and legal environment, normative market mechanism, reasonable industrial structure, multiple fields of investment, stable return on investment, and internationally leading technology and management experience. It is the bridge connecting Asian-Pacific Region and developed European with American countries.

(i) Industrial investment trend of China-invested enterprises in Australia

During 2005-2015, Australia became the second largest destination country for global direct investment of China. During 2013-2015, China became the first overseas direct investment source country of Australia. The industrial investment of China-invested enterprises in Australia experiences exploration process and gradual change of investment field for years.

1.1980-2005 (Starting Stage): China-invested enterprises carried out few investment activities in Australia. In this stage, the investment and cooperation of China in Australia was at a small scale. The typical cases contain Portland Aluminum Factory invested by CITIC Group, Rio Tinto Channar iron ore invested by Sinosteel Corporation, and Five Star Shipping Agency, China-Australia Joint Venture established by China COSCO Shipping Corporation Limited, cotton industry invested by Chinatex Corporation, and business recovery of Bank of China in Australia.

2.2006-2012 (Energy and mineral resource field): China-invested enterprises started investing in Australia at a large scale. In this stage, the investment cooperation projects in China were mainly in energy and mineral fields. About 73% of accumulated investment amount is for mineral industry, and 18% is for naturalgas industry, mainly in Western Australia and Queensland. The typical cases are LNG project of CNOOC, iron core project of CITIC Pacific, coal mine and port project of Yanzhou Coal Industry, and MMG procurement project of China Minmetals Corporation.

3.2013 to now (Tendency of diversification) :The investment of China-invested enterprises in Australia presents a tendency of diversity. In this stage, except energy and mineral fields, the investment projects of China-invested enterprises in Australia contain infrastructure, agriculture, manufacture, high-end food, leisure, retail industry, and logistics industry. The typical cases are JOHN.HOLLAND procurement by China Communications Construction, NEWCASTLE port 99 years lease right acquired by China Merchants Group, Darwin Port 99 years lease right acquired by Shandong Land Bridge Group, local power grid equity purchased by the State Grid Corporation of China, agricultural land of the Northern Territory purchased by Shanghai Zhongfu Group, dairy farm and dairy products processing plant invested by New Hope Group, and commercial real estate invested by well-known real estate enterprises such as Greenland Group, Australia cinema purchased by Wanda, seafood industry invested by Lenovo, and e-business platform arranged by Alibaba.

(ii) The linkage between Chinese and Australian strategies brings new opportunities for clustered development of China-invested enterprises

In November 2014, the strategic partnership between China and Australia is advanced to a comprehensive strategy partnership. On April 4,2016, President Xi Jinping, Premier Li Keqiang, and the Premier of Australia officially announced the linkage between the Belt & Road strategy of China and Developing

Northern Australia strategy, between innovation-driven development strategy of China and "National Innovation and Science Agenda" of Australia. The all-round strategy linkage of the governments of the two countries provides unprecedented opportunity for clustered development of China-invested enterprises in Australia.

Under the new situation, China-invested enterprises' building economic and trade cooperation zone in Australia can effectively boost clustered development, promote industry transformation and upgrading, and jointly improve the status in global value chain, industrial chain, logistics chain and innovation chain. Inside the economic and trade cooperation zone, the China-invested enterprises can not only share supporting infrastructures and various standard services, but also reduce transaction cost such as logistics due to nearby geological position between supporting and cooperative enterprises so as to play collective benefits, enjoy preferential policy support and convenient system arrangement of two governments, promote two countries to form new industrial cooperation chain and industrial cooperation cluster, boost enterprises of two countries to grow and develop, and become a new power for interaction and innovative cooperation among enterprises.

III. Analysis on cases and service function of Chinese Economic and Trade Cooperation Zone in Australia

(i) Analysis on cases of Chinese Economic and Trade Cooperation Zone in Australia

1.UNSW Torch Innovation Park Project

(1) Project profile

The University of New South Wales (UNSW) , founded in 1949 and located at Sydney, is a top research-intensive university in Asia Pacific. In January 2016, the President of UNSW visited Torque Center of Ministry of Science and Technology, and reached consensus on Torque Innovation Park construction in UNSW with Torque Center. The Torque Innovation Park will become a brand new platform for technology industry cooperation between China and Australia, and provide services for Chinese and Australian enterprises, scientific research experts, investors and pioneering youth in fields of energy and environment, advanced materials and biotechnology.

（2）Project schedule

The Torque Innovation Park will be constructed in two steps. Firstly, UNSW will provide 1000m^2 office site in Kensington main campus to build the business incubator, and attract Chinese enterprises to set up research office or carry out business in Australia; secondly, UNSW will use the 20,000m^2 land in Sydney campus to build a comprehensive science and technology industrial innovation zone including multiple innovation platforms such as enterprise sharing laboratory, pilot plant test base, marker space and enterprise incubator.

（3）Factors of the Chinese side

The Torch Center, founded in 1989 and belonged to the Ministry of Science and Technology of China, aims to "develop high technology, and realize industrialization", explores boldly, innovates ceaselessly, and keep promoting forward development of high and new technology industry in China. The Project is worth of AUD 100 million, and will lead China-invested enterprises to strengthen cooperation in scientific research fields in Australia by building a new science and technology park in UNSW.

（4）Contract signing

In April 2016, under the witness of Primer Li Keqiang and Premier

Turnbull who visited China, the Torch Center of Ministry of Science and Technology signed Memorandum of Understanding for Joint Construction of Torch Innovation Park in Australia with UNSW, and jointly started construction of UNSW Torch Innovation Park. The first batch of partners contains Fuchunjiang Group/Hangzhou Cable Co., Ltd., Fuzhou Danlaw Xicheng Electronic Technology Co., Ltd., Shenzhen Kohodo New Energy Co., Ltd., Shenzhen Intelligence Power Co., Ltd. and a batch of advantageous enterprises in photo voltaic energy field.

2.Australian Education City Project

（1）Project profile

Australian Education City project locates at the place 25km southwest to Melbourne. It plans to create the first international education and scientific research CBD in the Southern Hemisphere and the world first "cognition city". The floor area is 5km^2. Total building area is 604m^2, and downtown area is 1.3km^2. The Australian Education City Project orients at creating international education and scientific research CBD, the largest city building project in the past 50 years in Australia. It will create over 100,000 job opportunities and plan to invite the best research and development universities from China, UK, America and Australia to run universities jointly. In addition to the branches of best middle schools and technical training schools in Australia, there will be over 50,000 students.

（2）Unique advantages

Australia has 15 Nobel scholar winners, and over 50% universities rank world top 500 in academy and research. The quantity of global international overseas students ranks the world fourth. In May 2016, the Australian Government issued the first international education planning, aiming to double the overseas students in Australia in the next 10 years. Melbourne is a publicly recognized knowledge center and owns multiple world first-class universities and research institutions with ideas of development-type cooperation in running schools.

(3) Chinese side factors

China-invested enterprises participate in Australian Education City Project to provide teaching buildings and other teaching facilities for free and 25-year free rent to well-known universities of China planned to be invited. They will help the well-known Chinese universities to acquire all legal operation qualifications in Australia, employ excellent teachers all over the world according to requirements of universities, provide comprehensive services such as administrative management and non-teaching and research services, and promise to guarantee sources of local students and international overseas students.

3.Full Share Comprehensive Industrial Park Project

(1) Project profile

The Full Share Comprehensive Industrial Park is independently developed by Nanjing Full Share Industry Holding Group Co., Ltd. It locates at the north of Queensland, covering an area of about 30km^2. The preliminary planning is divided into ecological agriculture park, education and training park, health maintenance park, sports park, vacation resort and business and entrainment park. According to existing planning, the total building area of the project is over 800,000m^2, and the project sets about 860 quay berths, several apartments, three golf courses, one four-star hotel, and one five-star hotel. After completion, it can become a small town for over 15,000 permanent residents. The total construction period is about 15-20 years.

(2) Project schedule

The agricultural park and supporting facility Phase I Project will be carried out from 2016 to 2023, including storage dam, irrigation system, and crops procurement, plantation, pocking, storage, processing and transportation in agricultural park; the supporting infrastructure contains wharf, small private and cargo airport, sports park, park channel, road, water, electricity, network, pollution discharge system, drainage system, substation, water storage station transformation and upgrading. The education training Park Phase I project will be carried from 2017 to 2024. It plans to promote cooperation with Chinese universities and universities in Queensland, and sets up training schools for agriculture, airplane and yacht driving, medical service management, hotel, and golf, including early planning approval, campus construction, license verification, operation management, and supporting facility construction.

(ii) Analysis on service function of Chinese Economic and Trade Cooperation Zone in Australia

As an important platform for industrial agglomeration development, the Economic and Trade Cooperation Zone built by China-invested enterprises in Australia refer to industrial service guidance of ministries and commerce such as Ministry of Commerce, and successful experiences of other overseas economic and trade cooperation zones. It shall attach high importance to providing high quality comprehensive service to stationed enterprises.

1.Information consulting service, including policy consulting, legal service and product promotion

The Economic and Trade Cooperation Zone can establish a communication and coordination platform between enterprises stationed and Australian government departments and relevant organizations, and provide relevant policy consulting services including investment, trade, finance and industry to help enterprises stationed know laws and investment environment of Australia, seek and entrust legal service intermediary, help enterprises stationed participate in exhibition hall, product symposium, and trade fair, and set up a local cooperation platform for enterprises in Australia.

2.Operation and management services, including enterprise registration, financial affairs, customs declaration, human resources, financial services and logistics services

The economic and trade cooperation zone shall establish a communication and connection mechanism with Australian foreign capital management departments or investment promotion institutions, provide consulting services for enterprises about registration in Australia, help enterprises handle registration, environmental impact assessment and planning design approval; provide policy consulting in aspects of finance and tax, and help enterprises carry out financial management, trademark registration, tax application and payment; provide consulting services with regard to customs declaration, imported equipment customs clearance, warehousing and transportation, import/export procedures, certificate of origin and tariff application; provide policy consulting services with regard to employee management and personnel visa, and help enterprises stationed in the zone handle human resources affairs such as employee training, recruitment and talent exchange; provide financial consulting services such as investment, financing and insurances, and help enterprises stationed handle financial procedures, establish channel for connection between enterprises stationed and Chinese and Australian financial organs, and provide necessary logistic services such as transportation, storage, loading/unloading, handling, delivery and information processing according to the requirements of enterprises stationed.

3.Property management services, including lease service, plant construction, supporting facilities for production and life, maintenance service, and medical service

The Economic and Trade Cooperation Zone shall, according to laws and commercial traditions of Australia, provide lease service for standard workshop, office building, warehouse, exhibition hall and storage yard to enterprises stationed; provide necessary support when the enterprises build new plants; help handle relevant procedures including design, construction tender and bidding, construction license, commencement license and acceptance license; provide supporting convenience and services for production such as electricity supply, water supply, heating supply, communication, gas supply, security, waste water treatment, refuse disposal and toxic waste disposal; provide supporting facilities and services for life, such as employee dormitory, service flat, sports, fitness, culture, entertainment and various sewages; provide professional and efficient maintenance services to enterprises, and help them solve maintenance difficulties encountered in production and living; provide simple medical treatment service, and establish smooth emergency treatment channel with Australian hospitals.

4. Emergency services

The Economic and Trade Cooperation Zone shall cooperate with Australian government management organ closely, make emergency plans, effectively prevent from and cope with emergencies such as fire, flood, strike and destructive activity, implement emergency guarantee such as post-disaster relief and guarantee personal and property safety of the zone and enterprises stationed.

IV. Suggestions on ideas for Economic and Trade Cooperation Zone built by China-invested enterprises in Australia

(i) Distinct positioning, scientific planning, and leading international competitive advantages

The amount of investment in Economic and Trade Cooperation Zone Construction in Australia is large; the return cycle is long; enterprises participated in are many, and unpredictable difficulties are complex. Without distinct positioning and scientific planning, the constructing enterprises will face large investment risks. Therefore, the constructing enterprises shall make clear industry orientation, scientifically plan various conditions of industrial cluster development, coordinate relationships between government and market, between constructing enterprises and enterprises stationed, and between park environment and macroscopic environment of Australia, and better play the competitive advantages of China-invested enterprises in foreign investment. In recent years, based on accumulation since reform and opening up, the China-invested enterprises actively explores cluster development direction of high-end manufacture industry and technology and capital-intensive industry, and develops from cluster development mode featured by low cost, labor-intensive industry and middle and low end manufacture to brand new "country comparison competitive advantage" with Chinese characteristics. The China-invested enterprises shall aim at and insist on advanced international industrial competitive advantages when building Economic and Trade Cooperation Zone in Australia, form high-end industrial cluster with Chinese characteristics and strive for upstream status with high added values in labor divisions of new international industrial chain.

(ii) Take the opportunity of free trade agreement signed by China and Australia

Australia is the main exporter of global agricultural products and energy and mineral products, and the main developed economy with large global economic aggregate, mature market economy system and matching legal system and governance mode. In a few years, the economic complementarity between China and Australia will strengthen increasingly. In June 2015, the Chinese and Australian governments signed *Free Trade Agreement*. Firstly, in the field of goods, the products of respective party accounting for 85.4% of export volume will adopt zero tariff as soon as the agreement takes effect. After the transition period, the proportion of tax item with zero tariff and trade volume proportion in Australia will reach 100%, and in China will respectively reach 96.8% and 97%, far higher than the 90% tax lowering level in common free trade agreements. Secondly, in the field of service, the Australian side promises to open service department to the Chinese side by negative list mode after the agreement takes effect, and Australia is the first country in the world making service trade commitment to China by negative list. The Chinese side will open service department to the Australian side by positive list. Moreover, the Australian side also makes special arrangement for the Chinese side in aspects of holiday work mechanism. Thirdly, in the field of investment, both parties will offer the most-favored-nation treatment to each other after the agreement takes effect. Meanwhile, the Australian side will lower the review threshold for China-invested enterprises to invest in Australia, and offer convenient arrangement. Fourthly, the agreement also regulate promotion of exchange and cooperation of "21st Century Economic and Trade Topics" between both sides in fields of e-business, government procurement, intellectual property right and competition.

(iii)Complement advantages with local economy, and promote industrial upgrade

The science and technology innovation is always an important strategic support to improve social productivity and comprehensive national strength. The science and technology reform derives from the drive of social demand, and will greatly promote great development of social economy. The countries taking the preemptive opportunities from the new science and technology reform in the world will surely become the leader of the world economy. Australia is a great exporter of resources, energy, agricultural products and health products, while China is the largest consumption market and a great manufacturing county. It can be said that two countries are supplementary and practical in advanced manufacturing industry and science and technology innovation field. The cooperation between Chinese and Australian enterprises has great development space under the background of globalization. The development of China-invested enterprises and local Australian enterprises with supplementary economic advantages will help their industrial upgrade, and can jointly lead the world new technology reform to a higher level. The Economic and Trade Cooperation Zone featured by high technology industry development, as output of new technology reform and knowledge economy age, can efficiently realize "industry-university-research" integration development objects and greatly promote technology innovation and industrial transformation upgrade. The successful Economic and Trade Cooperation Zone can urge Chinese and Australian enterprises to form new industrial cooperation chain and industrial cooperation cluster, boost China-invested enterprises to increase, develop and grow, and become the engine for innovation and venture of China-invested enterprises.

(iv) Powerful combination: strengthen cooperation with domestic first-class industrial parks

To build Economic and Trade Cooperation Zone, the China-invested enterprises shall strengthen cooperation with domestic first-class industrial parks to form powerful combination and composition forces. Beijing Zhongguancun Industrial Park, Shanghai Zhangjiang Industrial Park and Jiangsu Suzhou Industrial Park have abundant operating experiences. In March 2016, under great support of the Belt & Road Office, Ministry of Science of Technology, Ministry of Foreign Affairs, and Zhongguancun Management Committee, the Zhongguancun the Belt & Road Industry Promotion Association is established. It will, based on the Belt & Road strategy and around contents of infrastructure interconnection between countries along the Belt & Road, the construction of key economic and trade industrial parks and technology industry transfer efficiently play advantages of innovation and high tech industry in Zhongguancun, and establish "going abroad" community by market operation mode, create the international cooperation service platform with the best global influence, and promote enterprises in different industrial fields and upstream and downstream enterprises of the industrial chain unit to go abroad by complementary advantages. It can effectively cope with challenges and risks for independent going abroad, and help enterprises expand the international market. In July 2016, Zhongguancun the Belt & Road Industry Promotion Association, China Development Bank Shanghai Branch and Nanjing Full Share Industry Holding Group signed the *Development-oriented Finance Cooperation Agreement*. The three sides agreed to bring intelligence and enterprise service platform advantages of Zhongguancun to play, and exert financing advantages of China Development Bank to support development and investment of Full Share Group in Queensland, and urge park construction projects to become the new field and a new direction for linkage between the Belt & Road strategy and Developing Northern Australia strategy.

(v) Set up financial platform to support construction of Economic and Trade Cooperation Zone

The capital market in Australia is highly developed, and the proportion of financial industry to national economic aggregate is the largest. Australia owns the second largest stock market in Asia Pacific Region, and the trading volume of AUD in the world ranks the fifth. To create a financial cooperation platform supporting Economic and Trade Cooperation Zone built by China-invested enterprises in Australia, the advantages and functions of various financial forms in China such as development-oriented finance, policy finance and commercial finance. The platform shall strengthen cooperation with local Australian banks such as Australia & New Zealand banking, National Australia Bank, Westpac Bank, and Commonwealth Bank, and financial institutions such as industrial investment fund, insurance company and risk capital, smoothen investment and financing cooperation channel, improve comprehensive operating ability and influence of China-invested banks in aspects of product development, risk control, information technology and operation management, comprehensively carry out integrated financial service such as project financing, trade financing, international settlement, financial consulting, offshore assets securitization, and syndicated loan, and provide all-round one-stop services to China-invested enterprises to jointly support China-invested enterprises to build Economic and Trade Cooperation Zone in Australia.

It shall be mentioned particularly that the development-oriented finance, different from commercial finance, does not aim at maximum profits. The development-oriented financial institution can serve as the forerunner and pioneer to firstly support China-invested enterprises in early stage to build Economic and Trade Cooperation Zone with early-low and later-high cash flow in Australia. In the initial stage of Economic and Trade Cooperation Zone, the return cycle is long, and the profit rate is low and fund gap is large; thus it is difficult for commercial finance to participate in. The development-oriented finance can provide early support and guarantee for other financial forms through own experiences, influence and capital input. The development-oriented institutions can support construction enterprises and China-invested enterprises stationed in the zone to actively explore multiple cooperation modes such as "EPC+F", PPP, BOT and PFI, promote significant infrastructure construction in the Economic and Trade Cooperation Zone, create favorable market environment and market rules for gradual station of commercial financial institutions, and optimize financial ecological environment supporting the development of the Economic and Trade Cooperation Zone.

References:

Hu Huaibang, "Serving the Belt & Road Strategy by Development-Oriented Finance", *China Banking Industry*, 2015（12）.

Conway H. M., L. L. Liston, R. J. Saul, *Industrial Park Growth: An Environmental Success Story*, Georgia: Conway Publicaitons,1979.

China Chamber of Commerce in Australia, *China-invested Enterprises in Australia*, China Renmin University Press.2015（12）.

Meng Gang, "Research on Financial Cooperation of Four Countries along the Southern Route of the 21st Century Marine Silk Road", *Journal of Development-Oriented Finance Research*, 2016（1）.

Meng Gang, "Approach of Australia Science and Technology Innovation Strategy

Integrating to China and Financing Cooperation", *Globalization*, 2016 (7).

Meng Gang, "Australia Northern Development Strategy Brings New Opportunity for Development-oriented Finance", *China Banking Industry*, 2016 (4).

Meng Gang, "Experiences of Infrastructure PPP Mode in Australia and Enlightenment to China", *Overseas Investment and Export Credit*, 2016 (4).

Meng Gang, "Study on International Capacity Cooperation of China in Australia", *Journal of Development-Oriented Finance Research*, 2016 (3).

Department of the Prime Minister and Cabinet, *Our North, Our Future: White Paper on Developing Northern Australia*. Australia, 2015.6.

National Innovation and Science Agenda, Australia commonwealth Government.

Australian Bureau of Statistics, Australia.

Xiao Wen, "Research on Development of Chinese Overseas Economic and Trade Cooperation Zone – Take Zhejiang Province Overseas Cooperation Zone as Example", *Master Dissertation of Zhejiang University*, 2014 (5).

Guan Lixin, *Comparison between China-Singapore Overseas Industrial Parks and Enlightenment*, 2012 (1).

Yu Suo, "Practices and Experiences of Overseas Industrial Park Developed by China-invested Enterprises", *Special Zone Economy*, 2014 (1).

Xun Kening, "New Opportunity for Overseas Park Development under Background of the Belt & Road", *Theory Journal*, 2015 (10).

Li Donghong, "Overseas Industrial Park: Industrial Cluster Goes Abroad under the Belt & Road Strategy", *Financial World*, 2016 (1).

Infrastructure PPP Mode Practice in Australia and Its Enlightenment to China

I. Introduction of infrastructure PPP mode in Australia

(i) Concept of PPP and global situations

PPP is short for Public-Private Partnership, i.e. government-social capital partnership. It is a partnership mechanism providing public products such as infrastructures to the public. UK is the origin of PPP mode. In accordance with the complexity and cooperation degree of PPP, some research institutions divide countries financing under PPP mode into three groups[①]. UK and Australia belong to the first group, and are deemed as countries with most mature

---

① One of themed PPP researches of China Bond Rating: PPP Definition and Overview of Domestic and Overseas Development, January 2015.Deloitte proposed PPP market maturity theory in 2007, and listed nine elements measuring PPP market maturity in each country, respectively understanding about risk transfer principle, PPP application experiences of public sectors, PPP application experience of private sectors, support of the public and stake holders, market size, atmosphere of stable and powerful support of public sectors, fund availability, awareness and realization of expected results and innovation, and legal framework and business institutions.

development of PPP mode. The Netherlands, Italy, New Zealand, Ireland, France, Canada, USA, Japan and Germany belong to the second group, with relatively high market maturity. India, Russia, South Africa, Brazil, Hungary, Czech, Belgium, Denmark and China belong to the third group, with low PPP market maturity and expecting further development. Analysis of PWF (Public Works Financing), a well-known PPP institution, shows during 1985-2011 the total investment in global PPP project has reached over USD 770 Billion, which accounts for 24.2% in Asia and Australia.

(ii) Basic characteristics of infrastructure PPP project

All countries in the world attach high importance to infrastructure construction. Infrastructure plays a role in supporting social economy and public life of one country fundamentally. As a mature concept commonly used internationally, the infrastructure PPP of all countries shares the common characteristics. Firstly, the projects are featured by social and public welfare nature with high investment cost, long construction period, low return rate, weak non-competitiveness and non-excludability, and strong public participation property. Secondly, governments attract social capital for project construction by transferring franchise right and naming right. The government plays the role as the project initiator while social investor plays the role as the project investor. Thirdly, the social capital effectively eases financial pressure of the government so as to transfer functions of government, improve public service levels and activate infrastructure construction. Fourthly, through cooperation, government and social capital can complement each other, and reasonably share risks.

(iii) Basic types of infrastructure PPP mode in Australia

The policy guide issued by the Australian government divides PPP modes of infrastructure into two types. The first type is "social infrastructure PPP", which means the main source of income or fund to repay social capital financing is the service (or use) fee paid by the government. This mode is usually used in social (i.e. non-profit) infrastructures such as scientific research institutions, schools, hospitals, cultural facilities and prisons. The second type is known as "economic infrastructure PPP", which means the main fund source is expense paid by infrastructure users, such as toll paid by highway users. This mode covers traffic facilities including bridge, highway, tunnel, railway, port, wharf and airport, as well as water and electricity supply facilities, drainage facilities and communication facilities. In Australia, the projects of these two infrastructure types are about half and half. In view of the total investment, the projects of economic infrastructure accounted for a majority proportion.

(iv) Participation of Australian social capital in Infrastructure PPP

From the angle of social capital, the most common PPP operation mode in Australia is a special SPV project company jointly established by several investors. SPV will sign PPP project agreement with a term of 20-30 years for project design, financing, construction and operation. The financing party generally has no recourse or limited recourse right for shareholders (investors) of SPV. The loan adopts bullet repayment mode, and will be prepaid at lump sum at maturity. During loan period, the financing party can transfer loan share by refinancing in financial market. SPV and government will sign agreement with other companies on various tasks about project implementation to confirm these companies can perform agreements. In case of performance failure risk, relevant liabilities will be held in accordance with relationship between rights and obligations agreed in the contract. SPV is given long-term franchise right and earning right of infrastructure projects. Therefore, they have enough power for rapid construction and efficient operation. Upon expiration, the project assets will be transferred to government voluntarily in general. Chances are that the agreement is renewed at proper price or in latest commercial conditions after negotiation between the government and investor.

II. Successful experiences of Australian infrastructure PPP mode

(i) Set special PPP government administrative institutions and release policy guide

Australia pays attention to coordination in the level of government. The Federal Government establishes nationwide infrastructure PPP management department, i.e. Department of Infrastructure and Regional Development. This department collects demands of various levels of government for infrastructure construction and issues guidance policy. Its services are not limited to PPP, but promotion of PPP is one of its important functions. In October 2015, Department of Infrastructure and Regional Development updated nationwide PPP policy framework of Australia launched in 2008, and introduced implementation policies of PPP project in details, including PPP project centralized procurement method, investor guide, business principle of social infrastructure, business principle of economic infrastructure, government operation guide, and financial computing method. Governments, on that basis, formulated local framework guide to regulate PPP project in details respectively. For instance, the State of Victoria makes special regulations on information disclosure of PPP project, and requires contracts of all PPP projects that State of Victoria PPP Center participated in, except projects dominated by state-owned enterprises, being released in three months after the financing program is finished.

(ii) Confirm the VFM principle of PPP project

The core access standard of PPP project confirmed by Australia is "Value for Money, VFM" . It checks whether PPP mode is better than traditional modes, and whether social capital can realize the VFM principle, i.e. the minimum cost, maximum output and expected effect. Government departments of Australia will, in initiation stage, formulate infrastructure and public sector development planning, and check necessity of project construction and application of PPP mode by full cost-benefit analysis method. The basic principle is to respectively calculate the cost and benefit of specific infrastructure projects under mode of public sector procurement and PPP procurement by technological, economic, and social analysis methods, and decide the optimal procurement method of the infrastructure project according to VFM principle and comparison method. In launching stage of PPP project, the government departments of Australia will adopt the Public Sector Comparator (PSC) method to compare the full life cycle cost of PPP mode and traditional modes. If the tender price cost of PPP mode is lower than the cost of traditional modes, the VFM mode is reflected. PSC refers to all costs required by traditional public sector procurement mode of infrastructure project including net cost of construction and operation, cost for transferable risks, cost of risk retention, and competitive neutral adjustment cost, assuming construction fund is not limited, PPP project construction period and output standards are the same, and cost difference of transactions under different procurement modes is considered,. When PPP mode shows VFM maximally through quantitative comparison, the government departments will finally select one most suitable enterprise (or combo comprised by several enterprises) to grant franchise right.

(iii) Formulate full-process performance assessment and supervision system

The Australian Government emphasizes the formulating of full-process performance and supervision system, and urges the social capital to guarantee product or service quality and improve efficiency by Output and Outcome-based Performance Specification. The key point supervised by Australia is the quality and quantity of products or services rather than intervention in the methods used by social capital to meet performance requirements so as to bring the initiative and creativity of social capital to full play. To be specific, the social capital takes charge of project quality management, management plan formulation, supervision data collection and supervision report preparation; the government department takes charge of project quality management review, technical standards formulation, social capital management plan and supervision report review, finance audit, and assessment, rewards and punishment implementation; the third party takes charge of independent audit, data collection and dispute treatment; product or service user has the right to feed using situations back to government departments and has channels to report profit damage situations. The supervision result shall be shown in reports. The supervision expenses are generally shared by government and social capital. However, if the results fail to meet supervision requirements, the expenses on re-detection will be covered by social capital.

(iv) Emphasize on guarantying reasonable profits of social capital

In PPP project, the power of active participation is to guarantee the reasonable profits of social capital. There are two cases for PPP projects driven by Australian Government. The first is profit of project, i.e. Usage-based or Availability-based mode. The usage-based mode is also known as Concession mode, which realizes reasonable profits such as highway, bridge and subway by charging users; for the availability-based mode, government pays social capital at lump sum or regularly according to requirement no regardless of actual demand and usage situations of the project after the project complied with government requirements and put into operation. In reality, the two cases are always combined to use. Government pays certain expenses and the remaining is collected from users. The second is that government surrenders part of the profits to social capital, such as additional profits of land. In PPP project of Royal Children's Hospital of Melbourne, in the beginning the State Government of Victoria negotiated with social capital that after the new hospital is completed and put into operation, the social capital can reconstruct and use former hospital to such as run supermarket or hotel. The income will belong to social capital, and tax preference can be enjoyed. However, the final ownership of land and all real estate property belongs to the government.

(v) Set public profit protection as preconditions to drive PPP mode

The Australian Government always sets public benefit protection as a precondition for PPP promotion. The PPP project promotion driven by government can help ease government fiscal restraint, improve product or service quality, optimize risk sharing, reduce construction cost, and promote economic growth and market economy, which is finally shown in protection of rights of all tax payers in Australia. Under the PPP mode, the social capital can more extensively participate in each stage including design, construction, financing, operation and maintenance to bring the technology, experience and initiative to full play. The government department lays the emphasis on comprehensive coordination, policy guidance, quality control and safety supervision, and targets at guaranteeing rights and profits of taxpayer to maximally improve public service quality. Compared with traditional infrastructure financing, the risks of construction period extension and over-spending budget are transferred to social capital. The expenditure of government on purchasing public service every year is fixed so as to improve certainty of government expenditure and further to improve controllability of government debts. Since the operation and maintenance of PPP project is undertaken by social capital, the social capital will actively improve project plan to control risks and costs rather than manufacturing in a rough way for limit of construction period. In that way, the legal rights and profits of the public are guaranteed on the whole.

III. Successful case of PPP mode in Australia - Plenary Group

(i) Company profile

Plenary Group is the pacemaker in the field of infrastructure PPP, and occupies about 30% of the Australian PPP project market. Since foundation in 2004, Plenary Group has built and been operating 37 key urban public infrastructure projects under PPP mode, with a total amount of AUD 24 billion. The bid winning rate is over 40%. The successful cases contain AUD 1.2 billion Australia Defense LEAP project, AUD 1 billion Gold Coast light rail, AUD 1.4 billion Melbourne Convention Center Project, AUD 1.7 billion Toowoomba Second Branch Line Project, AUD 1.27 Victoria State Cancer Center Project, AUD 288 million Biochemistry Research Center Project, and AUD 120 million Casey Hospital project. Plenary Group has won the honors of the Second Place of Global Sponsor (all PPP projects), Gold Price for Urban Construction, Best Project Sponsor, Annual Best Global PPP Project (W-N line of Sydney

Railway).

(ii) Analysis on company operation mode

In every PPP project, Plenary Group has participated in the entire process including design, construction, financing and maintenance as project sponsor, developer, financial advisor, long-term investor and assets manager. In bidding stage, firstly, Plenary Group, as sponsor, closely cooperates with government and partners to organize and finish bidding plan, and promotes completion of contract and financing; secondly, as the arranger of finance and business, Plenary Group coordinates relationship between the government, fund provider and partner, implements legal and business negotiation, and builds financial mode and taxation structure; thirdly, as the equity investor, Plenary Group absorbs social equity investor, and allies with partners and holds project equity. During construction and operation stage, in the aspect of construction and design, Plenary Group sets up SPV project company and the management level; in the aspect of service, the company plays the role of government and fund provider, and organizes specific project construction; in the aspect of parent company level, the company conducts well public relation and strategic media, normalizes business contract, guides project operation, and supervises financial operation of SPV project company.

(iii) Analysis on successful factors

The main factors for success made by Plenary Group are as follows: firstly, the management level of the Company has gotten abundant PPP project experiences from the beginning of 1990s, and finished over 40 urban construction infrastructure projects; secondly, Plenary Group has professional teams in project financing and investment field, owns many financial and investment consultants, and is supported greatly by business, engineering,

239

facility operation and public relation teams; thirdly, the Company holds equity in all projects, and strives to maintain long-term and active shareholder relation and serve as a sponsor, financial consultant, investor and assets manager of PPP project; fourthly, the Company designs long-term financial mode for PPP project, shows "profits and risks sharing" , and provides more accurate offer and more efficient financing; fifthly, the Company makes plan in time for possible problems of PPP project, and provides the most effective solutions; sixthly, Plenary Group has made a global deployment, and acquired vast success in important Asia- Pacific and Northern America markets.

IV. Insufficiencies of Australia PPP mode

(i) Access principle is difficult to control

The VFM principle of Australian PPP project is to sufficiently use respective advantages of government and social capital. However, it is a complex computation system to calculate VFM principle of PPP project by Public Sector Comparator method, and its application is difficult. This computing method values quantitative calculation and analysis, and depends on assumption or estimated data in aspects of investment, discount rate and risk sharing especially in the early stage when authentic and accurate data and materials are lacked. It is easy to generate deviation. Therefore, it is challengeable and difficult to control and quantize economic and social benefits of infrastructure construction project, sufficiently use respective advantages of government and social capital, and combine social responsibility, planning, coordination mechanism of the government and fund support, technical means, management efficiency and professional experiences of social capital to realize

VFM principle.

(ii) Project alternatives are less

Australia is a country with high PPP maturity. However, the projects under PPP mode are only dozens of percent in the infrastructure field. Although in many researches, PPP and privatization are divided, PPP is still deemed as a Trojan Horse for gradual privatization. For worries about privatization, PPP promotion and implementation is hindered to a certain degree. Moreover, under PPP mode, as restricted by contracts, the government is unable to adapt to the change of economic and social development speed, and to flexibly adjust to changes of public demands. Thus, PPP is not applicable to all fields, nor used to solve all problems. The project structure must be designed reasonably according to actual situations of the project.

(iii) Early effective communication of public-private side is difficult

The structure of PPP mode is more complex than that of the traditional mode, so in initiation stage, the Australian Government and social capitals need in-depth research or consulting, which will generate higher transaction costs and trend of opportunism. The government may, in order to attract social capital, firstly reduce various standards, and revise clauses after bidding is finished. Social capital may give favorable conditions to acquire project first, and negotiate after commencement. Many large-scale PPP projects in initiation stage in Australia, under concern of social public and pressure of supervision by public opinions, may spend a few years before enter actual operation stage due to the long communication and negotiation process of the government and social capital. Those may be potential risks for failure of PPP project, against long-term healthy development of PPP mode and actual guarantee of public benefits.

(iv) Financing support is insufficient

The financing cost of social capital in Australia is obviously higher than government debt cost. In Australian financial market, the repayment mode for 2-3 years refinancing arrangement of PPP projects is like the passing game, and 5-7 years refinancing problem is prominent. Among Australian PPP projects, the medium and long-term financing channel restrictions for social capital are more, and some projects cannot get stable medium and long-term fund support, which is bad for mobilizing enthusiasm of social capital to participate in PPP projects.

V. Enlightenment and recommendations on PPP mode in China

Under the new situation, the Chinese government faces the challenge of "three-stage overlapping" . On one hand, the Chinese government needs to digest adverse effects of early stimulation policies and control local government debts; on the other hand, it shall solve problems of employment and people's livelihood, and transfer economic growth mode. The third plenary session of the 18th CPC Central Committee proposed to make market play decisive role in resource configuration, and better bring government's role to full play. PPP mode is highly valued and becomes one of the ways to promote market-government cooperation. On May 19,2015, the General Office of the State Council forwarded the *Guiding Opinions on Promoting Public-Private Partnership Mode in Public Service Field* issued by the Ministry of Finance, Development and Reform Commission, and the People's Bank (known as the No.42 Document in the industry) to clarify application of PPP mode in public service fields such as energy, traffic and transportation, water conservancy, environmental protection, agriculture, forestry, science and technology, government-subsidized housing, medical care, hygiene, pension, education and culture, and lift PPP to a strategic high for market-government cooperation. Through the systematic research on experiences and insufficiencies of Australia infrastructure PPP mode field, the references to PPP mode promotion in China are provided in the following aspects.

(i) Strengthening top design from the national strategy level

Australia values linkage between PPP and target of national growth and social development. Infrastructure Australia emphasized repeatedly, in the report submitted to the Council of Australia Governments which particularly coordinates with federal, state and local government, that they should better make use of existing infrastructure construction, create new opportunity for capital investment, and eliminate bottleneck and gap hindering economic and social growth of Australia. For PPP mode promotion and application, China can extensively introduce social capital to participate in investment in public products and services, which copes with the national strategy of public innovation and venture, and is an important content of supply side structure reform. Therefore, China shall strengthen top design of PPP mode from the national strategy level, pay attention to implementation of national preferential project, economic benefits, social benefits and environmental benefits, balance the realization of public policy target and social capital profits target, show social public profits by public property of PPP mode and better urge realization of public policy target.

(ii) Reasonably confirming project selection standards

China follows the government-oriented market economic growth mode. Therefore, various levels of government affirm and appraise the public service demand extensively. Local government leaders own great power in project selection. The performance demand sometimes may be mixed up with public service demands, and relatively objective standards for project alternatives are lacked. On that basis, it is recommended to refer to experiences of PPP mode in Australia, issue special appraisal guidance on VFM for specific project, and compare government expenditure cost present value and public sector comparator during the entire life cycle to guarantee that PPP mode is the optimal choice to improve efficiency and reduce costs.

(iii) Sorting out government responsibilities

The success of Australian PPP mode lies in effective cooperation between government departments and social capital. In order to implement strategic decisions made by the Party Central Committee and the State Council, each level of government departments shall follow the same ideas, sufficiently know the important role of PPP in improving public service supply quality and promoting economic structure adjustment, actively transfer function orientation, control and supervise the responsible aspects, and particularly improve professional knowledge and skills of PPP. Moreover, it is necessary to strengthen coordination between ministries and commissions, and central and local departments, establish trans-department supervision mechanism, avoid overlapped supervisor, prevent from absence of supervisor, and improve government department segmentation. Only in this way can government departments and social capital truly cooperate, and adapt to great challenges brought by PPP mode for concept, governance structure, operation details and effective supervision in investment.

(iv) Perfecting legal and policy system

Although Australia applies Anglo-American legal system, through years' development, PPP mode has established complete and valid statutory law guarantee systems in terms of law and policy guidance rather than only being regulated by cases. China applies continental law systems, and shall sort out, revise, abolish existing and inapplicable laws, regulations or local provisions for PPP mode promotion and application in time, strive to issue unified PPP fundamental laws, and actively push higher level systematic legislation to solve unsmooth and conflicting problems of laws, regulations, department rules, local provisions and normative documents which seriously restrict the promotion of PPP mode.

(v) Introducing a third party to establish PPP project supervision and appraisal mechanism

In the whole-process PPP performance supervision system in Australia, the third party supervision and appraisal plays an important role. The Output and Outcome-based Performance Specification under joint efforts of the government, social capital and independent third party is used to make sure the quality of products or services provided by social capital and improve efficiency. The third party supervision and appraisal does not mean government supervision is unnecessary. The key point of government supervision is to formulate technical standards, check product or service quality, and review supervisory report and finance of social capital. The third party shall objectively and justly make independent audit, collect data and handle disputes. The systematic PPP project supervision and appraisal mechanism can combine profits demands of all stakeholders, strengthen information disclosure and social supervision, enhance transparency and public trust of PPP project and prevent possible moral hazards and black box operations.

References:

Report on Private Investment in Public Infrastructure: www.partnerships.vic.gov.au, 2012.9.12.

Meng Gang, "Research on Financial Cooperation of Four Countries along the South

Routine of the 21st Century Marine Silk Road", *Journal of Development-Oriented Finance Research*, 2016（1）.

Australian Ministry Of Finance, The Policy Principle About Using The Public-Private Partnership of Australian Government,2015（12）.

Linda M. English, "Public Private Partnerships in Australia: An Overview of Their Nature, Purpose, Incidence and Oversight", *UNSW Law Journal*, Volume 29（3）.

Liu Xiaokai, et al., "PPP from Global Perspective: Connotation, Mode, Practice and Problems", *International Economic Review*, 2015（4）.

Wu Shouhua, et al., "Analysis on Overseas PPP Situations and Restrictions", *Journal of Development-Oriented Finance Research*, 2015（1）.

Meng Gang, "Study on International Capacity Cooperation of China in Australia", *Journal of Development-Oriented Finance Research*, 2016（3）.

Miraftab F., "Public-Private Partnerships: The Trojan Horse of Neoliberal Development?", *Journal of Planning Education and Research*, Vol24, No.1, pp. 89-101,2004.

Glendinning R., "The concept of value for money", *International Journal of Public Sector Management*, 2007,01（01）.

Mo Xiaolong, et al., "Experience and Enlightenment of PPP Development in Australia," *China State Finance*, 2013（6）.

Xing Huiqiang, "Government Responsibilities in PPP Mode", *Law Science*, 2015(11).

Yu Benrui, et al., "Domestic and Overseas Practice and Enlightenment of PPP Mode", *Modern Management Science*, 2014（8）.

Meng Gang, "Approach of Australia Science and Technology Innovation Strategy Integrating to China and Financing Cooperation", *Globalization*, 2016（7）.

Dai Zheng zong, "Australia: PPP Beats Government Purchase", China Government Procurement News, Jan.20,2015.

Liang Qingxue, "Typical Domestic and Overseas PPP Project Case and Enlightenment", *Economics of Agricultural Engineering*, 2015（8）.

Meng Gang, "Australia Northern Development Strategy Brings New Opportunity for Development-oriented Finance", *China Banking Industry*, 2016（4）.

246

Research On Investment Cooperation of China-funded Enterprises in the Field of Energy and Mineral Resources in Australia

I. China-funded enterprises meet periodical investment opportunities in the field of energy and mineral resources

(i) The price of bulk energy and mineral resources commodities show a new round of inflection point of "bull market"

After the financial crisis in 2008, the price of global bulk commodities such as energy and mineral resources dropped seriously, and stepped into "bear market" . Since 2016, it could be seen that the new round "bull market" of bulk energy and mineral resource commodities is coming. Firstly, the price of crude oil, iron ore, coal, copper, lead-zinc, iron and steel rises sharply, and characteristics of short-term demands of bulk commodities are obvious. Secondly, according to analysing the long-term demand, the global economy develops steadily. Manufacturing industries in countries such as America become prosperous. And the economic growth rate of many important economies in the world doubled on Quarter-on-Quarter basis. China's suppiy-side structural reform has achieved initial success. the Belt & Road construction revitalizes global infrastructure construction. The demands of bulk commodities Demands have provided sustainable power for vigorous growth.

(ii) Foreign-trade dependence of strategic mineral resources in China is high

China's mineral resources highly rely on foreign trade, which has become a prominent bottleneck restricting economic and social development. In order to guarantee strategic demands of national economy, national defense safety and development of strategic emerging industry, the State Council passed *China Mineral Resources Planning (2016-2020)* in November 2016. 24 mineral products such as petroleum and natural gas were first listed into strategic mineral directory, these 24 mineral products include petroleum, natural gas, shale gas, coal, coal-bed mine, uranium, iron chrome, copper, aluminum, gold, nickel, tungsten, stamnun,molybdenum,stibium,cobalt ,lithium, rare earth, zirconium, phosphorus, sylvite, scaly graphite, fluorite. The Planning emphasizes to list 24 mineral products such as petroleum, natural gas, coal, rare earth and scaly graphite into strategic mineral product directory as key objects of mineral resources macro-control and supervision management. The planning systematically analyzes supply-demand and resources situations of foreign and domestic mineral products, and strengthens safety warning capacity coping to international serious conflict resources, and strengthens guiding and differential management in aspects of resource configuration, financial investment, significant projects and mining land to improve resource safety supply capacity and development and utilization level.

(III) China-funded enterprises Should hold the periodical opportunity for investing in the fields of energy and mineral resource

In a sense, the pricing right of global bulk commodities is decided by the enterprise groups with maximum resource occupation. Taking iron ore as an example. The current transactions in global maritime transportation of iron ore market is about 1.3 billion ton every year. As a great exporter of iron ore, Australia exports about 800 million ton every year. Brazil exports nearly 400 million ton, while China imports about 1 billion ton. The import amount of iron ore in China is less than that of crude oil, ranking the second of single bulk commodity import amount. However, China has no the pricing right, and greatly relys on foreign trade. Based on the historical trend analysis, the bull market situation of bulk energy and mineral resources commodities is featured by continuously growing market price. The rising period should keep for at least five years. The investment risk in the initial period of bull market is small. Therefore, in the new round trend of great global economy development, China-funded enterprises should consider the situation and hold the strategic opportunities of the time to take the initiative in global energy and mineral resources market from the origin, and break through the bottlenecks restricting economic and social development of China.

II. PEST analysis on investment of China-funded enterprises in Australian energy and mineral fields under the new situation

(i) Joint construction of the Belt & Road is the new situation under framework of China-Australia government cooperation

In November 2014, President Xi Jinping delivered a speech in Canberra, the Capital of Australia. He proposed South Pacific region is the natural extension of the "21st Century Maritime Silk Road", and meanwhile announced the strategic partnership between China and Australia became the comprehensive strategic partnership. China sincerely welcomes Australia to join in the construction of Maritime Silk Road, and promote greater development of economic and trade cooperation. In April 2016, President Xi Jinping and Premier Li Keqiang announced the linkage between the Belt & Road and "Developing North Australia", and linkage between Innovation-driven strategy of China and Scientific and Innovative strategy of Australia with Turnbull, Premier of Australia, who visited Beijing.

Australia is an important partner of China for investment in the field of energy and mineral resources. With vast land and less population, Australia stepped in a developed country early. In 2015, the GDP of Australia is about USD 1.598 trillion, and per capita GDP of Australia is about USD 66,580. Australia is the 12th largest economy in the world. Australia has a stable political and legal environment, a normalized market mechanism, a reasonable industrial structure, more investable fields, a stable return on investment, advanced intenational technologies and management experiences, hence, it plays the role as a bridge between Asian-Pacific region and European and American developed countries. In metal minerals field, China-funded enterprises mainly invest in Oceania and North America. Australia, belongs to Oceania, is the main destination country for overseas investment of China's metal mineral enterprises. During 2005-2015, Australia became the second largest destination for direct global investment of China. During 2013-2015, China became the first overseas direct investment source country of Australia.

Table 1 Macroscopic Economic Data of Australia in 2004, 2009 and 2014

Year	GDP (USD Billion)	Economic growth rate(%)	Population(Ten Thousand)	GDP Per Capita(USD)
2004	613	4.2	2,013	30,452
2009	900	1.5	2,169	41,494
2014	1,444.4	2.5	2,349	61,728

Data Source: IMF

(II) PEST analysis on investment of China-funded enterprises in the field of energy and minerals in Australia

In order to better study macro environment that China-funded enterprises invest in the energy and mineral field in Australia under new situations, the author will analyze macro environment that China-funded enterprises to invest in the energy and mineral field in Australia and the influence on formulation of strategic target in aspects of political factors, economic factors, social factors and technological factors.

1. Political factors: Comprehensive strategic cooperation between China and Australia brings new opportunities to China-funded enterprises

Under the background of the Belt & Road cooperation, leaders of both China and Australia attach high importance to build comprehensive strategic cooperation framework from the government level, and guarantee the maximum return on investment of enterprises. In Oceania, Australia and New Zealand are the earliest countries which establish a comprehensive strategic partnership with China. The China-Australia strategic economic dialogue gradually deeps in higher level. The governments of China and Australia have reached an agreement to further improve the fields and levels of cooperations by linkage of development strategies of the two countries, particularly to consolidate traditional cooperation between China and Australia in the energy and mineral resource field. In April 2016, Premier Turnbull of Australia visited China soon after took office, and deeply discussed economic and trade cooperation between China and Australia with President Xi Jinping and Premier Li Keqiang. In some sense, the linkage between the Belt & Road proposal of China and Developing Northern Australia, and the linkage between Innovative-driven development strategy of China and"National Innovation and Science Agenda" of Australia lay firm foundation for traditional cooperation between the two countries in the energy and mineral resource field. Under new circumstances, the comprehensive strategic linkage between governments of China and Australia brings unprecedented opportunities for China-funded enterprises' investment cooperation in the energy and mineral resource field in Australia.

2. Economic factors: free trade agreement brings new conveniences for investment of China-funded enterprises

In June 2015, governments of China and Australia signed a *Free Trade Agreement*. According to the FTA, firstly, in the field of goods, products of both sides accounting for 85.4% of export volume will implement zero tariff when FTA takes effect. After the transition period, the tax items proportion and trade volume proportion with zero tariff in Australia will reach 100%, while in China will reach 96.8% and 97% respectively, more higher than the 90% tax reduction level agreed in FTA. Secondly, in the field of services, the Australian make promises to open service department to China by the mode of negative list after FTA takes effect. It is the first country in the world making service trade commitment by negative list to China. China will open service department to Australia by positive list. Moreover, Australia also makes special arrangement for China in aspects of holidays and work mechanism. Thirdly, in the field of investment, both parties mutually offer most-favored-nation treatment after FTA takes effect. Meanwhile, Australia lowers the investment review threshold for Chinese enterprises in Australia and makes convenient arrangements. Fourthly, the FTA regulates to promote exchange and cooperation between two sides in dozens of fields of "21st Century Economy and Trade Topics" such as e-business, government purchase, intellectual property right and competition.

3. Social factors: multiple immigrant cultures create the new environment for the foundation and development of China-funded enterprises

Australia is a country of immigrants from the beginning of foundation. It has multiple foreign nations and cultures. Regardless of political and ideological elements made by minority negative politicians, the national culture is not exclusive in essence, and featured by vivid diversified immigrant cultures. There is no narrow nationalist culture centering at local culture in Australia. On the contrary, Australia is comprehensive and open, and it encourages residents to use their own languages and keep their own culture. In September 2016, a forum on racial diversity in political circle was held in Sydney, Australia. Eugenia Grammatikakis, the Acting Chairwoman of the Commonwealth Minority Ethnic Community Committee, said currently about 1/4 Australian were born overseas, and at least one parent of the other 1/4 Australian were born overseas. Thus, all political parties in Australia must make more endeavors to guarantee the profits of ethnic minorities that can be represented truly. Moreover, legal system of Australia is complete. In Australia, laws are available, fully observed and strictly enforced and that lawbreakers are duly punished in all aspects from food, housing to national economic life. Complete, justice and transparent laws can be used as basis for investment and operation, private property protection, consumer protection, criminal justice, civil dispute, foreign investment, traffic management, state election, public administration, diplomacy and protection of women and children's rights. The multiple immigrant culture and complete legal system in Australia, which create harmonious environment for foundation and development of China-funded enterprises. Therefore, China-funded enterprises will not be rejected due to their Chinese nationality, and can make local residents and government sufficiently realize their intention of investment is sincere with mutual benefits and win-win results through communication, integration and interaction, and they are not threatening and hazardous. In that way, they can create localized operating environment for long-term development.

4. Technological factors: technical innovation linkage creates the new atmosphere for technical cooperation between Chinese and Australian enterprises

In April 2016, President Xi Jinping, Premier Li Keqiang and Premier of Australia, who visited China, announced the linkage between China's innovation-driven development strategy and Australia's "National Innovation and Science Agenda". Australia plans to set five Landing Pads overseas such as Shanghai, San Francisco and Tel Aviv to help newly-founded Australian enterprises set foot in international markets and develop to enterprisewith high growth and high return. The Torch High Technology Industry Development Center, Ministry of Science & Technology jointly launched UNSW Torch Innovation Park project with University of New South Wales. According to several global scientific and technical revolutions, technological innovation is always the important strategic support for improving social productivity and comprehensive national strength. The scientific and technical revolution is driven by social demands, and it will promote great development of social economy.Countries seizing preemptive opportunities from the revolution will surely become leaders of world economy. Australia is a great exporter of resources, energy, agricultural products and healthy products, while China is the largest consumption market and has great manufacturing power. It should be mentioned that the cooperation between two countries in the field of technological innovation is complementary and practical. The powerful combination between Chinese and Australian enterprises is the necessary way to jointly lead new world scientific and technological revolution under the background of globalization.

III. Energy and mineral reserve of Australia is prominent in the world

(i) Global status of Australia in the field of energy and mineral resource

1. Multiple energy and mineral resources of Australia almost on the top of the world

Australia has abundant natural resources, and reserve of multiple energy and mineral resources almost on the top of the world. It is one of countries with the highest per capita occupation of the world's mineral resources. It takes lead in global mineral products production and export. Among the products, the production of bauxite, alumina, rutile and zirconite occupies the first place in the world, the production of gold, iron ore, lead, lithium, manganese ore, tungsten and zinc occupies the second place in the world, the production of ilmenite and uranium occupies the third place in the world, the production of black coal (also the largest exporter), nickel and silver occupies the fourth place in the world and the production of aluminum, lignite and copper occupies the fifth place in the world.

For reserve of proved mineral resources with economic mining value, the gold, iron ore, lead, nickel, rutile, silver, uranium, zinc and Zr resources occupies the first place in the world, reserve of bauxite, lignite, cobalt, ilmenite and tantalum occupies the second place in the world, reserve of copper and lithium resources occupies the third place in the world, thorium reserve occupies the fourth place in the world, reserve of black coal and manganese ore occupies the fifth place in the world, The reserve of bauxite is about 5.3 billion ton, of iron ore is 14.6 billion ton, of black coal is 40.3 billion ton, of lignite is 30 billion ton, of lead is 22.9 million ton, of nickel is 22.6 million ton, of silver is 41,400t, of tantalum is 40,800t, of zinc is 41 million ton, and of gold is 55.7 million ton. Besides, Australia has sedimentary basins covering area of 16 million square kilometers, and the area of coastal shelf is as twice as inland area. Its undersea oil and gas reserve is considerable. The proved reserve of crude oil is 1.108 billion barrels, and salable natural gas is 89 trillion c.f.

2. The cost of energy and mineral resource production in Australia at low level in the world

For the cost of the production, the production costs of large-scale mining enterprises in Australia are at a lower level in the world. Taking iron ore as an example. In the past 10 years, the grade of iron ore in Australia kept at 60% with low mining cost, more higher than the 33% average level in China. Mining cost of large-scale mines such as Rio Tinto and BHP Billiton is about USD 30/Ton. Before 2013, the mining cost of later development enterprises such as FMG is between USD 50-60/ton. In recent years, due to the decreasing cost and the increasing benefit, the current mining cost reaches nearly USD 30/

Ton. Comparatively, the iron ore mining cost in China is about USD 130/Ton.

Taking lead-zinc ore as another example. The grade of lead-zinc ore in Australia is high, and most of which can be mined in open air. Therefore, the mining cost is low. For instance, the Cannington Mine in northwest Queensland is the largest ag-pb mine in the world with the lowest cost, grade of lead is 10.4%, grade of zinc is 3.88%, and silver content is 455g/t. The Brucken Mountain lead-zinc-silver mine in New South Wales is of large reserve (lead and zinc metal content is 3.9579million ton), high grade (grade of zinc is 9.4%, grade of lead is 7.3%, grade of silver is 89g/ton), and easy exploitation. However, the price of crude oil and LNG in Australia is high, and has no competitiveness in the world. Development cost of mature oil field is about USD 60-70/bbl, and LNG cost is almost in the highest level in the world, about USD 12-16/MMBtu.

(II) The distribution of energy and mineral resources in Australia

1. Western Australia

Western Australia is the mining state of Australia. The mineral resources are of large reserve, extensive distribution, shallow burial and easy exploitation. The mining industry has formed scale, and mining equipment is of large size and high automation degree. The iron ore output of Western Australia occupies 1/4 of global output, bauxite output occupies about 1/3 of global output, copper and gold output occupies about 70%, nickel output occupies of 90%, crude oil and LNG respectively 66% and 57%, and natural gas about 92% of total output in Australia. Mining areas in Western Australia are Pilbara, Koolyanobbing, Cockatoo, Koolanooka and Jackfor iron ore, Jundee, Kalgoorlie,Kanowna, Plutonic,SunriseDam and YilgamSouth for gold, Hollandaire and De Grussa for copper, Yeelirrie for uranium ore, Mount Weld for rare earth ore. The Northwest Shelf, Gorgon, Browse, Wheatstone and Pluto are in fluential LNG projects in entire Australia.

2. Queensland

Queensland is the most important area of the black coal prodution (metallurgical coal and steam coal), and owns over 30 billion ton black coal, which accounts for 59% of total reserve in entire Australia. Moreover, Queensland owns 2/3 zinc ore resources of Australia, and 13% copper ore resources. Main mining areas in Queensland are coal mining areas in Bowen Basin, Galilee Basin and Surat Basin, lead-zinc-silver mining areas in Cannington, NWBrooks Range, Iberian Pyrite Belt, George Fisher, Black Star and Hilton, copper molybdenum mining area in Kalman and Mount Isa, and Weipa alumina mining area.

3. Northern Territory

Northern Territory has abundant resources of the uranium, bauxite, manganese and lead-zinc ore. 12 mines are under mining, which produce uranium, bauxite, manganese, gold, iron ore, and phosphate. Northern Territory possesses the world's second largest uranium mine in Ranger, leading manganese mine in Groote Eylandt and Bootu Creek, Callie, one of the largest gold mines in Australia, McCarthy River mine with largest zinc-silver reserve, and large-scale bauxite mine in Gove.

4. South Australia

South Australia has abundant copper and uranium resources. The cooper reserve is more than 10 billion ton, and uranium reserve makes up about 80% of total reserve in Australia and nearly 30% in the world. Main mining areas in South Australia are mainly world first Olympic Dam, Beverley and Honeymoon uranium ore, world third Olympic Dam copper mine.

5. New South Wales (NSW)

NSW owns gold, silver, copper, lead and zinc ores. Main mining areas are Cadia copper-gold mine and Northparkes copper mine. Ore products with exploitation opportunities in NSW are copper, gold, zinc-lead, silver, Sn-W, nickel, iron, rutile-zircon-ilmenite ore. Furthermore, coal resources such as black coal are abundant in Sydney-Gunnedah Basin. There are over 60 mines are in operation and over 30 development plans.

6. State of Victoria

State of Victoria has abundant gold and base metals, such as iron, steel, copper, nickel, aluminum, lead, zinc, Sn and tungsten. The main mining areas are BCD Resources NL copper mine, Jabiru Metals Ltd copper-lead-zinc mine, Stawell gold mine and Fosterville gold mine.

IV. Case analysis on investment cooperation of China-funded enterprises in the field of energy and mineral in Austraila

From 1980 to 2005, China-funded enterprises carried out few investment activities in Australia. In this stage, the investment cooperation of China in Australia had not formed to scale. Typical cases are joint venture project of Sinosteel Rio Tinto Channer Iron Mine, investment of CITIC in Portland Aluminum Manufacturer. From 2006 to 2012, China-funded enterprises started investing in Australia massively. In this stage, China's investment cooperation projects are centralized in energy and mineral fields. Accumulatively 73% of total investment was used for mining industry, 18% in natural gas, including Minmetals' purchasing OZ Australia, Yanzhou Coal Mining's purchasing Felix Resources Australia, CITIC Pacific Irone Mine Project in Western Australia, CNOOC Curtis LNG project. Since 2013, it is a depression and equalization period for China-funded enterprises to investment in Australia energy and mineral resources field.

(i) Sinosteel Rio Tinto Channer Iron Mine Joint Venture Project

From 1973, Rio Tinto, one of the top three mining giants in the world, became the first foreign enterprise exporting iron ore to China. So far, Rio Tinto has accumulatively supplied over 1.8 billion ton iron ore products to China. The Chinese market contributed 40% operating income of Rio Tinto. Sinosteel and Rio Tinto signed a cooperative agreement officially in 1987 for Channer iron ore joint venture project. In the joint venture project, Sinosteel owns 40% equity, and Rio Tinto owns 60% equity. This project locates at Pilbara Region, Western Australia. It is the earliest overseas mining investment project of Chinese enterprises, and also the project with the longest cooperation between Chinese and Australian enterprises.

This project is a typical case of successful cooperation between China-funded enterprises and global mining giants by mode of joint venture but not holding. It has been one of the most profitable businesses of Sinosteel Group. In the beginning of cooperation, the original output of the project should be 200 million ton iron ore, and the project should supply 100 million ton to Sinosteel every year. Later, 50 million ton output is expanded. In April 2016, under witness of Premier Li Keqiang and Premier Turnbull, this project is exended to the end of 2019. In accordance with the agreement, total output of Channer iron ore project will add another 30 million ton. On that basis, both parties also signed additional exclusive sales agreement. From 2016 to 2021, Sinosteel will sell no more than 40 million ton iron ore for Rio Tinto.

(ii) Minmetals is purchasing OZ of Australia

OZ Mining of Australia was newly incorporated in 2008 after acquisition andreorganization. It is the third mining company of Australia and the second manufacturer of zinc ore over the world. The total amount of zinc resources it owns is about 18.74% of proved zinc reserves in China, and the amount lead resources is about 6.28% of proved lead reserves in China. Moreover, it owns copper, gold and silver mine with large output. In June 2009, through great endeavors, Minmetals reassured Australian government, the shareholder of enterprise and local residents when Chinese investment and acquisition is not understood and supported by overseas countries, successfully acquired OZ Mining of Australia, and integrated target company to MMG. The Company realized profits of USD 192 million in current year, and USD 747 million in next year. This project is a typical case for overseas acquisition of China-funded enterprises. By successful acquisition, integration, operation and management, mutual benefits and win-win are realized by both parties. It becomes a symbolic bridge for investment cooperation in mining field between China and Australia.

The acquisition time of this project is in the dense period for acquisition carried out by Chinese companies in Australia. Hualing increased shares of FMG, Anshan Iron and Steel Group invested GINDALBIE, and Aluminum Corporation of China Limited invested Rio Tinto simultaneously. The large-scale acquisition of China-funded enterprises caused revolt of local nationalists in Australia. Leader of Australian Opposition Party firstly launched an attack in parliament, and called to "better distinguish main customers from owners" . Thus continuous fierce opposition broke out. Some media hyped "Chinese Resources Plunder" , and non-economic factors such as ideology and political factors were involved in market behavior. The management team of Minmetals strictly insisted on and abided by international business rules, declared themselves at

261

low profile, and sincerely mediated among Australian government, Board of Directors and Higher Management of OZ Mining, visited Australia Federation of Trade Unions, lobbied and gained support of the Opposition Party, and corresponded to foreign fund investment review commission to explain specific situations. Finally, it gained support of relevant Australian parties. By voting in Annual Shareholder's Meeting of OZ Mining, the acquisition transaction succeeded. The affirmative vote rate is as high as 92%.

(iii) Yanzhou Coal Mining's purchasing Felix Resources

Felix Resources is an Australian enterprise, which mainly engages in coal mining and exploitation. Products are mainly steam coal, PCI coal and coking coal; the coal assets are four coal mines in operation, two coal mines under development, and four coal exploration projects. The total quantity of resource shall be 2.5 billion ton, and total reserve shall be 500 million ton. Main customers are Asian, European, American and local Australian iron and steel manufacturers and power generators. Yanzhou Coal Mining is held by Yankuang Group. It was listed in Hong Kong, New York and Shanghai respectively in 1998. The total asset in 2008 was over 32 Billion Yuan. It is one of the leaders of coal industry in China. However, coal resources are short, which is a significant factor for restricting development of the company. The intensive desire for high quality coal resources is the inner motivation for Yanzhou Coal Mining to firmly carry out overseas acquisition.

During the acquisition process, all social sectors of Australia have a positive attitude. One of the important reasons is that the leading deep exploration technology of Yanzhou Coal Mining can make up blank of local technology and improve coal mining rate. In proved coal reserves in Australia, the thick coal seams over 6m is about 58%. Most of coal seams are mined by opencast working, generally to 4-6m. The recovery rate of thick coal seams is generally lower than 50%, and sometimes lower than 30%, causing serious wastes. Mining Society of Australian Institute of Energy has always promoted underground mining actively to improve coal recovery rate. Yanzhou Coal Mining is one of Chinese enterprises exporting most mining technologies overseas, and it owns over 60 domestic and overseas patents. The "fully mechanized top coal caving hydraulic support" technology is the core of fully mechanized top coal caving production process, and can solve worldwide technical difficulties of thick coal seam mining. It is the optimal technology for medium and thick coal seam mining. The new technology forms new competitive advantages between cooperative parties. Both the acquirer and acquiree wish to acquire the most desirable resources from each other. After the success of the acquisition transaction, Yanzhou Coal Mining and target company realized complementary effect in aspects of technology, market, patent, products, management and culture, and greatly improved competitive strength.

(iv) CNOOC Curtis LNG project

Curtis Project locates at Queensland, Australia, and is the first world-level LNG project with coal-bed mine as resources. The proved and controlled CBM reserves of the project is about 350m^3. After liquidation, the LNG will be sold to Asian Pacific countries such as China and Japan. BG Group is the largest shareholder of the project. CNOOC Gas & Power Group owns 25% equity of upstream assets and 50% equity of the first LNG production line of middle stream liquidation plant. It is the second largest equity owner and investor of the entire project. The Curtis project is developed by two phases. The first phase is from 2011 to the middle of 2015, the phase I project is constructed and put into operation; the second phase started in April 2014, and planned to end in 2018 by rolling development. The CBM generated from upstream will be transported to middle stream LNG plant by long-term pipeline for liquidation, storage and exportation.

Curtis Project is the first full industrial chain investment in overseas LNG project. CNOOC and BG Group reached an agreement to purchase 3.6 million ton LNG from LNG project of BG Group in Australia for 20 years. The Curtis Project will enhance China's rights of speech in LNG production and distribution, and be of great significance inguarantying energy safety, optimizing energy structure and improving global competitiveness of LNG industry. Although China does not lack of CBM resources, the exploration and development of CBM in China are very slow since many mining entities are not coal mining enterprises, and CBM and coal mining rights are overlapped. The competitive natural gas resources acquired from the world will make active contribution to natural gas industry development in China and guarantee clean energy supply in China.

(v) Western Australia iron ore project of CITIC Pacific

The SINO IRON project of CITIC Pacific in Western Australia is a project of China-funded enterprise suffering serious difficulties in overseas investment in energy and mineral resource field. The feasibility of this project in early stage is insufficient, and also the difficulty of magnetite mining in Australia is underestimated. MCC, as EPC of the project, constructed hurriedly, and budget is overspent at a large amount. The construction period delayed and operation is unsuccessful. The loss on exchange rate is large, and derivative trading is frustrated as well. Palmer, the Australian partner of the project, has large ethical risks. It publicly showed hostile attitude toward Chinese Partner and even China in interview, and generated litigation disputes with CITIC Pacific.

SINO IRON project pushed CITIC Pacific to improve technical level and management capacity. CITIC Pacific strived to reverse the passive situation by cost decreasing and benefit increasing. This project has started to export concentrated ore and iron fines to domestic special steel plant of CITIC Pacific and other Chinese iron and steel enterprises. Currently, all six production lines of the project have fully put into operation stage. The target of CITIC Pacific is to improve output. In order to realize scale benefits and become one of the lowest cost concentrated fines manufacturers in China. Apparently, China-funded enterprises may not be smooth when investing overseas. However, by summarizing experiences of failures, they can generate motivation under pressure so as to improve comprehensive capacity.

V. Suggestions on driving investment cooperation of China-funded enterprises in Australia energy and minerals' field

(i) Accurately master essence of supply side structural reform, and make progress steadily

In business circles five contents of supply side structural reform are "removing low-profit and high-pollution capacity, inventory and lever, lowering cost and making up shortcoming", and investment project overseas energy and mineral resources shall suspend to promote. The author believes, to certain degree, such opinion misunderstands the nature and essence of the five contents. They may miss the best opportunity to go bottom fishing when bulk global energy and mineral commodity price bottoms out. In short, the key points of the five contents are lowering cost and making up shortcoming except first three aspects with regard to the removing. If China-funded enterprises decisively merge overseas high quality energy and mineral resources at proper price of bulk energy and mineral commodities, they will surely effectively reduce industrial economy cost of enterprises, make up shortcomings of national economy and even control pricing right of global bulk energy and mineral commodities. The author works in Australia since the end of 2012, and has witnessed the fluctuation cycle for bulk energy and mineral commodity price, and seen various cost decreasing and benefit increasing measures adopted by energy and mineral resources transnational groups to cope with periodic fluctuation. Taking iron ore price as an example, the price reached about USD 170/ton in the end of 2012, and then dropped to USD 40/ton in the beginning of 2016. During iron ore price falling, several energy and mineral transnational groups such as Rio Tinto and BHP Billiton, instead of passive waiting, adopted a series of cost decreasing and benefits increasing measures such as technical improvement, output regulation and market expansion. After consolidation for a long time, the price of iron ore has rebounded to USD 80/ton by the end of 2016. During the snow-slide periodic fluctuation of bulk commodities' price such as iron ore, the transnational groups are not knocked down, but instead, they improved their ability of operation, management and risk handling. The more disconcerting problem is that these transnational groups still control large amount of high quality energy and mineral resources. Therefore, the pricing right of bulk energy and mineral commodities is still firmly controlled by the transnational groups of supply side.

For "Progress in stability", the key point is "stability", the purpose is "progress", and mode is overall planning in an alternative way. The author believes important energy and mineral resources with high foreign-trade dependence and concerning national interest and people's livelihood shall be systematically coordinated by national authorities, with extensive participation of China-funded enterprises and scientific research institutions. It shall be clarified to rights and obligation relationship between each party involved, unified decision making and action mechanism. All parties shall observe and study periodic fluctuation actively, listen to opinions of front-line workers, make repeated research and scientific verification, cooperate with each other for overseas business, and decisively control overseas high quality energy and mineral resources by reasonable price. After all, the decision of "bottom fishing" cannot be accomplished in an action, but can be made by resolute decision making and decisively make actions after long-term observation and mastering rules. The author wrote a paper "Research on Financial Cooperation of Four Countries along the Southern Route of the 21st Century Marine Silk Road" in the end of 2015, and believed the sharp falling of international bulk commodities price would bring more problems to resource exporters, including sharp currency devaluation, foreign exchange shortage, inflation or weakening external loan redemption ability by sovereignty. However, according to analysis from another point of view, the global energy and mineral market is depressed currently. Quite a lot of energy and mineral resources are priced reasonably and even underestimated seriously. This is a precious opportunity for China-funded enterprises to participate in cooperation and competition in global energy and mineral market under the Belt & Road strategy. Stable funds of bulk commodities such as energy and minerals are recommended to support China-funded enterprises to carry out business cooperation by the mode of equity investment priority under mutual benefits and win-win situations; while help ease collapse impact of bulk commodity price falling on economy of exporter, enhance right of speech and even dominant right of China-funded enterprises in pricing of international bulk commodities such as energy and mineral resources.

(ii) Form resultant force targeting to participate in and lead pricing right

Most industry prospective believe fair value of iron ore shall be USD 40-50 (CIF fair value), and in next 2 or 3 years, the iron ore will keep the trend of over supply. On that basis, although commodity price may fluctuate up and down around fair value and deviation from fair value in a short time, the current price of iron ore is greatly higher than fair value under excessive supply for demand; besides, energy and mineral transnational groups such as upstream iron ore traders gain super profits while downstream steel mills are at loss. Such circumstance is abnormal. Apparently, the pricing right mechanism of iron ore goes against protection of downstream steel mills' profits. The pricing right is generally for commodity manufacturer, and refers to price increase ability of manufacturers without affecting demand quantity. As for buyers, the ability to lower purchase price or acquire more preferential conditions under certain purchase quantity is known as "bargaining ability". Therefore, pricing right is controlled by enterprises occupying high quality energy and mineral resources, fundamentally.

The several energy and mineral resources transnational groups in the world are of a relation, which both competition and cooperation exists. For instance, CVRD and Rio Tinto reached cross-shareholding agreement with clear purpose to control pricing right so as to gain unreasonable monopoly profits from supply side. Chinese enterprises shall clearly know such situation, and aim for pricing right of energy and mineral resources such as iron ore. China-funded enterprises shall cooperate with each other to strive for profits, and take actions decisively in proper time to occupy high quality energy and mineral resources, control pricing right, and at least improve right of speech. In the case of China-funded enterprises occupy higher proportion of quality energy and mineral resources, supply side will change, and several energy and mineral transnational groups are forced to change unreasonable pricing right mechanism, so as to urge energy and mineral resource price approaching fair value. In a word, it is necessary to sufficiently play advantages of government-oriented market economy in China, coordination skills of government department and powerful executive capacity of state-owned enterprises. Command, strategic departments and execution departments shall cooperate to plan first, form resultant force, and reach the expected target of effectively affecting energy and mineral resource pricing right mechanism to the maximum degree.

(iii) Investment plan shall be practical, and technical details shall be controlled by expert team

When investing in energy and mineral resource fields in Australia, China-funded enterprise must rely on expert group, and formulate practical investment plan. The technical details shall be controlled by experts.

The first is to deeply study and master the target country and market. The investment environment of target country decides whether is suitable for entering of foreign capital. The openness degree, political pattern, legal environment, industrial access threshold, foreign exchange and labor policies, religious custom, trade usage and resident communities in target country shall be studied deeply. In Australia, the political system is stable, regime change is legal and ordered, investment environment is favorable, economy is highly developed, and industrial structure is reasonable. However, the "China Threat Theory" affects relationship between China and Australia to a certain degree. Minority politicians censured China for islands construction without basis, made gestures on South Sea issue, and even thought selling key assets to China-funded enterprises may cause boycott of the public. Therefore, China-funded enterprises shall sufficiently communicate with government department such as foreign capital review committee, main parties, labor union organizations and social residents to avoid a wild goose chase after inputting large amount of costs in early stage.

Secondly, early stage feasibility study report shall be highly emphasized. The first is to sufficiently know energy and mineral resources situations to be merged, such as endowment of minerals, grade and mineable degree; technical teams shall work on information collection, filtration and verification to guarantee mineral resource endowment and authentic and reliable grade. The second is to study relevant issues involved in operation of mineral development project, such as climate, hydrology, vegetation and other geographical conditions where deposit locates, whether meet the requirement of infrastructure conditions such as road, wharf and bridge for project implementation, and whether transportation conditions match with output. The third is to pay attention to environment and labor protection. Must be sure to follow the green, friendly and sustainable development way, and attach high importance to ecological benefits and social benefits. Problems such as vegetation reclamation, sewage treatment, waste residue stacking, environmental cost accounting, sufficient local labor, source and visa of technicians introduced shall be considered. It also shall be guaranted the life of local residents free from influence of development behaviors of the project.

Thirdly, expert group shall be trusted and depended on. The features of energy and mineral resource project are more aspects and complex problems involved, large investment in infrastructure construction period, step by step, long development time and unforeseeable accidents. Therefore, the problems incurred may not only affect each other, but also affect the situation as a whole. The responsibility of management level is in charge of decision-making of China-funded enterprises and finally make decisions on operation after comprehensively considering factors of all aspects. The decision-making level shall know how to judge and use people. A powerful expert team shall be treated as think tank for decision making, such as experts in technology, finance, law, public relation, negotiation as well as intermediaries familiar with local situations. The program design for entire project development, investment, construction, operation, transportation and sales shall extensively involved in and repeatedly demonstrated by expert team to guarantee scientific, accurate and serious decision made by leaders.

(IV)Setting up bank-enterprise cooperation platform to avoid funding mismatch and guarantee the stable cash flow

The field of mineral resources is a typical fund, technology and management intensive industry, and particularly needs long-term stable supports of large-amount capital. With deepening of "going abroad" strategy and implementation of the Belt & Road strategy, policy-based financial institutions, such as China Development Bank, Export-Import Bank of China and the Silk Road Fund as well as commercial banks, create innovated financial products to China-funded enterprises for investing overseas coal and mineral resources field, provide more convenient comprehensive financial services. China-funded enterprises shall master the essence of open-up policies, foreign capital approval and supporting policies of China, use encouragement policies sufficiently and favorably, and strive for great support of financial institutions to the largest degree.

When investing overseas energy and mineral resource field, China-funded enterprises shall avoid funding mismatch, long-term use of short-term loan and technical tight cash flow caused by manmade reasons during the project construction period. The capital market of Australia is highly developed, and the proportion of financial industries for grossing national economic aggregate is the largest. It owns the second largest stock market in Asian Pacific area. The global trade volume of AUD ranks the fifth. When investing energy and mineral resource field in Australia, China-funded enterprises shall play advantages and role of development-oriented finance, policy-based finance in China and commercial finance between China and Australia, actively set up bank-enterprise cooperation platform and smoothen channel for investment and financing cooperation.

It is particularly necessary to point out that, different from commercial finance, the development-oriented financial institutions, represented by CDB, do not aim at maximum profits. They have comprehensive operating advantages of investment, loan, debt, lease and security, and can firstly support China-funded enterprises to invest in energy and mineral resources field in the early stage. The common commercial finance is difficult to participate in large project because of long-term pay back period, low profit rate and large financing gap. The development-oriented finance can be invested by own experiences, influence and capital, provide support and guarantee in early stage for entering of other financial form, create favorable market environment and market rules for commercial finance to step in gradually, and optimize ecological and financial environment for China-funded enterprise to invest in Australian energy and mineral resource field.

(V) Strengthen operation and management, pay attention to talent cultivation, and promote sustainable development

Operation and management of overseas energy and mineral project is one of the most important factors deciding success of China-funded enterprises' investment. Under different legal systems, cultures and religious customs in different countries, it is the key of long-term stable operation of overseas energy and mineral resources for China-funded enterprises to communicate, manage and coordinate dispatched employees, local employees and foreign employees, improve transnational thinking transfer ability and adapt ability to external environment changes. In accordance with regulations in Labor Visa Law of Australia, when foreign companies invest in Australia, the labors and workers shall be preferentially hired from local residents or residents with long-term residence permit, unless management talents and special technicians required by company development must be hired. Therefore, the Australian energy and mineral resource projects of China-funded enterprises will hire large amount of local workers. Currently, Minmetals MMG project, Yanzhou Coal Mining project in Australia, CITIC Pacific iron mine project in Western Australia and Anshan Iron & Steel Group Karara Iron Ore Project all assign higher level management personnel from China, while hire mid-level and basic management personnel as well as large amount workers locally. The operation and management experiences of such large-scale China-funded enterprises show such mode is feasible and practical, and has gained favorable effects, trained dispatched management team from China and cultivated a batch of expert team knowing international operation and management.

If too many project management personnel are dispatched from China, it is difficult to reach ideal management effect due to cultural difference; in case of great contradiction between them and local employees, it may cause larger risks of operation and reputation. Thus, the management team dispatched from China must be fewer but better, and able to bear great responsibility and pressure. They should not only adapt to local environment as soon as possible, get along with local employees, but also gain trust and respect of local employees from management communication and operation experiences. In a certain sense, the entire country and all social resources are integrating force to support China-funded enterprises to invest overseas energy and mineral resources project. Therefore, the China-funded enterprises shall particularly treasure the opportunity to participate in investment and operating management of overseas energy and mineral resources project. They should not only prevent from risks and guarantee maximum economic benefits, but also take long-term profits of China as mission, and highly emphasize soft strength improvement during implementation of overseas mineral resources project, create a high level, composite international energy and resource project team skilled in operation management, from aspects of better communication skill, professional technical strength, development and operation management experiences and cross-cultural management ability so as to promote sustainable and healthy development of energy and mineral enterprises and the entire national economy from a higher level and a longer angle.

References:

Hu Huaibang, "Serving the Belt & Road Strategy by Development-Oriented Finance", *China Banking Industry*, 2015 (12).

Zheng Zhijie, "Seize Historical Opportunity, Serve the Belt & Road Building by Development-oriented Finance", *People's Daily*, Aug. 4, 2016.

Department of the Prime Minister and Cabinet, "Our North, Our Future: White Paper on Developing Northern Australia", *Australia*, 2015.

Meng Gang, "Research on Financial Cooperation of Four Countries along the Southern Route of the 21st Century Marine Silk Road", *Journal of Development-Oriented Finance Research*, 2016(1).

Yang Shuang, *Thinking On Yanzhou Coal Mining's Purchasing Felix Resources Limited Australia*, 2011(4).

National Innovation and Science Agenda, Australia commonwealth government.

Department of the Prime Minister and Cabinet, "Green Paper on Developing Northern Australia", *Australia*, 2014.6.

Australian Bureau of Statistics, Australia.

Meng Gang, "Approach of Australia Science and Technology Innovation Strategy Integrating to China and Financing Cooperation ", *Globalization*, 2016 (6).

He Xianhu, "Thinking on China Minmetals' Purchasing OZ Mining Australia", *Master's Thesis of Capital University of Economics and Business*, 2014(3).

China Chamber of Commerce in Australia, "China-invested Enterprises in Australia", *China Renmin University Press*. 2015 (12).

Jin Yingmei, "Sinosteel-Rio Tinto Channar Iron Ore Mine Joint Venture Contract Renews: Sinosteel Gains Favorable Conditions, 21st Century Business Herald", April 14,2016.

Gao Wei, "Evolution of International Direct Investment Theory and Enlightenment to China", *Doctoral Dissertation of Jilin University*, 2011(12).

Meng Gang, "Research on Linkage between the Belt & Road and Developing Northern Australia by Development-oriented Finance", *Globalization*, 2016(11).

Jiang Qunying, "Studies on Current Status and Countermeasures for Direct Foreign Investment of China-funded Enterprises", *Doctoral Dissertation of Fudan University*, 2003(4).

Lin Sha, "Difference between China Enterprises Greenfield Investment and Cross-border Acquisition – Analysis on Experiences of 223 Domestic Enterprises", *Management Review*, 2014 (9).

Zhuo Lihong, "Study on China-Foreign Productivity Cooperation New Pattern under the Belt & Road Strategy", *Dongyue Tribune*, 2015(10).

Wu Wenqing, "Made in China Catches Dream of 2025 Investment Boosting International Capacity Cooperation", *China Tendering*, 2015 (27).

Meng Gang, "Study on International Capacity Cooperation of China in Australia", *Journal of Development-Oriented Finance Research*, 2016 (3).

附件1

推动共建丝绸之路经济带和 21 世纪海上丝绸之路的愿景与行动
国家发展改革委　外交部　商务部
（经国务院授权发布）
2015 年 3 月

目录

前言

2000 多年前，亚欧大陆上勤劳勇敢的人民，探索出多条连接亚欧非几大文明的贸易和人文交流通路，后人将其统称为"丝绸之路"。千百年来，"和平合作、开放包容、互学互鉴、互利共赢"的丝绸之路精神薪火相传，推进了人类文明进步，是促进沿线各国繁荣发展的重要纽带，是东西方交流合作的象征，是世界各国共有的历史文化遗产。

进入 21 世纪，在以和平、发展、合作、共赢为主题的新时代，面对复苏乏力的全球经济形势，纷繁复杂的国际和地区局面，传承和弘扬丝绸之路精神更显重要和珍贵。

2013 年 9 月和 10 月，中国国家主席习近平在出访中亚和东南亚国家期间，先后提出共建"丝绸之路经济带"和"21 世纪海上丝绸之路"（以下简称"一带一路"）的重大倡议，得到国际社会高度关注。中国国务院总理李克强参加 2013 年中国—东盟博览会时强调，铺就面向东盟的海上丝绸之路，打造带动腹地发展的战略支点。加快"一带一路"建设，有利于促进沿线各国经济繁荣与区域经济合作，加强不同文明交流互鉴，促进世界和平发展，是一项造福世界各国人民的伟大事业。

"一带一路"建设是一项系统工程，要坚持共商、共建、共享原则，积极推进沿线国家发展战略的相互对接。为推进实施"一带一路"重大倡议，让古丝绸之路焕发新的生机活力，以新的形式使亚欧非各国联系更加紧密，互利合作迈向新的历史高度，中国政府特制定并发布《推动共建丝绸之路经济带和 21 世纪海上丝绸之路的愿景与行动》。

一、时代背景

当今世界正发生复杂深刻的变化，国际金融危机深层次影响继续显现，世界经济缓慢复苏、发展分化，国际投资贸易格局和多边投资贸易规则酝酿深刻调整，各国面临的发展问题依然严峻。共建"一带一路"顺应世界多极化、经济全球化、文化多样化、社会信息化的潮流，秉持开放的区域合作精神，致力于维护全球自由贸易体系和开放型世界经济。共建"一带一路"旨在促进经济要素有序自由流动、资源高效配置和市场深度融合，推动沿线各国实现经济政策协调，开展更大范围、更高水平、更深层次的区域合作，共同打造开放、包容、均衡、普惠的区域经济合作架构。共建"一带一路"符合国际社会的根本利益，彰显人类社会共同理想和美好追求，是国际合作以及全球治理新模式的积极探索，将为世界和平发展增添新的正能量。

共建"一带一路"致力于亚欧非大陆及附近海洋的互联互通，建立和加强沿线各国互联互通伙伴关系，构建全方位、多层次、复合型的互联互通网络，实现沿线各国多元、自主、平衡、可持续的发展。"一带一路"的互联互通项目将推动沿线各国发展战略的对接与耦合，发掘区域内市场的潜力，促进投资和消费，创造需求和就业，增进沿线各国人民的人文交流与文明互鉴，让各国人民相逢相知、互信互敬，共享和谐、安宁、富裕的生活。

当前，中国经济和世界经济高度关联。中国将一以贯之地坚持对外开放的基本国策，构建全方位开放新格局，深度融入世界经济体系。推进"一带一路"建设既是中国扩大和深化对外开放的需要，也是加强和亚欧非及世界各国互利合作的需要，中国愿意在力所能及的范围内承担更多责任义务，为人类和平发展作出更大的贡献。

二、共建原则

恪守联合国宪章的宗旨和原则。遵守和平共处五项原则，即尊重各国主权和领土完整、互不侵犯、互不干涉内政、和平共处、平等互利。

坚持开放合作。"一带一路"相关的国家基于但不限于古代丝绸之路的范围，各国和国际、地区组织均可参与，让共建成果惠及更广泛的区域。

坚持和谐包容。倡导文明宽容，尊重各国发展道路和模式的选择，加强不同文明之间的对话，求同存异、兼容并蓄、和平共处、共生共荣。

坚持市场运作。遵循市场规律和国际通行规则，充分发挥市场在资源配置中的决定性作用和各类企业的主体作用，同时发挥好政府的作用。

坚持互利共赢。兼顾各方利益和关切，寻求利益契合点和合作最大公约数，体现各方智慧和创意，各施所长，各尽所能，把各方优势和潜力充分发挥出来。

三、框架思路

"一带一路"是促进共同发展、实现共同繁荣的合作共赢之路，是增进理解信任、加强全方位交流的和平友谊之路。中国政府倡议，秉持和平合作、开放包容、互学互鉴、互利共赢的理念，全方位推进务实合作，打造政治互信、经济融合、文化包容的利益共同体、命运共同体和责任共同体。

"一带一路"贯穿亚欧非大陆，一头是活跃的东亚经济圈，一头是发达的欧洲经济圈，中间广大腹地国家经济发展潜力巨大。丝绸之路经济带重点畅通中国经中亚、俄罗斯至欧洲（波罗的海）；中国经中亚、西亚至波斯湾、地中海；中国至东南亚、南亚、印度洋。21世纪海上丝绸之路重点方向是从中国沿海港口过南海到印度洋，延伸至欧洲；从中国沿海港口过南海到南太平洋。

根据"一带一路"走向，陆上依托国际大通道，以沿线中心城市为支撑，以重点经贸产业园区为合作平台，共同打造新亚欧大陆桥、中蒙俄、中国—中亚—西亚、中国—中南半岛等国际经济合作走廊；海上以重点港口为节点，共同建设通畅安全高效的运输大通道。中巴、孟中印缅两个经济走廊与推进"一带一路"建设关联紧密，要进一步推动合作，取得更大进展。

"一带一路"建设是沿线各国开放合作的宏大经济愿景，需各国携手努力，朝着互利互惠、共同安全的目标相向而行。努力实现区域基础设施更加完善，安全高效的陆海空通道网络基本形成，互联互通达到新水平；投资贸易便利化水平进一步提升，高标准自由贸易区网络基本形成，经济联系更加紧密，政治互信更加深入；人文交流更加广泛深入，不同文明互鉴共荣，各国人民相知相交、和平友好。

四、合作重点

沿线各国资源禀赋各异，经济互补性较强，彼此合作潜力和空间很大。以政策沟通、设施联通、贸易畅通、资金融通、民心相通为主要内容，重点在以下方面加强合作。

政策沟通。加强政策沟通是"一带一路"建设的重要保障。加强政府间合作，积极构建多层次政府间宏观政策沟通交流机制，深化利益融合，促进政治互信，达成合作新共识。沿线各国可以就经济发展战略和对策进行充分交流对接，共同制定推进区域合作的规划和措施，协商解决合作中的问题，共同为务实合作及大型项目实施提供政策支持。

设施联通。基础设施互联互通是"一带一路"建设的优先领域。在尊重相关国家主权和安全关切的基础上，沿线国家宜加强基础设施建设规划、技术标准体系的对接，共同推进国际骨干通道建设，逐步形成连接亚洲各次区域以及亚欧非之间的基础设施网络。强化基础设施绿色低碳化建设和运营管理，在建设中充分考虑气候变化影响。

抓住交通基础设施的关键通道、关键节点和重点工程，优先打通缺失路段，畅通瓶颈路段，配套完善道路安全防护设施和交通管理设施设备，提升道路通达水平。推进建立统一的全程运输协调机制，促进国际通关、换装、多式联运有机衔接，逐步形成兼容规范的运输规则，实现国际运输便利化。推动口岸基础设施建设，畅通陆水联运通道，推进港口合作建设，增加海上航线和班次，加强海上物流信息化合作。拓展建立民航全面合作的平台和机制，加快提升航空基础设施水平。

加强能源基础设施互联互通合作，共同维护输油、输气管道等运输通道安全，推进跨境电力与输电通道建设，积极开展区域电网升级改造合作。

共同推进跨境光缆等通信干线网络建设，提高国际通信互联互通水平，畅通信息丝绸之路。加快推进双边跨境光缆等建设，规划建设洲际海底光缆项目，完善空中（卫星）信息通道，扩大信息交流与合作。

贸易畅通。投资贸易合作是"一带一路"建设的重点内容。宜着力研究解决投资贸易便利化问题，消除投资和贸易壁垒，构建区域内和各国良好的营商环境，积极同沿线国家和地区共同商建自由贸易区，激发释放合作潜力，做大做好合作"蛋糕"。

沿线国家宜加强信息互换、监管互认、执法互助的海关合作，以及检验检疫、认证认可、标准计量、统计信息等方面的双多边合作，推动世界贸易组织《贸易便利化协定》生效和实施。改善边境口岸通关设施条件，加快边境口岸"单一窗口"建设，降低通关成本，提升通关能力。加强供应链安全与便利化合作，推进跨境监管程序协调，推动检验检疫证书国际互联网核查，开展"经认证的经营者"（AEO）互认。降低非关税壁垒，共同提高技术性贸易措施透明度，提高贸易自由化便利化水平。

拓宽贸易领域，优化贸易结构，挖掘贸易新增长点，促进贸易平衡。创新贸易方式，发展跨境电子商务等新的商业业态。建立健全服务贸易促进体系，巩固和扩大传统贸易，大力发展现代服务贸易。把投资和贸易有机结合起来，以投资带动贸易发展。

加快投资便利化进程，消除投资壁垒。加强双边投资保护协定、避免双重征税协定磋商，保护投资者的合法权益。

拓展相互投资领域，开展农林牧渔业、农机及农产品生产加工等领域深度合作，积极推进海水养殖、远洋渔业、水产品加工、海水淡化、海洋生物制药、海洋工程技术、环保产业和海上旅游等领域合作。加大煤炭、油气、金属矿产等传统能源资源勘探开发合作，积极推动水电、核电、风电、太阳能等清洁、可再生能源合作，推进能源资源就地就近加工转化合作，形成能源资源合作上下游一体化产业链。加强能源资源深加工技术、装备与工程服务合作。

推动新兴产业合作，按照优势互补、互利共赢的原则，促进沿线国家加强在新一代信息技术、生物、新能源、新材料等新兴产业领域的深入合作，推动建立创业投资合作机制。

优化产业链分工布局，推动上下游产业链和关联产业协同发展，鼓励建立研发、生产和营销体系，提升区域产业配套能力和综合竞争力。扩大服务业相互开放，推动区域服务业加快发展。探索投资合作新模式，鼓励合作建设境外经贸合作区、跨境经济合作区等各类产业园区，促进产业集群发展。在投资贸易中突出生态文明理念，加强生态环境、生物多样性和应对气候变化合作，共建绿色丝绸之路。

中国欢迎各国企业来华投资。鼓励本国企业参与沿线国家基础设施建设和产业投资。促进企业按属地化原则经营管理，积极帮助当地发展经济、增加就业、改善民生，主动承担社会责任，严格保护生物多样性和生态环境。

资金融通。资金融通是"一带一路"建设的重要支撑。深化金融合作，推进亚洲货币稳定体系、投融资体系和信用体系建设。扩大沿线国家双边本币互换、结算的范围和规模。推动亚洲债券市场的开放和发展。共同推进亚洲基础设施投资银行、金砖国家开发银行筹建，有关各方就建立上海合作组织融资机构开展磋商。加快丝路基金组建运营。深化中国—东盟银行联合体、上合组织银行联合体务实合作，以银团贷款、银行授信等方式开展多边金融合作。支持沿线国家政府和信用等级较高的企业以及金融机构在中国境内发行人民币债券。符合条件的中国境内金融机构和企业可以在境外发行人民币债券和外币债券，鼓励在沿线国家使用所筹资金。

加强金融监管合作，推动签署双边监管合作谅解备忘录，逐步在区域内建立高效监管协调机制。完善风险应对和危机处置制度安排，构建区域性金融风险预警系统，形成应对跨境风险和危机处置的交流合作机制。加强征信管理部门、征信机构和评级机构之间的跨境交流与合作。充分发挥丝路基金以及各国主权基金作用，引导商业性股权投资基金和社会资金共同参与"一带一路"重点项目建设。

民心相通。民心相通是"一带一路"建设的社会根基。传承和弘扬丝绸之路友好合作精神，广泛开展文化交流、学术往来、人才交流合作、媒体合作、青年和妇女交往、志愿者服务等，为深化双多边合作奠定坚实的民意基础。

扩大相互间留学生规模，开展合作办学，中国每年向沿线国家提供 1 万个政府奖学金名额。沿线国家间互办文化年、艺术节、电影节、电视周和图书展等活动，合作开展广播影视剧精品创作及翻译，联合申请世界文化遗产，共同开展世界遗产的联合保护工作。深化沿线国家间人才交流合作。

加强旅游合作，扩大旅游规模，互办旅游推广周、宣传月等活动，联合打造具有丝绸之路特色的国际精品旅游线路和旅游产品，提高沿线各国游客签证便利化水平。推动 21 世纪海上丝绸之路邮轮旅游合作。积极开展体育交流活动，支持沿线国家申办重大国际体育赛事。

强化与周边国家在传染病疫情信息沟通、防治技术交流、专业人才培养等方面的合作，提高合作处理突发公共卫生事件的能力。为有关国家提供医疗援助和应急医疗救助，在妇幼健康、残疾人康复以及艾滋病、结核、疟疾等主要传染病领域开展务实合作，扩大在传统医药领域的合作。

加强科技合作，共建联合实验室（研究中心）、国际技术转移中心、海上合作中心，促进科技人员交流，合作开展重大科技攻关，共同提升科技创新能力。

整合现有资源，积极开拓和推进与沿线国家在青年就业、创业培训、职业技能开发、社会保障管理服务、公共行政管理等共同关心领域的务实合作。

充分发挥政党、议会交往的桥梁作用，加强沿线国家之间立法机构、主要党派和政治组织的友好往来。开展城市交流合作，欢迎沿线国家重要城市之间互结友好城市，以人文交流为重点，突出务实合作，形成更多鲜活的合作范例。欢迎沿线国家智库之间开展联合研究、合作举办论坛等。

加强沿线国家民间组织的交流合作，重点面向基层民众，广泛开展教育医疗、减贫开发、生物多样性和生态环保等各类公益慈善活动，促进沿线贫困地区生产生活条件改善。加强文化传媒的国际交流合作，积极利用网络平台，运用新媒体工具，塑造和谐友好的文化生态和舆论环境。

五、合作机制

当前，世界经济融合加速发展，区域合作方兴未艾。积极利用现有双多边合作机制，推动"一带一路"建设，促进区域合作蓬勃发展。

加强双边合作，开展多层次、多渠道沟通磋商，推动双边关系全面发展。推动签署合作备忘录或合作规划，建设一批双边合作示范。建立完善双边联合工作机制，研究推进"一带一路"建设的实施方案、行动路线图。充分发挥现有联委会、混委会、协委会、指导委员会、管理委员会等双边机制作用，协调推动合作项目实施。

强化多边合作机制作用，发挥上海合作组织（SCO）、中国—东盟"10+1"、亚太经合组织（APEC）、亚欧会议（ASEM）、亚洲合作对话（ACD）、亚信会议（CICA）、中阿合作论坛、中国—海合会战略对话、大湄公河次区域（GMS）经济合作、中亚区域经济合作（CAREC）等现有多边合作机制作用，相关国家加强沟通，让更多国家和地区参与"一带一路"建设。

继续发挥沿线各国区域、次区域相关国际论坛、展会以及博鳌亚洲论坛、中国—东盟博览会、中国—亚欧博览会、欧亚经济论坛、中国国际投资贸易洽谈会，以及中国—南亚博览会、中国—阿拉伯博览会、中国西部国际博览会、中国—俄罗斯博览会、前海合作论坛等平台的建设性作用。支持沿线国家地方、民间挖掘"一带一路"历史文化遗产，联合举办专项投资、贸易、文化交流活动，办好丝绸之路（敦煌）国际文化博览会、丝绸之路国际电影节和图书展。倡议建立"一带一路"国际高峰论坛。

六、中国各地方开放态势

推进"一带一路"建设,中国将充分发挥国内各地区比较优势,实行更加积极主动的开放战略,加强东中西互动合作,全面提升开放型经济水平。

西北、东北地区。发挥新疆独特的区位优势和向西开放重要窗口作用,深化与中亚、南亚、西亚等国家交流合作,形成丝绸之路经济带上重要的交通枢纽、商贸物流和文化科教中心,打造丝绸之路经济带核心区。发挥陕西、甘肃综合经济文化和宁夏、青海民族人文优势,打造西安内陆型改革开放新高地,加快兰州、西宁开发开放,推进宁夏内陆开放型经济试验区建设,形成面向中亚、南亚、西亚国家的通道、商贸物流枢纽、重要产业和人文交流基地。发挥内蒙古联通俄蒙的区位优势,完善黑龙江对俄铁路通道和区域铁路网,以及黑龙江、吉林、辽宁与俄远东地区陆海联运合作,推进构建北京—莫斯科欧亚高速运输走廊,建设向北开放的重要窗口。

西南地区。发挥广西与东盟国家陆海相邻的独特优势,加快北部湾经济区和珠江—西江经济带开放发展,构建面向东盟区域的国际通道,打造西南、中南地区开放发展新的战略支点,形成21世纪海上丝绸之路与丝绸之路经济带有机衔接的重要门户。发挥云南区位优势,推进与周边国家的国际运输通道建设,打造大湄公河次区域经济合作新高地,建设成为面向南亚、东南亚的辐射中心。推进西藏与尼泊尔等国家边境贸易和旅游文化合作。

沿海和港澳台地区。利用长三角、珠三角、海峡西岸、环渤海等经济区开放程度高、经济实力强、辐射带动作用大的优势,加快推进中国(上海)自由贸易试验区建设,支持福建建设21世纪海上丝绸之路核心区。充分发挥深圳前海、广州南沙、珠海横琴、福建平潭等开放合作区作用,深化与港澳台合作,打造粤港澳大湾区。推进浙江海洋经济发展示范区、福建海峡蓝色经济试验区和舟山群岛新区建设，加大海南国际旅游岛开发开放力度。加强上海、天津、宁波—舟山、广州、深圳、湛江、汕头、青岛、烟台、大连、福州、厦门、泉州、海口、三亚等沿海城市港口建设，强化上海、广州等国际枢纽机场功能。以扩大开放倒逼深层次改革，创新开放型经济体制机制，加大科技创新力度，形成参与和引领国际合作竞争新优势，成为"一带一路"特别是21世纪海上丝绸之路建设的排头兵和主力军。发挥海外侨胞以及香港、澳门特别行政区独特优势作用，积极参与和助力"一带一路"建设。为台湾地区参与"一带一路"建设作出妥善安排。

内陆地区。利用内陆纵深广阔、人力资源丰富、产业基础较好优势，依托长江中游城市群、成渝城市群、中原城市群、呼包鄂榆城市群、哈长城市群等重点区域，推动区域互动合作和产业集聚发展，打造重庆西部开发开放重要支撑和成都、郑州、武汉、长沙、南昌、合肥等内陆开放型经济高地。加快推动长江中上游地区和俄罗斯伏尔加河沿岸联邦区的合作。建立中欧通道铁路运输、口岸通关协调机制，打造"中欧班列"品牌，建设沟通境内外、连接东中西的运输通道。支持郑州、西安等内陆城市建设航空港、国际陆港，加强内陆口岸与沿海、沿边口岸通关合作，开展跨境贸易电子商务服务试点。优化海关特殊监管区域布局，创新加工贸易模式，深化与沿线国家的产业合作。

七、中国积极行动

一年多来，中国政府积极推动"一带一路"建设，加强与沿线国家的沟通磋商，推动与沿线国家的务实合作，实施了一系列政策措施，努力收获早期成果。

高层引领推动。习近平主席、李克强总理等国家领导人先后出访20多个国家，出席加强互联互通伙伴关系对话会、中阿合作论坛第六届部长级会议，就双边关系和地区发展问题，多次与有关国家元首和政府首脑进行会晤，深入阐释"一带一路"的深刻内涵和积极意义，就共建"一带一路"达成广泛共识。

签署合作框架。与部分国家签署了共建"一带一路"合作备忘录，与一些毗邻国家签署了地区合作和边境合作的备忘录以及经贸合作中长期发展规划。研究编制与一些毗邻国家的地区合作规划纲要。

推动项目建设。加强与沿线有关国家的沟通磋商，在基础设施互联互通、产业投资、资源开发、经贸合作、金融合作、人文交流、生态保护、海上合作等领域，推进了一批条件成熟的重点合作项目。

完善政策措施。中国政府统筹国内各种资源，强化政策支持。推动亚洲基础设施投资银行筹建，发起设立丝路基金，强化中国—欧亚经济合作基金投资功能。推动银行卡清算机构开展跨境清算业务和支付机构开展跨境支付业务。积极推进投资贸易便利化，推进区域通关一体化改革。

发挥平台作用。各地成功举办了一系列以"一带一路"为主题的国际峰会、论坛、研讨会、博览会，对增进理解、凝聚共识、深化合作发挥了重要作用。

八、共创美好未来

共建"一带一路"是中国的倡议，也是中国与沿线国家的共同愿望。站在新的起点上，中国愿与沿线国家一道，以共建"一带一路"为契机，平等协商，兼顾各方利益，反映各方诉求，携手推动更大范围、更高水平、更深层次的大开放、大交流、大融合。"一带一路"建设是开放的、包容的，欢迎世界各国和国际、地区组织积极参与。

共建"一带一路"的途径是以目标协调、政策沟通为主，不刻意追求一致性，可高度灵活，富有弹性，是多元开放的合作进程。中国愿与沿线国家一道，不断充实完善"一带一路"的合作内容和方式，共同制定时间表、路线图，积极对接沿线国家发展和区域合作规划。

中国愿与沿线国家一道，在既有双多边和区域次区域合作机制框架下，通过合作研究、论坛展会、人员培训、交流访问等多种形式，促进沿线国家对共建"一带一路"内涵、目标、任务等方面的进一步理解和认同。

中国愿与沿线国家一道，稳步推进示范项目建设，共同确定一批能够照顾双多边利益的项目，对各方认可、条件成熟的项目抓紧启动实施，争取早日开花结果。

"一带一路"是一条互尊互信之路，一条合作共赢之路，一条文明互鉴之路。只要沿线各国和衷共济、相向而行，就一定能够谱写建设丝绸之路经济带和21世纪海上丝绸之路的新篇章，让沿线各国人民共享"一带一路"共建成果。

附件 2

国务院关于推进国际产能和装备制造合作的指导意见
国发〔2015〕30 号

各省、自治区、直辖市人民政府，国务院各部委、各直属机构：

近年来，我国装备制造业持续快速发展，产业规模、技术水平和国际竞争力大幅提升，在世界上具有重要地位，国际产能和装备制造合作初见成效。当前，全球产业结构加速调整，基础设施建设方兴未艾，发展中国家大力推进工业化、城镇化进程，为推进国际产能和装备制造合作提供了重要机遇。为抓住有利时机，推进国际产能和装备制造合作，实现我国经济提质增效升级，现提出以下意见。

一、重要意义

（一）推进国际产能和装备制造合作，是保持我国经济中高速增长和迈向中高端水平的重大举措。当前，我国经济发展进入新常态，对转变发展方式、调整经济结构提出了新要求。积极推进国际产能和装备制造合作，有利于促进优势产能对外合作，形成我国新的经济增长点，有利于促进企业不断提升技术、质量和服务水平，增强整体素质和核心竞争力，推动经济结构调整和产业转型升级，实现从产品输出向产业输出的提升。

（二）推进国际产能和装备制造合作，是推动新一轮高水平对外开放、增强国际竞争优势的重要内容。当前，我国对外开放已经进入新阶段，加快铁路、电力等国际产能和装备制造合作，有利于统筹国内国际两个大局，提升开放型经济发展水平，有利于实施"一带一路"、中非"三网一化"合作等重大战略。

（三）推进国际产能和装备制造合作，是开展互利合作的重要抓手。当前，全球基础设施建设掀起新热潮，发展中国家工业化、城镇化进程加快，积极开展境外基础设施建设和产能投资合作，有利于深化我国与有关国家的互利合作，促进当地经济和社会发展。

二、总体要求

（四）指导思想和总体思路。全面贯彻落实党的十八大和十八届二中、三中、四中全会精神，按照党中央、国务院决策部署，适应经济全球化新形势，着眼全球经济发展新格局，把握国际经济合作新方向，将我国产业优势和资金优势与国外需求相结合，以企业为主体，以市场为导向，加强政府统筹协调，创新对外合作机制，加大政策支持力度，健全服务保障体系，大力推进国际产能和装备制造合作，有力促进国内经济发展、产业转型升级，拓展产业发展新空间，打造经济增长新动力，开创对外开放新局面。

（五）基本原则。

坚持企业主导、政府推动。以企业为主体、市场为导向，按照国际惯例和商业原则开展国际产能和装备制造合作，企业自主决策、自负盈亏、自担风险。政府加强统筹协调，制定发展规划，改革管理方式，提高便利化水平，完善支持政策，营造良好环境，为企业"走出去"创造有利条件。

坚持突出重点、有序推进。国际产能和装备制造合作要选择制造能力强、技术水平高、国际竞争优势明显、国际市场有需求的领域为重点，近期以亚洲周边国家和非洲国家为主要方向，根据不同国家和行业的特点，有针对性地采用贸易、承包工程、投资等多种方式有序推进。

坚持注重实效、互利共赢。推动我装备、技术、标准和服务"走出去"，促进国内经济发展和产业转型升级。践行正确义利观，充分考虑所在国国情和实际需求，注重与当地政府和企业互利合作，创造良好的经济和社会效益，实现互利共赢、共同发展。

坚持积极稳妥、防控风险。根据国家经济外交整体战略，进一步强化我国比较优势，在充分掌握和论证相关国家政治、经济和社会情况基础上，积极谋划、合理布局，有力有序有效地向前推进，防止一哄而起、盲目而上、恶性竞争，切实防控风险，提高国际产能和装备制造合作的效用和水平。

（六）主要目标。力争到 2020 年，与重点国家产能合作机制基本建立，一批重点产能合作项目取得明显进展，形成若干境外产能合作示范基地。推进国际产能和装备制造合作的体制机制进一步完善，支持政策更加有效，服务保障能力全面提升。形成一批有国际竞争力和市场开拓能力的骨干企业。国际产能和装备制造合作的经济和社会效益进一步提升，对国内经济发展和产业转型升级的促进作用明显增强。

三、主要任务

（七）总体任务。将与我装备和产能契合度高、合作愿望强烈、合作条件和基础好的发展中国家作为重点国别，并积极开拓发达国家市场，以点带面，逐步扩展。将钢铁、有色、建材、铁路、电力、化工、轻纺、汽车、通信、工程机械、航空航天、船舶和海洋工程等作为重点行业，分类实施，有序推进。

（八）立足国内优势，推动钢铁、有色行业对外产能合作。结合国内钢铁行业结构调整，以成套设备出口、投资、收购、承包工程等方式，在资源条件好、配套能力强、市场潜力大的重点国家建设炼铁、炼钢、钢材等钢铁生产基地，带动钢铁装备对外输出。结合境外矿产资源开发，延伸下游产业链，开展铜、铝、铅、锌等有色金属冶炼和深加工，带动成套设备出口。

（九）结合当地市场需求，开展建材行业优势产能国际合作。根据国内产业结构调整的需要，发挥国内行业骨干企业、工程建设企业的作用，在有市场需求、生产能力不足的发展中国家，以投资方式为主，结合设计、工程建设、设备供应等多种方式，建设水泥、平板玻璃、建筑卫生陶瓷、新型建材、新型房屋等生产线，提高所在国工业生产能力，增加当地市场供应。

（十）加快铁路"走出去"步伐，拓展轨道交通装备国际市场。以推动和实施周边铁路互联互通、非洲铁路重点区域网络建设及高速铁路项目为重点，发挥我在铁路设计、施工、装备供应、运营维护及融资等方面的综合优势，积极开展一揽子合作。积极开发和实施城市轨道交通项目，扩大城市轨道交通车辆国际合作。在有条件的重点国家建立装配、维修基地和研发中心。加快轨道交通装备企业整合，提升骨干企业国际经营能力和综合实力。

（十一）大力开发和实施境外电力项目，提升国际市场竞争力。加大电力"走出去"力度，积极开拓有关国家火电和水电市场，鼓励以多种方式参与重大电力项目合作，扩大国产火电、水电装备和技术出口规模。积极与有关国家开展核电领域交流与磋商，推进重点项目合作，带动核电成套装备和技术出口。积极参与有关国家风电、太阳能光伏项目的投资和建设，带动风电、光伏发电国际产能和装备制造合作。积极开展境外电网项目投资、建设和运营，带动输变电设备出口。

（十二）加强境外资源开发，推动化工重点领域境外投资。充分发挥国内技术和产能优势，在市场需求大、资源条件好的发展中国家，加强资源开发和产业投资，建设石化、化肥、农药、轮胎、煤化工等生产线。以满足当地市场需求为重点，开展化工下游精深加工，延伸产业链，建设绿色生产基地，带动国内成套设备出口。

（十三）发挥竞争优势，提高轻工纺织行业国际合作水平。发挥轻纺行业较强的国际竞争优势，在有条件的国家，依托当地农产品、畜牧业资源建立加工厂，在劳动力资源丰富、生产成本低、靠近目标市场的国家投资建设棉纺、化纤、家电、食品加工等轻纺行业项目，带动相关行业装备出口。在境外条件较好的工业园区，形成上下游配套、集群式发展的轻纺产品加工基地。把握好合作节奏和尺度，推动国际合作与国内产业转型升级良性互动。

（十四）通过境外设厂等方式，加快自主品牌汽车走向国际市场。积极开拓发展中国家汽车市场，推动国产大型客车、载重汽车、小型客车、轻型客车出口。在市场潜力大、产业配套强的国家设立汽车生产厂和组装厂，建立当地分销网络和维修维护中心，带动自主品牌汽车整车及零部件出口，提升品牌影响力。鼓励汽车企业在欧美发达国家设立汽车技术和工程研发中心，同国外技术实力强的企业开展合作，提高自主品牌汽车的研发和制造技术水平。

（十五）推动创新升级，提高信息通信行业国际竞争力。发挥大型通信和网络设备制造企业的国际竞争优势，巩固传统优势市场，开拓发达国家市场，以用户为核心，以市场为导向，加强与当地运营商、集团用户的合作，强化设计研发、技术支持、运营维护、信息安全的体系建设，提高在全球通信和网络设备市场的竞争力。鼓励电信运营企业、互联网企业采取兼并收购、投资建设、设施运营等方式"走出去"，在海外建设运营信息网络、数据中心等基础设施，与通信和网络制造企业合作。鼓励企业在海外设立研发机构，利用全球智力资源，加强新一代信息技术的研发。

（十六）整合优势资源，推动工程机械等制造企业完善全球业务网络。加大工程机械、农业机械、石油装备、机床工具等制造企业的市场开拓力度，积极开展融资租赁等业务，结合境外重大建设项目的实施，扩大出口。鼓励企业在有条件的国家投资建厂，完善运营维护服务网络建设，提高综合竞争能力。支持企业同具有品牌、技术和市场优势的国外企业合作，鼓励在发达国家设立研发中心，提高机械制造企业产品的品牌影响力和技术水平。

（十七）加强对外合作，推动航空航天装备对外输出。大力开拓发展中国家航空市场，在亚洲、非洲条件较好的国家探索设立合资航空运营企业，建设后勤保障基地，逐步形成区域航空运输网，打造若干个辐射周边国家的区域航空中心，加快与有关国家开展航空合作，带动国产飞机出口。积极开拓发达国家航空市场，推动通用飞机出口。支持优势航空企业投资国际先进制造和研发企业，建立海外研发中心，提高国产飞机的质量和水平。加强与发展中国家航天合作，积极推进对外发射服务。加强与发达国家在卫星设计、零部件制造、有效载荷研制等方面的合作，支持有条件的企业投资国外特色优势企业。

（十八）提升产品和服务水平，开拓船舶和海洋工程装备高端市场。发挥船舶产能优势，在巩固中低端船舶市场的同时，大力开拓高端船舶和海洋工程装备市场，支持有实力的企业投资建厂、建立海外研发中心及销售服务基地，提高船舶高端产品的研发和制造能力，提升深海半潜式钻井平台、浮式生产储卸装置、海洋工程船舶、液化天然气船等产品国际竞争力。

四、提高企业"走出去"能力和水平

（十九）发挥企业市场主体作用。各类企业包括民营企业要结合自身发展需要和优势，坚持以市场为导向，按照商业原则和国际惯例，明确工作重点，制定实施方案，积极开展国际产能和装备制造合作，为我拓展国际发展新空间作出积极贡献。

（二十）拓展对外合作方式。在继续发挥传统工程承包优势的同时，充分发挥我资金、技术优势，积极开展"工程承包＋融资"、"工程承包＋融资＋运营"等合作，有条件的项目鼓励采用BOT、PPP等方式，大力开拓国际市场，开展装备制造合作。与具备条件的国家合作，形成合力，共同开发第三方市场。国际产能合作要根据所在国的实际和特点，灵活采取投资、工程建设、技术合作、技术援助等多种方式，与所在国政府和企业开展合作。

（二十一）创新商业运作模式。积极参与境外产业集聚区、经贸合作区、工业园区、经济特区等合作园区建设，营造基础设施相对完善、法律政策配套的具有集聚和辐射效应的良好区域投资环境，引导国内企业抱团出海、集群式"走出去"。通过互联网借船出海，借助互联网企业境外市场、营销网络平台，开辟新的商业渠道。通过以大带小合作出海，鼓励大企业率先走向国际市场，带动一批中小配套企业"走出去"，构建全产业链战略联盟，形成综合竞争优势。

（二十二）提高境外经营能力和水平。认真做好所在国政治、经济、法律、市场的分析和评估，加强项目可行性研究和论证，建立效益风险评估机制，注重经济性和可持续性，完善内部投资决策程序，落实各方面配套条件，精心组织实施。做好风险应对预案，妥善防范和化解项目执行中的各类风险。鼓励扎根当地、致力于长期发展，在企业用工、采购等方面努力提高本地化水平，加强当地员工培训，积极促进当地就业和经济发展。

（二十三）规范企业境外经营行为。企业要认真遵守所在国法律法规，尊重当地文化、宗教和习俗，保障员工合法权益，做好知识产权保护，坚持诚信经营，抵制商业贿赂。注重资源节约利用和生态环境保护，承担社会责任，为当地经济和社会发展积极作贡献，实现与所在国的互利共赢、共同发展。建立企业境外经营活动考核机制，推动信用制度建设。加强企业间的协调与合作，遵守公平竞争的市场秩序，坚决防止无序和恶性竞争。

五、加强政府引导和推动

（二十四）加强统筹指导和协调。根据国家经济社会发展总体规划，结合"一带一路"建设、周边基础设施互联互通、中非"三网一化"合作等，制定国际产能合作规划，明确重点方向，指导企业有重点、有目标、有组织地开展对外工作。

（二十五）完善对外合作机制。充分发挥现有多双边高层合作机制的作用，与重点国家建立产能合作机制，加强政府间交流协调以及与相关国际和地区组织的合作，搭建政府和企业对外合作平台，推动国际产能和装备制造合作取得积极进展。完善与有关国家在投资保护、金融、税收、海关、人员往来等方面合作机制，为国际产能和装备制造合作提供全方位支持和综合保障。

（二十六）改革对外合作管理体制。进一步加大简政放权力度，深化境外投资管理制度改革，取消境外投资审批，除敏感类投资外，境外投资项目和设立企业全部实行告知性备案，做好事中事后监管工作。完善对中央和地方国有企业的境外投资管理方式，从注重事前管理向加强事中事后监管转变。完善对外承包工程管理，为企业开展对外合作创造便利条件。

（二十七）做好外交服务工作。外交部门和驻外使领馆要进一步做好驻在国政府和社会各界的工作，加强对我企业的指导、协调和服务，及时提供国别情况、有关国家合作意向和合作项目等有效信息，做好风险防范和领事保护工作。

（二十八）建立综合信息服务平台。完善信息共享制度，指导相关机构建立公共信息平台，全面整合政府、商协会、企业、金融机构、中介服务机构等信息资源，及时发布国家"走出去"有关政策，以及全面准确的国外投资环境、产业发展和政策、市场需求、项目合作等信息，为企业"走出去"提供全方位的综合信息支持和服务。

（二十九）积极发挥地方政府作用。地方政府要结合本地区产业发展、结构调整和产能情况，制定有针对性的工作方案，指导和鼓励本地区有条件的企业积极有序推进国际产能和装备制造合作

六、加大政策支持力度

（三十）完善财税支持政策。加快与有关国家商签避免双重征税协定，实现重点国家全覆盖。

（三十一）发挥优惠贷款作用。根据国际产能和装备制造合作需要，支持企业参与大型成套设备出口、工程承包和大型投资项目。

（三十二）加大金融支持力度。发挥政策性银行和开发性金融机构的积极作用，通过银团贷款、出口信贷、项目融资等多种方式，加大对国际产能和装备制造合作的融资支持力度。鼓励商业性金融机构按照商业可持续和风险可控原则，为国际产能和装备制造合作项目提供融资支持，创新金融产品，完善金融服务。鼓励金融机构开展PPP项目贷款业务，提升我国高铁、核电等重大装备和产能"走出去"的综合竞争力。鼓励国内金融机构提高对境外资产或权益的处置能力，支持"走出去"企业以境外资产和股权、矿权等权益为抵押获得贷款，提高企业融资能力。加强与相关国家的监管协调，降低和消除准入壁垒，支持中资金融机构加快境外分支机构和服务网点布局，提高融资服务能力。加强与国际金融机构的对接与协调，共同开展境外重大项目合作。

（三十三）发挥人民币国际化积极作用。支持国家开发银行、中国进出口银行和境内商业银行在境外发行人民币债券并在境外使用，取消在境外发行人民币债券的地域限制。加快建设人民币跨境支付系统，完善人民币全球清算服务体系，便利企业使用人民币进行跨境合作和投资。鼓励在境外投资、对外承包工程、大型成套设备出口、大宗商品贸易及境外经贸合作区等使用人民币计价结算，降低"走出去"的货币错配风险。推动人民币在"一带一路"建设中的使用，有序拓宽人民币回流渠道。

（三十四）扩大融资资金来源。支持符合条件的企业和金融机构通过发行股票、债券、资产证券化产品在境内外市场募集资金，用于"走出去"项目。实行境外发债备案制，募集低成本外汇资金，更好地支持企业"走出去"资金需求。

（三十五）增加股权投资来源。发挥中国投资有限责任公司作用，设立业务覆盖全球的股权投资公司（即中投海外直接投资公司）。充分发挥丝路基金、中非基金、东盟基金、中投海外直接投资公司等作用，以股权投资、债务融资等方式，积极支持国际产能和装备制造合作项目。鼓励境内私募股权基金管理机构"走出去"，充分发挥其支持企业"走出去"开展绿地投资、并购投资等的作用。

（三十六）加强和完善出口信用保险。建立出口信用保险支持大型成套设备的长期制度性安排，对风险可控的项目实现应保尽保。发挥好中长期出口信用保险的风险保障作用，扩大保险覆盖面，以有效支持大型成套设备出口，带动优势产能"走出去"。

七、强化服务保障和风险防控

（三十七）加快中国标准国际化推广。提高中国标准国际化水平，加快认证认可国际互认进程。积极参与国际标准和区域标准制定，推动与主要贸易国之间的标准互认。尽早完成高铁、电力、工程机械、化工、有色、建材等行业技术标准外文版翻译，加大中国标准国际化推广力度，推动相关产品认证认可结果互认和采信。

（三十八）强化行业协会和中介机构作用。鼓励行业协会、商会、中介机构发挥积极作用，为企业"走出去"提供市场化、社会化、国际化的法律、会计、税务、投资、咨询、知识产权、风险评估和认证等服务。建立行业自律与政府监管相结合的管理体系，完善中介服务执业规则与管理制度，提高中介机构服务质量，强化中介服务机构的责任。

（三十九）加快人才队伍建设。加大跨国经营管理人才培训力度，坚持企业自我培养与政府扶持相结合，培养一批复合型跨国经营管理人才。以培养创新型科技人才为先导，加快重点行业专业技术人才队伍建设。加大海外高层次人才引进力度，建立人才国际化交流平台，为国际产能和装备制造合作提供人才支撑。

（四十）做好政策阐释工作。积极发挥国内传统媒体和互联网新媒体作用，及时准确通报信息。加强与国际主流媒体交流合作，做好与所在国当地媒体、智库、非政府组织的沟通工作，阐释平等合作、互利共赢、共同发展的合作理念，积极推介我国装备产品、技术、标准和优势产业。

（四十一）加强风险防范和安全保障。建立健全支持"走出去"的风险评估和防控机制，定期发布重大国别风险评估报告，及时警示和通报有关国家政治、经济和社会重大风险，提出应对预案和防范措施，妥善应对国际产能和装备制造合作重大风险。综合运用外交、经济、法律等手段，切实维护我国企业境外合法权益。充分发挥境外中国公民和机构安全保护工作部际联席会议制度的作用，完善境外安全风险预警机制和突发安全事件应急处理机制，及时妥善解决和处置各类安全问题，切实保障公民和企业的境外安全。

国务院

2015 年 5 月 13 日

跋

　　近年来中国一直是澳大利亚最大的贸易伙伴，双边经贸合作不断深化，相互投融资关系充满活力。2014 年 11 月，国家主席习近平成功对澳大利亚进行了国事访问，明确欢迎澳大利亚等南太平洋地区国家参与"一带一路"建设，共同推动区域经济一体化。对此，澳方反应积极，行动迅速。在 2015 年"中澳战略经济对话"中，双方就中方"一带一路"倡议与澳方"北部大开发"计划对接等建议达成共识，政府相关部门成立了工作组，澳方还成立了澳中"一带一路"产业合作促进会；澳中组织和学者发表了多篇专题报告，在澳各地举办了相关研讨活动，澳洲一些地方政府部门同我国家开发银行等单位还开展了联合规划调研，合作势头良好，前景十分广阔。

　　在各界的努力下，中澳全面战略伙伴关系掀开了新的一页：2015 年《中澳自由贸易协定》签署并生效，至今已经实施了三轮降税；双边农产品贸易增长迅猛，中国成了澳洲葡萄酒最大出口市场；服务贸易潜力进发，双向投资十分活跃；澳大利亚作为创始成员国加入了亚洲基础设施投资银行；两国政府还签署了澳肉牛输华卫生检疫议定书。2016 年两国签署了进一步开放民航市场协议，厦航、国航、东航、南航、首都航空分别开通了厦门、昆明、成都、青岛、沈阳、广州等城市直飞墨尔本、悉尼、阿德莱德新航线；国家电投收购了太平洋水电和塔拉贾风电公司；月亮湖投资收购了塔州范迪门土地公司；华润、绿叶集团分别参股澳洲医疗企业；海航、南山参股维珍航空公司；富源牧业收购了布拉乳品公司；上海中福收购了卡尔顿山牧场；中投汇通参股墨尔本港；明加尔金源参股卡古利金矿；中房置业参与收购基德曼公司。中澳经贸合作硕果累累，金融机构的支持功不可没。

国家开发银行是我国对外投融资合作主力银行之一，目前在澳大利亚贷款规模名列前茅，为促进中澳在能源、矿产、基础设施、规划等领域的合作做出了积极贡献。孟刚博士作为国家开发银行在澳洲和南太地区工作组的负责人，做了大量卓有成效的工作，分别促成国家开发银行和我驻澳相关总领馆与昆士兰州政府、维多利亚州政府就对接"一带一路"建设签署会议纪要，和兖煤澳洲等上市公司达成"一带一路"建设专项财务顾问协议，和中关村"一带一路"产业促进会与澳方教育城公司及丰盛澳洲综合产业园区公司签署共建经贸合作园区谅解备忘录，融资支持澳大利亚白石风电项目并荣获上海市最佳银团贷款项目及最佳牵头行奖。

推动中澳"一带一路"投融资合作具有深远的战略意义和迫切的现实需要，孟刚博士对此进行了系统调研和深入思考，并拿出了高质量的著作：《中国在澳大利亚"一带一路"投融资合作研究》，令人敬佩，可喜可贺。在澳大利亚中资企业的诸多高管人员中，我和孟刚博士交往已久，相处愉快，赞赏他勤奋好学、谦虚严谨的优秀品质，佩服他爱国实干的敬业精神。在此书撰写过程中，作者曾将其文稿发我阅评，与我讨论其中的观点及各种思路，征求不同看法。我以为，本书具有理论创新和补白意义，是一部有水平、接地气的佳作。孟刚先生用自己呕心沥血的实际行动，为推动中澳"一带一路"框架下的互利合作做着积极的贡献。我衷心祝贺孟刚博士的新书顺利出版！祝愿他在新的征途上取得更好的成绩！

黄任刚

中华人民共和国驻澳大利亚大使馆公使衔经济商务参赞

2017 年 3 月于堪培拉

策划编辑：徐庆群

特约编辑：李倩文　董馨怡　徐庆颖

图书在版编目（CIP）数据

中国在澳大利亚"一带一路"投融资合作研究/孟刚 著 . — 北京：
　人民出版社，2017.4
ISBN 978 - 7 - 01 - 017390 - 0

I.①中…　II.①孟…　III.①对外投资 - 直接投资 - 研究 - 中国②外商投资 -
直接融资 - 研究 - 澳大利亚　IV.① F832.6 ② F836.114.8

中国版本图书馆 CIP 数据核字（2017）第 030657 号

中国在澳大利亚"一带一路"投融资合作研究
ZHONGGUO ZAI AODALIYA YIDAIYILU TOURONGZI HEZUO YANJIU

孟　刚　著

人民出版社 出版发行
（100706　北京市东城区隆福寺街 99 号）

北京集惠印刷有限责任公司 新华书店经销

2017 年 4 月第 1 版　2017 年 4 月北京第 1 次印刷
开本：710 毫米 × 1000 毫米 1/16　印张：19.75
字数：269 千字

ISBN 978 - 7 - 01 - 017390 - 0　定价：49.00 元

邮购地址 100706　北京市东城区隆福寺街 99 号
人民东方图书销售中心　电话：（010）65250042　65289539